Tagore's Heroines

Assessing the Portraits of Gender Orientation

Tagore's Heroines

Assessing the Portraits of Gender Orientation

Bina Biswas

AUTHORSPRESS

Worldwide Circulation through Authorspress Global Network
First Published 2013
by
Authorspress

Editorial
Q-2A Hauz Khas Enclave
New Delhi-110 016

Marketing
E-35/103, Jawahar Park
Laxmi Nagar, Delhi-110 092

e-mails: authorspress@rediffmail.com; authorspress@hotmail.com
Website: www.authorspressbooks.com

Tagore's Heroines: Assessing the Portraits of Gender Orientation
ISBN 978-81-7273-744-3

Printed in India at Salasar Imaging Systems, Delhi-35

To
My father and mother

Foreword

Dr. Nibir K. Ghosh

Long years ago when Khushwant Singh was in his heyday (I guess it has always been like that for him), I had read somewhere of his visit to some Sen family in Calcutta. After a wonderful Bengali dinner followed by coffee, the lively conversation moved towards writers in Bengal. Khushwant Singh, in his usual style, stunned his hostess, Mrs. Sen, by referring to Rabindranath Tagore as a sub-standard writer. Shell-shocked, Mrs. Sen was visibly angry. She told him in no uncertain terms, "How can you say such awful things about Gurudev? We worship him in Bengal!" Khushwant quickly retorted, "Don't worship him. Read him." Though it is quite customary for all Bengalis to worship Tagore even without reading him, I – who had developed an admiration, bordering on worship, reading stories like "Homecoming," "Castaway" and "Cabuliwalah" when I was an adolescent myself (like Pathik Chakravarty, Neelkant or Mini) – have no hesitation whatsoever in saying that had Khushwant himself taken the trouble of reading Tagore, he would have definitely volunteered to be one among the millions in the queue of Tagore's worshippers.

Dr. Dwijendranath Maitra (a Resident Surgeon at Mayo Hospital, Calcutta), whom W.B. Yeats mentions in his "Preface" to *Gitanjali*, had stated, "I read Rabindranath every day; to read one line of his is to forget all the troubles of the world." At the end of his "Introduction" to *Rabindranath Tagore: The Centenary Volume – 1861-1961*, published in 1961, Jawaharlal Nehru wrote: "He was in line with *rishis*, the great sages of India, drawing from the windows of the ancient past and giving it a practical garb and a meaning in the present.... This great and highly sensitive man was not only a poet of India, but also a poet of humanity and freedom everywhere.... Even as he tried to create an atmosphere in his school at Santiniketan, so he tried to produce that atmosphere in the whole of India. I earnestly trust that living message will always be with us, guiding us in our life and our endeavours." In recent time – in a letter written from her house arrest in 2001 to her fellow Nobel Laureates – Aung San Suu Kyi, the international symbol of peaceful resistance against oppression, spoke of Tagore thus: "During my years of house arrest I have learnt my most precious lesson from a poem by Rabindranath Tagore, many of whose verses reach out to that innermost, elusive land of the spirit that we are not always capable of exploring ourselves.... There are no words of comfort in the poem. No assurances of joy and peace at the end of the harsh journey. There is no pretence that it is anything but evil luck to receive no answer to your call, to be deserted in the middle of the wilderness, to have no one who would hold up a light to aid you through a stormy night. It is not a poem that offers heart's ease, but it teaches you that a citadel of endurance can be built on a foundation of anguish."

He was indeed a poet-prophet who could spontaneously participate in the joys and sorrows of life with equanimity and grace, one who could sing simultaneously of royalty as much as of ordinary mortals carved out of common clay. His poetic sojourns excluded nothing. He loved the company of the tiller "tilling the hard ground" or the pathmaker "breaking stones" as much as he desired to be with the millions of living beings who made up the "vast fair" on planet Earth. He could say with ease and felicity, "I am none of the wheels of power but I am one with the living creatures that are crushed by it."

Tagore's identification with common people and his sympathy for the oppressed and enslaved makes him concerned for the other half of the human society—the women. Long before the world saw the struggle for the emancipation of women take concrete shape, Tagore had emphatically pointed out that without fullest development of women's personality and potentiality, full fledged advancement of the society is not possible. If Tagore could visualize an Eden in the Western paradigm where Adam and Eve could create an Eden of their own on earth, he was no less aware of the harsh realities of the gender divide in his own enlightened Bengal.

Like Nora in Henrik Ibsen's *A Doll's House,* Mrinal in Tagore's "The Wife's Letter" (1914) blows the clarion call for women's liberty from the fetters of domesticity. Endowed with "the intellect that the other wives in the house lacked," Mrinal voices the many injustices in the daily commerce of a woman's life: "its set rules, set habits, set phrases, set blows." At the end of the story Mrinal is seen militantly writing to her husband: "I will never again return to your house at number 27, Makhan Baral Lane. I have seen Bindu. I have learnt what it means to be a woman in this domestic world. I need no more of it....Today I see there is no longer any need to maintain your family's dignity or self-pride." As creator of both the "home" and the "world," Tagore knew that the permanent significance of home "lies not in the narrowness of its enclosure, but in an eternal moral idea. It represents the truth of human relationship." In view of his ability to inspire the human system with his life and work, it must be acknowledged that he was not a poet who could be content with remaining hidden in the light of thought and singing unbidden songs like Shelley's Skylark.

Though much water has flowed through all the Indian rivers before and after Tagore penned the story mentioned above, we can easily see the likes of Mrinal, though made weak by time and fate, yet strong in will, striving to create a world free of gender bias. The stirrings of women emancipation and empowerment that Tagore so successfully foregrounded in his stories, poems, novellas, dance-dramas, essays, novels, in fact in every conceivable genre, speaks volumes of his intimate understanding of the proverbial "half the sky."

Images of woman in Indian literature usually move between the Sita and the Draupadi syndromes. The Sita variant silently suffer with utmost loyalty to their husbands, always ready to subject themselves to acid tests or fire sermons. The Draupadi types, on the contrary, refuse to be at the receiving end and dare to challenge the male hegemony in various ways. Rather than move between iconizations of these two bold and primordial figures, Tagore's women steer clearly away from such stereotyped portrayals that characterize majority of renderings in Indian literature. It will not be presumptuous to say that it was primarily Tagore who had not only envisioned the significance of empowerment of women through education and social awareness but also challenged demeaning mindsets that saw them merely as mother, wife, mistress or sex objects.

Yet, despite the proliferation of material on Rabindranath Tagore, it is difficult to locate any comprehensive study that brings to the fore the heroic tales of women that our first Nobel Laureate so effortlessly narrated in his monumental works. For those of us who are even remotely sensitive to the delicacy of gender issues, Dr. Bina Biswas's illuminating revelation of

Tagore's Heroines – Chandara, Charulata, Kumudini, Sohini, Damini, Harasundari, Kadambini, Mrinal, Binodini, Bimala, Anandomoyi, Mrinmoyee, Labanyo, "Mashi," "Didi" and many others – promises a lucid foray into hitherto veiled territories of human concern. Both individually and collectively, these protagonists reveal the diversity of women and the diversity within each woman as they, in myriad ways, attempt to redefine and reformulate existing spaces in the realms of domesticity and beyond it. Through in-depth analysis and critical evaluation of the major works of Tagore from a womanist perspective, and through interesting comparisons with women protagonists from Henrik Ibsen, Anton Chekhov, Tennessee Williams et al, the book, infused with sweetness and light, succeeds in showcasing the universal appeal of Tagore's portrayal of women beyond the limited regions of time and space.

In all fairness, it may be expected that those alien to the vibrant world of Tagore may be drawn by the lucid narrative of this book to enjoy and appreciate the acknowledged genius from Bengal, Khushwant Singh notwithstanding.

Dr. Nibir K. Ghosh, D.Litt., is Head, Department of English Studies & Research at Agra College, Agra. He was Senior Fulbright Fellow (2003-04) at the University of Washington, Seattle, USA. Former Executive Member of the Board of Directors for the American Studies Research Centre in Hyderabad, he is an Associate of the Indian Institute of Advanced Study, Shimla and the Chief Editor of ***Re-Markings****, an international biannual journal of research in English (www.re-markings.com). His most recent work is titled* ***Rabindranath Tagore: The Living Presence*** *(Authorspress, 2011).*

Preface

Rabindranath Tagore's short stories have lived through ages. His stories are as poetic as poetry and as dramatic as drama. Above all they have a vision. His stories portray the pains and pathos, sorrows and happiness, and unfulfilled dreams of the common men and women of his age. Through their portrayal he reveals the truths of human life and existence.

Tagore was an idealist and his abundant humanism was from the spirit of the West. His feelings were not for the strong but for the sufferers, not for the landlord but for the land-tiller, and not for the materialistic woman but for the woman of substance, for the woman who has an identity of her own—the New Woman. Like other educated Bengalis of his time, he also encountered the secular, democratic and republican liberalism of the nineteenth century literature and politics of Europe. But then his stories do not suffer from any myopic vision. They are rooted in the Indian soil with common themes from the socio-familial arena. His life-God (*jiban-debata*) is his guiding spirit.

Tagore created a new genre in Indian literature through short stories, and wrote over 90 of them during his long literary career. This versatile genius – poet, novelist, painter, and musician – the grand master of Bangla culture, was acclaimed as India's first-ever Romantic poet, and his stories also have elements of that same Romanticism in them.

Though born in an affluent zamindar family, Tagore could easily break in through the veils of aristocracy and superficiality of his class because his heart went out to the poor, to the tormented souls and to the victims of age-old patriarchal conventions which have chained humanity for ages.

This book makes a modest attempt to critically assess his stories with gender orientation. As it has been said of Shakespeare, Tagore also has no heroes but only heroines in his stories, and they suffer the brunt of society and then are reborn in an emancipated new role, as a new women. They are rebels and they are even ready to flee society to achieve the enlightenment of their souls, to fulfil their emotional quest, and for them material needs are not predominant.

The heroines of Tagore are always curious, sensitive, emotionally strong and modern with a vengeance. An attempt has been made here to compare his heroines to the heroines in the plays of Henrik Ibsen and Tennessee Williams, to those in the stories of Anton Chekov and to women portrayed in other writers' works.

According to the simplest definition of feminism, it attempts to discover clearly what it stands for, and carve itself out as a powerful discourse, discipline and project. It has a social, economic and political plank which is to establish equality for women in all fields including health, education and employment. But when we come to the arts, its emphasis falls on rediscovering the lost heritage and history of women artists and in literature of woman writers, in all religions and cultures, making them to resurface their voices that were not only marginalised but literally erased.

Feminism has had to, sometimes, consequently, in the absence of female voices as writers, use the technique or strategy of 'appropriation', that is, to make women characters in the works of male patriarchal writers of earlier ages thus speak for women, regarding their position and suffering in that scenario of the past. My interpretation is feminist in this concrete sense. I look at Tagore's women and the heroines in his work, even as I find that many of the other women there are also to me as heroines, as those through whose words and actions I arrogate by analysis of feminism in varying stages in Tagore's development as a writer. The twin edges of my interpretation are thus that Tagore himself is a proto- ornascent feminist or pro-feminist who rapidly evolves into quite a strident one by finally making characters like Sohini and Damini, and he was thus far ahead of his age in his position on women. Along with this thread of thought that weaves in and out of the book systematically, my own views also appear in radicalising many of his women characters, even touching on themes like sexual liberty and orientation, a radicalisation that is inevitable in writing in 2013, after the three waves of feminism and post-feminisms have happened, not to mention varieties of feminism like womanism and Indian feminisms.

The context of India, then and now, is different from what it is in an American or Eurocentric world but literature is also humanist and universal, especially regarding the plight of women, so in my analysis I have naturally borrowed on psychoanalytical criticism by including Freudian, Jungian and more consciously, 'Deutschian' views on Tagore's stories. Bringing in such comparisons to women thinkers and quotes from people like Londre and studies on women characters by great writers as I mentioned earlier, like Hedda of Ibsen, Stella of Tennessee Williams and Anna of Chekhov, and women writers like Alice Walker of Colour Purple fame and by referencing black Afro-American womanism etc., I show that Tagore was intuitive and his greatness lies in the malleability and flexibility of his texts in their ability to include both his contemporary Indian scene, today's India, and at the same time, speak to us even on the feminist issues that are still being contended with all over the world. This proves that he was much ahead of his time. This is no doubt the power of the discourse of literature, especially of fiction, specifically exemplified by his heroines.

To call the latter Tagore a feminist may or may not be 'not' required but to point out his leaning towards women as people worth portraying as oppressed and in need of emancipation is an absolute necessity, regarding his stance on their exploitation, widowhood and a myriad other such topics, as I have pointed out in my first chapter and throughout, as a worthy successor of Raja Rammohan Roy, Ishwạr Chandra Vidyasagar, Maharshi Debendranath Tagore etc. While reading the great feminist writers of Eurocentric feminism one is often stymied by their use of dense theoretical jargon like that of a Judith Butler, and the plus point in bringing Tagore into the picture is that his stories and novellas and novels, not to mention his letters or essays from which also I have quoted, can and do often make the same points in refreshingly aesthetic language, clothed in apt cultural similes and metaphors close to Indian hearts, right from the days in which he speaks of Kadambari's suicide and the reasons for it obliquely, to the end of his writing career.

While it is possible to connect Tagore to Marxism or any other 'ism', even as I have partly made linkages in his work to caste, religion, class and subalternity and not just gender, the most important fact to notice about his oeuvre while talking of it in terms of assessing his heroines as portraits of gender orientation, is to remember that for him his 'jiban debata' was purely and wholly feminine in essence, form, shape and inspiration. This is what made him write relentlessly of women in short story after short story and novelette and novel and colour his imagination to the point where he makes Bimala in *Home and the World* say: "... his language had caught fire from my eyes, we woman are not only the deities of the household fire, but the flame of the soul itself". In other words, to put it in a slightly deconstructive manner, Tagore is as great as he is because he is made great as much by the credited and uncredited women in his life and his women characters. In the same way he makes them so through his influence and creations. In short, the curve of his writing is not just a one-sided discourse but a multiple network of give and take and a fascinating world of emotionally and intellectually creative intercourse.

Finally, the books uphold the vision of the great story-teller Tagore and establishes that his heroines Tagore stand against time as they emerge stronger facing their challenges and confrontations with their society.

I offer my heartfelt gratitude to Dr Nibir Ghosh who encouraged me by writing a foreword to this book. I owe my thanks to Dr Ampat Varghese Koshy for his insightful criticism, Mr Sudarshan Kcherry for having faith in me and finally, to Mr Rakesh Sharma for his guidance and mentoring.

I thank my family for their unfailing support without which the book would not have been possible.

Bina Biswas

Contents

1

Tagore and the Milieu

Literature upholds human spirit. It gives intellectual enlightenment and aesthetic pleasure. The relation between aesthetics and literature is intimate, at the same time very complex. Philosophy adds richness to the relationship. To understand the philosophy, the artistry involved in Tagore's work, an estimate of the social, political cultural environment is absolutely necessary. No author writes in a vacuum. The contemporary world has a definite impression on the works. Societies, art, religion, faith—all influence the age and are manifested in the literature of the age. Rabindranath Tagore in *The Religion of Man* has said:

> From the time when Man became truly conscious of his own self he also became conscious of a mysterious spirit of unity which found its manifestation through him in his society. It is a subtle medium of relationship between individuals, which is not for any utilitarian purpose but for its own ultimate truth… .

An extract from Gurudev's essay *A Vision of History* will be valuable before having a glance through the colonial past of Bengal: "The history of India has been the history of struggle between the mechanical spirit of conformity in social organisation and creative spirit of man which seeks freedom and love in self-expression."

A few memorable and historical dates may prove helpful here in the study of this age of transition from the old to the new India.

The Battle of Plassey fought in 1757 was of extraordinary significance not only to the East India Company but it also showed the utterly corrupt political life in Bengal. It also revealed that the Hindus were absolutely frustrated with the Muslim rule in the province. But still it cannot be proved that the Battle of Plassey firmly established the British power in India or in Bengal. The British had still to fight for another 50 years or more to secure that position.

Mir Jafar remained the Nawab of Bengal after Siraj-ud-Daula, and when he died in 1765, the Calcutta Council put his son named Najam-ud-Daulah on the throne of Bengal. However, all the powers passed into the hands of the English Company. At this time, the condition of Bengal was chaotic. There was anarchy, confusion, bribery, corruption and extortion everywhere. Such was the state of affairs when Clive came to India in 1765 as the Governor of Bengal for the second time.

Clive was sent the second time specifically to reform the entire government of the company. He was the founder of the British Empire in India, and was also the architect of the ruin of the people of Bengal. Warren Hastings was appointed the Governor of Bengal in 1772. He was succeeded by Lord Cornwallis who remained the Governor General for seven years. The Permanent Settlement of Bengal, Bihar and Orissa was one of the great achievements of Cornwallis. This settlement created a limited proprietary right of the *zamindars*. Magisterial powers were taken away from them *zamindars*. Pathuriaghat Tagores were also affected by this settlement. Here, it will be quite interesting to note an excerpt from Tagore's *The Religion of Man*, "I was born in what was once the metropolis of British India." Gurudev told an audience at Oxford University in 1930. When he was almost 70 years old:

> My ancestors came floating to Calcutta upon the earliest tide of the fluctuating fortune of the East India Company. The unconventional code of life for our family has been a confluence of three cultures, Hindu, Mohammedan and British. My grandfather belonged to that period when amplitude of dress and courtesy and generous leisure were gradually being clipped and curtailed into Victorian manners.... I came to a world in which the modern city-bred spirit of progress had just triumphed over the lush green life of our ancient village community. Though the trampling process was almost complete..., something of the past lingered over the wreckage.

Lord Wellesley was appointed the Governor-General of Bengal. Lord Hastings succeeded Lord Wellesley and completed his work. Lord Amherst took over from Lord Hastings. The most important events of the reign of Lord Amherst were the First Burmese War and the capture of Bharatpur.

The arrival of Lord William Bentinck marked the beginning of a new era in many ways. He was a man of resolution, capacity and spirit. He is well-known not for his conquests but for the large number of reforms carried out by him in various fields. Besides financial, judicial, administrative and educational reforms his social reforms were noteworthy. He was responsible for the abolition of sati and thugee. Both these customs involved death. The death in the case of sati took place voluntarily. The source of the custom of sati is unknown. Undoubtedly, it was an old practice which prevailed among the higher castes. It was considered to be a privilege and honour, and that is why it was accompanied by the recitation of sacred hymns. The widowed woman burnt herself along with her husband. She was made to put on all her clothes and ornaments, and after the act of burning was over, the Brahmins were able to put all the gold into their pockets. This created vested interests and hence the custom continued in spite of protests from time to time. Even Mughal Emperor Akbar tried to suppress the custom of sati. William Bentinck made it a penal offence. He was helped in the task by Raja Rammohan Roy. By a regulation in 1829, Bentinck declared its practice as illegal and punishable as "culpable homicide".

The renaissance in modern Indian literature, in culture and spiritual awakening began with Raja Rammohan Roy. He was the first of the Indian masters of English prose, but he was so great in so many other fields that he belongs to Indian history more than to Indo-Anglian literary history.

The Brahmo Samaj was founded in 1828 by Raja Rammohan Roy. He aspired to set up a strict monolatrous worship of the Supreme Being, and the Brahmo Samaj advocated the worship of one God and the brotherhood of man. After the premature death of Raja Rammohan Roy the Brahmo Samaj was left without any organisation, constitution, membership, covenant or pledge. It was revived by Maharshi Debendranath who put a new life into the organisation and introduced a regular form of church service, including thanksgiving, praise and prayer. Debendranath did not officially become a Brahmo until 21 December 1843. There was a deep influence of Raja Rammohan Roy on him, who was, according to Tagore, "the best friend of my grandfather."

Roy was a unique linguist who drew upon sources written in Sanskrit, Arabic, Persian, Hebrew, Greek, English, French and Bengali. He was also the greatest Indian intellectual of the nineteenth century. Tagore placed him amongst the greatest Indians. Today Roy is remembered mainly for his stand against sati and widow remarriage. He aimed at getting rid of the contemporary Hindiusm of inauthentic traditions and meaningless rituals. After his death, this Society became the most influential and important movement of religious and social reforms in the nineteenth century India. One of its leaders was Prince Dwarkanath's son, Debendranath Tagore.

Rabindranath Tagore was born on 7 May 1861 at number 6, Dwarkanath Tagore's Lane, Jorasanko in Calcutta. He was the fourteenth child of Maharshi Debendranath. His father was an amazing man in many ways. Tagore himself says, "My father I saw very seldom; he was away a great deal, but his presence pervaded the whole house and was one of the deepest influences on my life… ." Debendranath was popularly called Maharshi or the great saint for his deep piety, his severe adherence to moral principles in conduct and for his deep piety, for his stout advocacy of the worship of the Invisible God, which meant a rejection of the idolatry practices prevalent amongst the Hindus. About five years before the birth of the poet, the Maharshi had left all his earthly pursuits and recreations, and after wandering about from place to place, had decided on settling in the Simla hills where he could immerse himself in religious contemplation, far off from worldly cares, chases and temptations.

After about two years' sojourn, the Maharshi was one day watching a beautiful hill-stream which was flowing towards the plains. He realised that though in the paths of its descending flight it might be polluted with dirt, yet it would fulfil its mission by fertilising the earth. There in the movement of the stream, he saw the ideal of his own life, too—the deliverance that might come through rejection and renunciation of the worldly life that appeared to be sheer vanity to him. He felt that if he had learnt any divine truth he must live it in practical life, in the welter of earthly endeavours. He left the hills and once more became a man among men, seeking the bliss of eternity in the midst of temporal and worldly activities.

The Maharshi was a believer in the One Invisible God whom he found in the teachings of the *Upanishads*; but he differed from the monistic interpretation of the scriptures made by the *Advaita* School of philosophy. The *Advaitin* believes in the absolute and complete identity of the individual self (*jiva*) and God, but the Maharshi reacted strongly from the philosophy in which the individual is submerged in the Absolute. His religion had a good deal of eclecticism and had undergone a gradual evolution. At first he argued that the Absolute is as different from the individual consciousness as the individual consciousness is from matter. He wrote, "We had no faith in *Vedanta* philosophy, because Shankaracharya seeks to prove therein that Brahma and all created beings are one and the same." Later on, he reached a more dynamic conception of the relation between the individual and the Absolute and he says, "This universe is the outcome of perfect truth. This universe is relative truth; its Creator is the Truth of Truth, the Absolute Truth." In his book on Brahma Dharma, there is no place for the doctrines of *Advaithavada* (Monism), *Avataravada* (Incarnation) and *Mayavada* (Illusion). In his religion, the individual soul and God are separate entities; they are like friends, but the difference between them is not unbeatable and unbridgeable. God is the Supreme Spirit, and the world is the result of a spontaneous overflow of His creative energy. He wills it, and it is there. This attitude to the world and God, which has a tinge of Vaishnavas' thought and religion—for the early Tagores were devout and religious Vaishnavites—reaches frontward to Tagore's philosophy of life.

The Tagore family became prosperous and affluent in the days of the East India Company in Calcutta, as merchants and *zamindars*, and the poet's grandfather Prince Dwarkanath, who was famous for the splendour of his living, was a friend of Raja Rammohan Roy, the founder of the Brahmo religion and "the herald of a new age." The Tagores were Brahmins, but the orthodox and the mainstream Brahmins demurred to accept them as belonging to their fold, because they were called Piralis. The Tagores were Vaishnavas in their religious outlook and stance, inclining to vegetarianism in diet; they were enlightened and free-thinking, and Prince Dwarkanath, who had assisted Raja Rammohan Roy in social reform, had visited England where he died in 1846.

In the course of a lecture in China, Tagore refers to the significance of the age in which he was born and the part taken by his family members in the three revolutionary movements which stirred the country in those days. The first movement was religious, and its founder was Rammohan Roy, who carried the ceaseless and perpetual war on superstitions and proclaimed oneness of God. One of the leaders of this movement for spiritual revival was Maharshi Debendranath Tagore. The second movement was in the field of literature where Bankimchandra rescued Bangla language from the muddle of dead forms, brought a new critical attitude and made Bangla a vehicle for the expression of ebullient imagination that would tolerate no discipline imposed from the outside. The third movement was the national movement; it was partly political and partly cultural. "It was a voice of indignation at the humiliation constantly heaped upon us by people who were not Oriental," and while not opposed to the importation of Western thought, it discouraged indiscriminate rejection of traditional Indian culture and habits. This movement is reflected in the life of the Maharshi whom many of his countrymen thought as bad as a Christian, but who, more than anyone else in his day, emphasised the study of the

Upanishads, and spared no pains to stem the tide of conversion into Christianity in Bengal.

In order to run its business efficiently, the British East India Company created a clerical group amongst the Bengal literati, who were taught the basics of the spoken English. Thus the Bengali middle-class was born—the Babu, who could communicate in English and imitate the Victorian mannerism. This was the cradle which nurtured the Bengali intelligentsia in the years to come, that would give birth to the Bengali national spirit later. Soon there emerged from this middle class a group of people who were prolific in the English language, and European ways and thinking. This was a quantum leap forward. Bengal had always been rich in its cultural and literary heritage. Now, with the influx of fresh ideas, new intellectuals came into being ushering in the Bengal Renaissance. The scene of the other provinces of the country was not different either.

The Bengal Renaissance refers to a social reform movement in Bengal, starting with Raja Rammohan Roy (1775-1833) and ending with Rabindranath Tagore (1861-1941), although there have been many stalwarts thereafter embodying particular aspects of this unique intellectual and creative output. Nineteenth century Bengal had an unequalled combine of religious and social reformers, scholars, literary giants, journalists, patriotic orators and scientists, all merging to form the image of a renaissance that marked the transition from the 'medieval' to the 'modern'.

The Renaissance, after the Indian uprising of 1857, saw a veritable explosion of great Bengali literary efforts. Raja Rammohan Roy and Pandit Ishwar Chandra Vidyasagar were the trailblazers. Others, like Bankim Chandra Chattopadhyay, followed suit and built upon this solid foundation. Later, along with the development and increase of the national spirit, social problems began to be dealt with, and the language became more colloquial and acceptable to the masses. The foremost amongst these greats was Sarat Chandra Chattopadhyay. Regarding the Bengal Renaissance, Historian Romesh Chander Dutt said:

> The conquest of Bengal by the English was not only a political revolution, but ushered in a greater revolution in thoughts and ideas, in religion and society... Nowhere in the annals of Bengali literature are so many and so bright names found crowded together in the limited space of one century as (these)... . Within the three quarters of the present century, prose, blank verse, historical fiction and drama have been introduced for the first time in the Bengali literature... .

As an educationist, Rammohan Roy co-founded the Hindu College in Calcutta (1817), along with several other schools and colleges. He supported the Western style of teaching and advocated education in English, science, Western medicine and technology. He published many journals and magazines in different languages, notable amongst which were *Brahminical Magazine* in English (published in 1821), *Sambad Kaumadi* in Bengali (1821) and *Mirat-ul-Akbar* in Persian (1822).

Ishwar Chandra Vidyasagar (1820-1891) was a philosopher, academic, educator, writer, translator, printer, publisher, entrepreneur, reformer and philanthropist par excellence. Though best known for his social reforms in proposing and pushing through the Widow Remarriage Act XV, 1856, and his support towards education of the girl children, it was he who was instrumental towards reconstructing the Bengali alphabet and reforming Bengali typography into an alphabet of 12 vowels and 40 consonants. His efforts to simplify and modernise Bangla prose were significant. He also rationalised and simplified the Bengali alphabet and type, which had remained unchanged since Charles Wilkins and Panchanan Karmakar had cut the first wooden Bangla type fonts in 1780.

Debendranath did not become a Brahmo until the death of his beloved grandmother in 1838. She passed away on the bank of the Ganges, amidst the funeral chanting accompanied by her grandson. It left him in a trance and a strange feeling overcame him. Aversion to wealth arose in him. He described it in the spiritual autobiography he wrote in an old age: "a strange sense of the unreality of all things suddenly entered my mind. I was as if no longer the same man. A strong aversion to wealth arose within me. The coarse bamboo mat on which I sat seemed to be my fitting seat, carpets and costly spreadings seemed hateful, in my mind was awakened a joy unfelt before."

"Cast-iron probity of behaviour, combined with his spiritual search in the Himalayas, like the 'rishis', laid the foundation of Debendranath's awesome reputation in the late nineteenth century Bengal. Dwarkanath was known as 'Prince', his eldest son became Maharshi [Great Sage]". E.M. Forster in 1941, reviewing the Maharishi's autobiography, remarked that Brahmoism was "not so much a creed as an attitude of mind, and would particularly appeal to a spiritual rebel."

Nirad C. Chaudhuri, who was born in 1897, was not a Brahmo, but absorbed Brahmo values as a child. He wrote:

> In this period, under Brahmo and related reforming influences, the Hindu middle-class showed "greater probity in public and private affairs, attained greater fulfillment of cultural aspirations, and put forth greater creativeness" than at any time in recent centuries.

A Bengali of the next generation Satyajit Ray, whose family were eminent Brahmos, though he himself was not, also valued the period. "Brahmos of that time," said Ray, "were very powerful figures, very demanding figures with lots of social fervour in them: the willingness, the ability and the eagerness to do good to society, to change society for the better." Having discarded idolatrous Hindu Shastra, a verse from the sacred *Upanishads* made a deep sense on Debendranath and subsequently on Tagore and MK Gandhi which was translated into English by Tagore, "All that is changing in this changeful world, know that it is enveloped by Him who is the Lord of all things. Therefore take your enjoyment in renunciation. Never covet wealth."

The zeniths of Brahmoism overlapped with roughly the second half of Debendranath's life and the first half of Tagore. Debendranath became a religious rebel, though he was fairly conformist in social matters. He was unable to agree on the issue that, at a later date, Keshub Chandra Sen raised and insisted that "no minister or preacher of the Samaj should retain any mark of caste or sectarian distinction whatsoever."

It is worthwhile to quote from *Rabindranath Tagore: The Myriad-Minded Man*:

> In matters of social custom, neither father nor son was by nature an iconoclast, unlike grandfather Dwarkanath, who dined with the Sahibs, drank alcohol and bluntly refused to make public atonement for crossing the 'black water's' between India and Europe. The Maharshi wore a sacred thread until he died and invested Tagore with one in 1873; and Tagore in turn invested his son Rathindranath in 1898. But whereas Debendranath, like most men became more conservative with age, Tagore in later life became more and more radical. The first part of Tagore's life was undoubtedly dominated by his father's austere spirituality—but the second part, which made him world-famous, owed as much, if not more, to the influence of his worldly, pleasure-loving grandfather.

With such a divine and puritanical parentage, Tagore could not only easily abandon the worldly pleasures and seek truth in God, but devoted his life to sing His praises and justify His ways to man in his *Gitanjali* (*Songs Offering*). The myriad-minded man, Rabindranath Tagore, the Great Sentinel, at the height of great fame, wrote:

> I have this paradox in my nature that when I begin to enjoy my success I grow weary of it in the depth of my mind.

Thus spoke Tagore in *Gitanjali*:

> Thou hast made me endless, such is thy pleasure. This frail vessel thou emptiest again and again, and fillest it ever with fresh life.
>
> This little flute of a reed thou hast carried over hills and dales, and hast breathed through it melodies eternally new.
>
> At the immortal touch of thy hands my little heart loses its limits in joy and gives birth to utterance ineffable.
>
> Thy infinite gifts come to me only on these very small hands of mine. Ages pass, and still thou pourest, and still there is room to fill.

Works Cited

Chauduri, N.C.: *Autobiography*, p.221.

Dutta, Krishna & Robinson, Andrew: *Rabindranath Tagore: The Myriad-Minded Man*, Rupa & Co., 2003, p.33.

Forster, E.M.: *Daily News and Leader*, 11 Nov. 1914.

Mahajan, V.D.: *India Since 1526*, S. Chand & Co., 2001, p.135.

Ray, Satyajit: *Brahmos of that time: Robinson*, p.15.

Sengupta, S.C.: *The Great Sentinel: A Study of Rabindranath Tagore*, p.4.

Sisirkumar, Ghose: *Makers of Indian Literature, Rabindranath Tagore*, Sahitya Akademi, 1990, p.124.

Tagore, Debendranath: *Atmajibani, Autobiography*, Calcutta, 1909, p.148.

____ : *Atmajibani*, p.14, *Autobiography*, p.57.

____ : *Atmajibani*, p.2, *Autobiography*, p.38.

Tagore, Rabindranath: "A Poet's School" *Towards Universal Man*, p.290.

____ : "Ideals of Education", *Vishwa Bharathi Quarterly*, April-July 1929, p.72.

____ : "Letter to Edward Thompson", *Chinnapatrabali* (*Torn Leaves*), Shantiniketan, 1921.

____ : *My Reminiscences*, p.31/ *Rabindra Rachanabali*, 17, p.286.

____ : Rabindranath Tagore on his father Debendranath Tagore: *Vishwa Bharathi Quarterly*, No. 1, 1961, p.1.

____ : *Religion of Man*, "Man's Nature", Rupa & Co., 2005, p.128.

____ : *The Religion of Man*, pp., 128,170.

2

Short Story, Novella and Novel: A Glimpse

The short story, like the novel, is a story told in prose, which may seem to be a brief edition of the novel, the technique and substance being widely divergent. There cannot be any intricate analysis of character, long explanation of plot or any exhaustive commentary on life. Its commencement is very near its end. There is no scope for detailed investigation and that is why it selects only such incidents or such traits of characters which may disclose some unrevealed, unconsummated aspect of life. There remains an impression of terseness and revelation.

The sole purpose of the short story is to tell and amuse. A story should be capable of creating awareness of life in people. The author conveys his message to the reader not directly but by developing short-cuts to the situations of life and thereby sieving the truths of life from fictitious elements. According to Edgar Allan Poe, "A short story is a prose narrative requiring from half an hour to one hour in perusal."

A short story can be read at a single sitting. The definition of a short story is that it is a brief, concentrated revelation or elucidation of some fact of life. But nevertheless, short story offers an analysis of life. It conveys the message and entertains the reader by projecting the glances of the society in which he lives and the conditions—social, cultural, political, emotional, and familial and religious—are reflected in them. It should also have universal appeal. It should be able to rise above the unities of time, place and character.

The short stories, like the modern novel, have its origin in the West. Although it is difficult to spot the first story, it can certainly be said that various writers contributed to its growth and development in America, Europe and Asia. With a few exceptions, many novelists are successful short story writers: Edgar Allan Poe, Nathaniel Hawthorne, O. Henry, Charles Lamb, Jack London, Stephen Crane, Katherine Mansfield, William Faulkner, Rudyard Kipling, Somerset Maugham, James Joyce, H.G.Wells, Graham Greene, Maupassant, Anton Chekov, Dostoevsky and Tolstoy; and in Indian English literature, Bankim Chandra Chatterjee, the so-called 'Scott of Bengal', Ishwar Chandra Vidyasagar, Michael Madhusudan Dutt, Lal Behari Dey, Aurobindo and Tagore-all wrote on social matters in powerful and precise language that harmonised the classical and the vernacular.

In modern Indian English literature, R.K. Narayan, Raja Rao, Mulk Raj Anand, Anita Desai are a few names which need to be mentioned in connection with short story and novels. Poet, critic and short story writer Edgar Allan Poe is famous for his cultivation of the mysterious and the macabre in fiction. He is one of the writers who is widely appreciated and read. He is the writer who fetched international repute for this genre, and his idealism and musical gifts as a poet, his dramatic art as a story-teller secured him a major position among the universally known men of letters. In his masterpieces, there is assorted content of his temper; his mind and his art are fused into one, single whole of tone, structure and movement. He devised rules for short stories in which he sought the traditional unities. The short story should relate complete action and take place within one day at one place. To these unities he added the "unity of mood or effect".

The second writer of significance is O. Henry whose real name is Sidney Porter. His tales romanticised the common place in life, and in particular the life of ordinary people in New York City. His stories express the effect of coincidence and suspense through humorous, grim or satirical modes with unexpected surprise endings.

Charles Lamb is considered not only as an essayist but also as a short story writer. His essays serve both the purpose of essays and short stories. His essays are remarkable as short stories essay form.

There are some British writers who published a collection of short stories based on the life of India. Rudyard Kipling's few short stories tend to become highly philosophical because of his genuine moral involvement with Indian consciousness, and he was deeply influenced by the national character of India.

By the beginning of the nineteenth century short stories and short novels constituted the output of many writers. Even the novelists turned to short stories because they could feel the suitability of certain themes only for short stories. The modern short story moves towards a more symbolic and metaphorical presentation. In 1899 Maugham produced his collection of short stories to this effect. Katherine Mansfield had a major influence on the evolution of the short story. James Joyce published 'Dubliners' which became a landmark in the history of the short story. D.H. Lawrence, between 1914 and 1934, published a large number of stories. Joseph Conrad's short stories are more relentless towards "human terms or moral ambiguities of ethical dilemmas of baffling mysteries."

Miss Elizabeth Bowen, a great story-teller herself, gives a lot of importance to 'tautness'. It does not sprawl, it concentrates on a single point—which is the focus of the story. The writer makes use chiefly of irony and anticlimax; the end brings out some unexpected facet of reality.

The name of H.G. Wells needs to be mentioned to illustrate directions in which short story travelled. H.G. Wells is fascinated by the concept of omniscient narration and this is the reason for his commercial success. His stories are evidence of a new talent and novel subject matter.

The Russian writers like Gogol, Chekov, Tolstoy and Dostoevsky had great influence on the short story. Chekov is one of the major Russian playwrights, foremost master of the modern short story and an outstanding representative of the late nineteenth century Russian realistic school. He experimented with serious writings also apart from writing anecdotes for humorous journals. His stories provide serious studies of human in misery and despair. Village life became an important theme in his work, notably the 'peasants'. His brilliant sketches of the rustic life created a stir in Russia. Leo Tolstoy, the writer of novels of an epic scale, is also a delightful short story writer. In his stories he exhibits a great love for humanity and studies the foibles and foolishness of mankind with a great amount of sympathy.

Short story developed in the hands of Henry James, and the characters of this writer are farmers, clerks, priests and prostitutes living ordinary lives. There is a similarity between the Western writers and Indian short story writers in English. The Indian short story writers took to Maupassant tradition. It is natural because the Maupassant short story shares certain qualities of the ancient Indian tale, like uninterrupted narration, preservation of curiosity ultimately resulting in portraiture of a clear picture of life. Although the Indian writers borrowed from writers abroad, a sense of realism—understanding of human situation in contemporary society through firm character delineation—is true to our own soul and rooted firmly to the Indian soil.

The ancient Indian tradition took broadly two forms—the fable and the popular tale or folktale. The fable form is the best exemplified in the tales of *Panchatantra, Jataka Tales, Brihatkatha Manjari* and *Kathasaritsagara.* Most of these are animal fables in which the characters are animals symbolising human beings. These fables are more akin to the modern short story than the popular tale of ancient India. Both the ancient Indian fable and the ancient Indian popular tale have helped the Indian short story writer in English in giving his story a definite shape. The Indian short story writers have tried a synthesis of the salient features of both the fable and the tale. The fable and the popular tale have also this virtue of striking the curiosity of the reader by imparting some useful knowledge in the most interesting way.

The short story does teach some practical wisdom as to how to achieve immediate gain in any given situation, often through sheer courage and perseverance. The didactic tale and the popular tale, however, have something in common—they impress the reader with their suspense and narration. The plot of a typical *Panchatantra* story shows how well the writer knew the curiosity of the listener, and preserved it till the end.

Stories are found in the *Upanishads* and epics like the *Ramayana*, the *Mahabhharata* and the *Bhagavad Gita.* The ancient tale form was later revived and preserved in the literatures of various Indian languages as a part of the bigger work.

Raja Rammohan Roy wrote and spoke English with mastery years before Macaulay wrote his Minute. As far as English education was concerned the Indo-Anglican writers of verse and prose—the Cavally Brothers, Derozio, Kashiprosad Ghose, Hasan Ali, P. Rajagopaul, Mohan Lal—belonged to the pre-Macaulay period. Michael Madhusudan Dutt came immediately afterwards. He was an extremely gifted writer. In his initial years as an author he tried his hand at English prose, verse and even drama. His narrative poem, 'The Captive Ladie' had strong influence of the English romantics. Swami Vivekananda arrived on the scene after the death of the Messiah Ramakrishna Paramahansa, his spiritual Guru, and conquered the world. He spoke with knowledge and conviction. He wrote verses in English and his writings are spread over many volumes.

Toru Dutt was the next poet to come onto the scene to write poems mainly of the ancient tales and carried forward the Romantic tradition. Romesh Chander Dutt and Manmohan Ghose (the elder brother of Sri Aurobindo) were both Bengalis but their literary activities were not restricted to Bengal alone. One finds the quintessence of Indian romantic poetry, expressed in the English language in their works.

The second half of the nineteenth century of the English literature made a great impact on the Indian writing. In English prose works were attempted. Newer forms like lyric, novel, short story began to appear in the Indian languages. By the end of the century short stories in the English language itself began to be written by the Indian writers. The modern Indian short story is a synthesis of age old cultural traditions of India and modern trends like realism and humanism.

The first name that comes to the mind in connection with the short story is Gurudev Rabindranath Tagore. It is rather strange that Tagore did not write any story originally in English. He wrote them in Bangla. His sympathy for the weak and the downtrodden, his flair for satire and his sense of humour as in the *Babus of Nayanjore* were obviously shared by our early short story writers in English.

It is interesting to note that by 1911-12 a fair number of Tagore's stories had been published in English translation in India (the first one as far back as 1901), without making much impact on the English readers—but hardly any poetry. But slowly among the Calcutta literati he began to be known as' the Bengal Shelley; Michael Madhusudan Dutt was the Milton of Bengal; Bankim Chatterjee was the Scott; someone else was the Byron.'

Tagore himself has written a popular poem while defining a short story and its impact, and the end of the poem goes like this:

> *Antare atripti rabe,*
> *Sango kori mone hobe,*
> *Sesh hoye hoilo na sesh*
>
> There will be an unsatisfied,
> unfulfilled urge even after the story is over,
> The end comes but appears to have not come. (Translated)

The short story basically emphasises on surprise and, in a nutshell, throws light on the larger intrigues of life. In Tagore's short stories there are surprises, turn of events, and in these tides there await surprises revealing a critical insight into human nature.

What Tagore wrote was basically meant for entertainment with a long lasting effect but unlike other writers of the age there was no moral preached, there was no illumination. But there was definitely a social criticism of life present in the stories.

J.C. Ghosh, a famous linguist in Bangla literature, wrote:

> The influence of Sanskrit on Bangla and on Bangla literature was similar to the influence of Latin on English, but much greater, because Sanskrit was not a foreign tongue and was alive at the time when Bangla was born i.e. during three or four centuries before the Muslim conquest of Bengal around A.D.1200, after which Sanskrit ceased to be a living language. The conquest led to introduction of many Persian, Arabic and Turkish words into Bangla. Two centuries later, with the

> coming of the Europeans, English words as well as Portuguese, French and Dutch words infiltrated Bangla.

All these vernacular writers (mentioned earlier) were steeped in Sanskrit. The ancient fable and the ancient popular tale have helped in moulding the thought process of these writers. Tagore frequently referred to Sanskrit literature. Like all Hindu children he enjoyed reading the great epics, *The Ramayana* and *the Mahabharata* in Bangla in his childhood, though he read them in original Sanskrit in his teens.

Kalidasa stirred him especially. He loved Jayadeva, a court poet of the last Hindu King of Bengal before the Muslim conquest. He read Jayadeva's *Gita Govinda*. The *Gitagovinda* has been called the Indian *Song of Songs*. In it the songs celebrate the divine love of Krishna and Radha. The combination of physical passion, sensuous imagery and verbal music definitely influenced Tagore. The Tagore family, being Brahmos, disapproved of it—but undoubtedly Vaishvanism left an indelible impression on Gurudev's mind which impresses upon his poetry at a later date in *Gitanjali*.

Tagore is, above everything else, a lyric poet, one of the greatest in the world, and his stories bear the impress of his lyrical and mystical genius. Indeed, in his best stories he seems to create a new literary genre in which the art of the lyric poem and that of the stories are united. They combine the element of surprise, so essential to the short story, with rich emotionalism which is the soul of the lyric. In describing his experience in the Great Illumination, which marked the turning point in his life, he says that he seemed to realise then for the first time that things which, on a surface view, appear to be detached from one another are really united by an inner harmony. This illumination not only gave him an idea of the unity of life but also enabled him to see behind the veil, to penetrate the surface into the deeper reality lying hidden from view. It is this perception of this deeper reality in various fields of life, which is the keynote of his short stories. It may, indeed, be said that the long novel with its analyses, descriptions and commentaries show the logic of life; but the short story with its emphasis on surprise throws light on the illogicality which, too, is a large part of life.

Tagore's stories divulge the fact that he had a great insight into women's heart. Srinivasa Iyengar writes about Tagore's women, "The women in his stories, of course, are splendidly womanly, frail and fair, yet wise and strong; always—or almost always—more sinned against than sinning. Tagore plumbs the depths of the womanly heart, and behind the seeming wiles and the helpless gestures he sees reserves of devotion and sacrifice". Women occupy the central roles in most of his stories.

The creative mastery of Tagore's stories is visible in their victorious endings. Like Chekhov, Tagore believed that the endings of the stories should have an element of incompleteness and surprise. Having heard the end of the story the reader must feel that though that was the end, the story did not end there. This 'incompleteness' helped the writer to show the incessant flow of life and make the reader think over problems of life.

The major themes in his stories are the problems of the joint-family system, social criticism in a wider sense, love obsessive or placid, extramarital relations or born of conjugal bonds, and love in its defiance and strangeness. William Radice in his *Introduction to Tagore's Selected Short Stories* states, ". . . we find in Tagore's stories ample evidences of his reflections on child-marriage and dowry-system; bigoted orthodoxy or casteism; changing landlord-tenant relations; the political frustrations of a rising educated class; the growing gulf between town and country;

man's intimate relation with nature; ruinous litigation; dehumanising poverty; cruel and corrupt officialdom". These themes are handled with pathos and sympathy.

Tagore's characters are never sham beings. They are everyday men and women, and children whom he met in his life on the estate. His stories show a wide picture of veracity through which one can have a glimpse of the widest sections of society, like peasants, petty officials, poor workers, intelligentsia living in city and villages, impoverished landlords, Brahmin priests, petty traders and so on. Through these characters he shows life as it flows in the society. The characters have their own personalities. At the same time they are typical of the nineteenth century Bengal. The tragic conditions of women in all roles of life—wife, mother, daughter, sister—are drawn through a number of characters in his stories. The spineless intelligentsia of Bengal during his days makes central characters in some of his stories.

The protagonist in many of his stories is a petty, jaunty, egoistic person, who is changed and intensified by the events of the story, or by a story told to him by someone else. Tagore very often starts his stories with one or two characters seen as living men and women, moving about him: then he proceeds to tell about incidents in their lives, incidents separated, sometimes, by years. The technician of today would criticise this lack of unity of action. "But in these short stories it is the men [it is often the women], who matter and the reader is to be told as much about them as is possible within the limits of a short story".

The events in the stories are usually narrated in one of two ways—first person narration, or the omniscient spectator's or the third person narration. The former method is appealing to the reader because he is much closer to the heart of the leading character, and he is allowed to see the working of the protagonist's mind and heart. Tagore in his later stories used this method to focus the interest of the reader on one person and on everything that was nearest to him. When the narration is in third person there is perfect neutrality, and all experiences, including thoughts, are revealed by an all-knowing, invisible onlooker. In the transmission of others' speech and thought the omniscient narrator's task is easier than that of the protagonist. The protagonist finds it difficult to communicate whatever has not been said by him or to him. Tagore in his later stories used this technique of third person narration with maturity, and much space was given to thought processes, which he tried to understand and communicate.

Nature is depicted in Tagore's stories to fulfil various functions. As a lyrical poet he could feel the pulse of nature. That is why in most of his stories one finds an integral link between man and nature. A true picture of Bengal with all its natural beauties is presented to the readers through the stories. "The author ponders over the fate of those who live in the midst of this rich nature. Tagore could feel subtle nuances of the beauty of nature and link it with human life". Tagore uses nature for the creation of a particular mood. This element of nature gives his stories a poetic quality. Human feelings get deepened and completed as the author reveals them through nature. Nature plays a definite role in the plot of his stories. He is realistic in the portrayal of nature. "In the stories of Tagore nature often, as in real life, is an unconcerned witness of human drama". Unlike Wordsworth, he never tries to make nature lyrical or takes it as a shelter from worldly maladies.

The style of Tagore's stories is simple, terse and some are melodious. No attempt is there in the stories to make surprises for readers or to artificially reinforce certain special episodes. Similarly, one does not find the author's sudden intervention with comments or any authorial voice. Tagore does not idealise or exaggerate.

The characters in his stories are not distinguished men but they leave a lasting impression in our minds. Like all the classical works of art, his stories demand a deeper study from the readers that make the readers introspect.

In most of the stories of the first two decades Tagore used an artificial literary language. It was not the colloquial language of his characters. If he wanted to be realistic he would have to use at least half a dozen dialects. He had found in England that even though there were several dialects there, the students were taught only the literary language. Hence he preferred literary language in his stories.

Though many of his stories are available as translated into English by different scholars, they are never inferior to the original Bengali versions. As Jaya Chaliha wrote in *India Today*:

> The translators, well-known in their own spheres, capture the simplicity, pathos and poignancy of Tagore's prose, be it in descriptions of the daily life of the common man in the delta, the seasons, particularly the monsoon, women's emancipation, western occult studies and the changing pattern of urban social life in Victorian Bengal. They have put themselves behind the stories and each piece emerges as an individual frame woven together in a fine tapestry.

Though Tagore lived in the colonial period, he can be classified as a postcolonial writer. Many of his heroines and heroes try to uphold the noble values, culture, ethos, beliefs, traditions, rituals and practices of Hinduism and India, and are willing to sacrifice their lives for them.

Pathos is the main current of Tagore's short stories. Tagore of the poetry is a visionary and mystic whereas he is a realist in his short stories. Srinivasa Iyengar writes on the themes of Tagore's short stories, "The recurring theme of the stories is the 'tears in things,' the heartaches at the core of life; . . . the truth that defiles the lie, or the sheer mad thrill of pain. The old 'stale' tales of Mother Earth and Mother Humanity, the pity and poetry of it all, the poetry being the pity—no painstaking 'modernity' at all" (*Indian Writing in English* 71).

In addition to the realistic portrayal of men and society, one can hear the poetic voice of the author. The reader can feel the loving mind of the writer, his deep feeling for mankind. Almost all the stories of 1890's were full of pathos. The reason for it is obvious because Tagore was then living amidst the suffering, miserable, ordinary villagers. "Sympathetic and human attitude to human personality, to his suffering and happiness gives a deep lyrical characteristic to the stories of Tagore and Chekhov". In Tagore as well as in Chekhov the personal feelings of the heroes went beyond the narrow framework of personal life, and acquired a broader framework of the problem of humanity as such.

His obsession with pathos is not the result of his tragic vision of life or pessimism. He is highly optimistic in his poetry, especially in *Gitanjali*. He wrote a majority of his stories immediately after his marriage, when he did not have any personal problems in his life. Then what grieved him much might be the miseries of the people whom he met around him. He portrayed their lives realistically.

Tagore takes small incidents in social and domestic life. He finds rifts in apparently unbroken surface of life and loads them with life and emotions. The revelation at the end of a story comes unobtrusively and emphatically, and is held before the gaze of the reader.

One finds elements of naturalism in Tagore's short stories, and his realism is basically realism of feeling. This is what he felt he had clearly achieved, and this is why he was not prepared to dismiss as unrealistic even the supernatural stories—"Skeleton", "In the Middle of the Night", "The Hungry Stones" etc. Such stories are just as full of pathos, grief, anguish and terror as the more naturalistic tales. They are also full of humour and irony—and this is another aspect of his realism which is found in both his 'supernatural' and 'natural' stories. In many, the narrator of the tale is a gay, shallow, self-regarding individual, who is changed and deepened by the events of the story, or by a story told to him by someone else. This 'Ancient Mariner' technique is a particular characteristic of the supernatural tales as if Tagore wanted to juxtapose the fantastic and the other-worldly with the ordinary and realistic. The same tone is found even in the natural stories like *Kabuliwallah* (Cabuliwalah), *Sampadak* (The Editor) or *Thakurda* (The Babus of Nayanjore) and the author's capacity for skepticism, mockery and hard-hitting rationality contributed as much to his realism as does his awareness of grief, pain and suffering.

To understand Tagore's realism one has to go beyond naturalism to something deeper, into the exact nature of knowledge of the customs, agriculture, dialect and religion of the villagers who were his tenants. In many ways his rural characters are generalised rather than specific and the language they speak is standard Bengali: only very rarely does he attempt to give his dialogue a truly peasant flavour. It has been said by some critics that his characteristic view of East Bengal was, as if it were 'through a window' of his houseboat: the life of the people passed before his eyes like the banks of Padma, distanced by his status of *zamindar*, his aristocratic lineage and mien, his refinement and education. He could never really know the ordinary people, and his stories are unrealistic as a result. This charge the author vigorously denied. In a speech at a felicitation ceremony in 1940 he said:

> "People have often ganged up against me to say: 'He is a rich man's son. He was born—as the English put it—'with a silver spoon in his mouth'. How can he know about villages?" But I can honestly say that those who say that know less than I do. How can they know anything? Conventional wisdom isn't true knowledge. In true knowledge there is love: the heartfelt love with which I have observed village life has opened the door for me. It might sound like boasting, but I would say that very few writers in Bengal have looked at their country with as much feeling as I have.

The importance of short stories and novels of Tagore is great, because here the scope for presentation of the problems of life, man-woman relationship and their possible solutions is far greater, and as a matter of fact, he has been able to portray his feminist outlook and his modernist point of view on women's progress in the social set-up of his own times against the context of the age old patriarchal concept of practice. This book focuses on the female protagonists of Tagore's few select short stories, with a view to analysing these women characters in the light of their emotional possibilities in the drab, unromantic milieu of domestic life.

Tagore's stories teem with people of various hues, men and women of homogeneous nature and contrary attitudes, of strong bearing and weak standpoints. There are egregious women and indifferent men, loving wives and cruel husbands, surrogate mothers and greedy fathers. All these definitely make an interesting picture of different shades. His short stories have definite feminist tilt. The problem of the women—physical, mental, circumstantial—have caught his attention. His mind was exercised over the question of women's emancipation since quite a few years before his epoch making short story *Streer Patro* (The Wife's Letter) was published in *Sabujpatra* (A Journal). There were scathing attacks from almost all corners of the society—his views were at once denounced a 'progressivist thinking of the West'.

At the outset of the twentieth century, the middle-class society of the urban Bengal had swayed with a force of 'Individualism'. From this life-force had evolved the desire of independent existence for the woman. The independence from the age-old traditions imposed only on the fair-sex by the patriarchal society, the freedom of thinking and fantasising, the sexual freedom—all became inevitable results of the twentieth century concept of individualism.

Tagore wielded his bludgeon and portrayed Mrinal of *Streer Patro* (The Wife's Letter) in the anti-establishment bravura image, the near catastrophic image of Binodini, the young love-starved widow of *Chokher Bali* (The Eyesore), the rebel-woman Damini of *Chaturanga* (The Four Aspects), the fatalist motherly love of Dakshyani in *Taraprosonner Kirti* (Taraprasanna's Achievement), the silently rebellious image of Anila of *Poila Number* (The Number One). Most of the Stories of Tagore have clear gender orientation and they are *Streer Patro* (The Wife's Letter), *Protihingsha* (The Revenge), *Ghater Katha* (The River Stairs), *Samapti* (The Conclusion), *Denapowna* (Dowry), *Haimanthi* (Haimanthi), *Aparichita* (The Unknown Woman), *Tyag* (The Sacrifice), *Manbhajan* (Breaking of the Ice), *Nastaneer* (The Broken Nest), *Madhyabartini* (The In-Between Girl), *Shashti* (The Punishment), *Drishtidaan* (Restoring the Eyesight), *Bostomi* (The Vaishnava Woman), *Subha* (Subha), *Subhadrishti* (The Auspircious Vision), *Jibito O Mrito* (The Living or Dead), *Didi* (The Elder Sister), *Samapti* (The End), *Khata* (The Exercise Book), *Anadhikar Probesh* (The Tesspassing), *Rabibar* (Sunday),

Laboratory (Laboratory), *Prayashchitto* (The Penance), *Bicharok* (The Judge), *Adhyapak* (The Professor), *Rashmoneer Chele* (Rashmonee's Son), *Shesher Ratri* (The Last Night), *Mushalmanir Galpo* (The Story of a Muslim Woman), *Jogajog* (Communication), *Postmaster* (The Postmaster), *Mashi* (The Aunt), *Damini* (Damini) *Aekti Namnjoor Galpa* (An Unapproved Story), *Sanskar* (Reform), *Ramkanayer Nirbudhdhita* (Ramkanai's Folly), *Thakurda* (Babus of Nayajore), *Taraprasanner Kirthi* (Taraprasanna's Fame) and these stories suffice to study the great storyteller's understanding of the women's emotions, their feelings and, above all, the pain and suffering that the patriarchal society inflict on them.

Tagore's representation of women is pre-eminently feminist but non-reformist, especially in the post *Sabujpatra* phase of writing. Tagore is not a feminist by tag. Society's centuries-old conservatism which dies hard against change is attacked in his writings at the slightest opportunities and, his writings—all genres—mirror the condition of women who live in the male-dominated patriarchal society.

He was already criticised for the highbrow angle of his writings, and in a poem a he confesses to his alleged lack of rapport with the masses being relegated to the narrow window-side position of honour in the high stratum of the society. The allegation regarding the absence of the picture of those living in the lowest stratum of social hierarchy cannot be totally denied. He came in contact with the people from all the rungs of the society during his Selidah stay, and he in his various letters and interviews and comments on the stories gave the following explanation:

> To begin with I only wrote poetry—I didn't write stories. One day my father called me and said, 'I want you to take charge of the estates.' I was astonished. I was a poet, a scribbler—what

> did I know about such matters? But father said, 'Never mind that—I want you to do it.' What could I do? Father had ordered me, so I had to go. Managing the 'jamidari' gave me the opportunity to mix with various kinds of people, and this was how my story-writing began. (Found in the Appendix to Pramathanath Bishi's study of Tagore's short stories, *Rabindranather Chota Galpa*, Calcutta 1954)

Tagore wrote over 90 short stories during his long and abundant literary career. In the essay called *Sahityabichar* (Appreciating Literature) in *Sahityer Swarup* (What is Literature?) he writes:

> Now it is time I gave a reply to those who complain that they fail to find any trace of middle—classism in my writings... Once month after month, I wrote stories on village life. I believe, before that, pictures of village life were not published in a systematic form in Bengali literature. At that time there was no dearth of middleclass writers, but almost all of them were not engrossed in contemplation of Pratap Singh or Pratapaditya. I am afraid, one day *Galpaguccha* would be found untouchable as bad literature for its association with a 'bourgeois writer.'

Tagore's prediction about *Galpaguccha* came to be untrue, for even more than a half century after his death; his short stories have not lost their appeal and relevance. The fact is that middleclass life comes alive through the pages of *Galpaguccha*, and his perception of this middle class life at that time reveals a social consciousness which, instead of cutting out any reformist image for him, is concerned with the ills that plagued the society. His object is to point out the defects and rouse people's conscience.

In the stories, Tagore has portrayed social problems and their impact on the life of individual, the interaction of the individual and the family, the fight of the individual to free himself from the numerous ill-begotten customs and many such problems afflicting the life of the individual and society. He was specially committed to the short story during the 1890s and 59 stories belong to this period. From 1891 to 1895 he wrote 44 i.e., almost one story a month. From 1896-97 and again in 1899, he stopped writing short stories but interest in storytelling was sustained in the narrative and dramatic poems of *Katha O Kahini* (Lyrics and Tales). He wrote these stories basically for the periodicals with which he was associated and the readership demanded them. Most of the Bangla literature of the nineteenth century reached out to its readers through these periodicals.

The leading literary figure of the 1870s and 1880s, Bankim Chandra Chatterjee, established new artistic, intellectual standards in his journal *Bangadarshan* serialising his novels in it. Tagore also contributed to this thereby establishing his name in the Calcutta's literary magazine culture. His flair for writing the short stories found an easy outlet in a number of journals—*Hitabadi*, *Sadhana*, *Bharathi*, *Prabasi*, *Sabujpatra* etc. some of which he himself edited. It was in *Hitabadi* that he started writing short stories. In his own words: "The journal called *Hitabadi* was born before *Sadhana*.... In that journal I wrote a short story every week, reviews and literary essays. My short story writing began in that journal. I wrote for six week". (In a letter written to Padmini Mohan Neogi, 1928)

Thirty-six of Tagore's short stories were published in *Sadhana*. He would not have written them at all if the magazine had not existed. His story-writing paused when it closed down and revived again when he reluctantly became the editor of another monthly journal, *Bharathi*, from May 1898 to April 1899. In an interview given in 1935, when asked about the background of his short stories, he replied:

> It was when I was quite young that I began to write short stories. Being a landlord I had to go to villages, and thus I came in touch with village people and their simple modes of life. I enjoyed the surrounding scenery and beauty of rural Bengal.

> The river system of Bengal, the best part of this province, fascinated me and I used to be quite familiar with those rivers. I got glimpses into the life of the people, which appealed to me very much indeed. At first I was quite unfamiliar with the village life as I was born and brought up in Calcutta and so there was an element of mystery for me. My whole heart went out to the simple village people as I came in close contact with them. They seemed to belong to quite another world, so very different from that of Calcutta. My earlier stories have this background, and they describe this contact of mine with the village people. They have the freshness of youth. Before I had written these short stories there was not anything of that type in Bengali literature. No doubt Bankimchandra had written some stories but they were of the romantic type; mine were full of the temperament of the rural people.... There is a note of universal appeal in them, for man is the same everywhere. My later stories haven't got that freshness, that tenderness of the earlier stories.

This explanation which Tagore gave of the origins of his short stories has been widely accepted by Bengali readers and critics. This is somewhat true and the readers of the marvellous letters that he wrote describing his life as manager of the family estates will find passages that relate quite exactly to characters, feelings and places in the short stories.

But some of the passages quoted often as the sources for the short stories do not seem to be sources at all. Many of the characters in the stories are "not simple village people", but of the middle or gentry class. Some are more urban than rural; some are supernatural fantasies; and many of them contradict Tagore's statement that he had 'no social or political problems in mind' when he wrote them. There is no doubt his stay at Selidah was crucial to his emotional, intellectual and spiritual development. This unmapped village at the confluence of two great branches of the Ganges was his headquarters during some of his most fruitful periods as a writer. (Here in 1912 he began the translations that won him the Nobel Prize.)

His pantheism, his involvement with rural economic improvement, his dislike of the city, his calls for Hindu-Muslim unity, his interest in folk-literature and the songs of wandering mendicants, were all rooted in these vital years away from the cultured but yet oppressive atmosphere of Jorasanko, the Tagore house in Calcutta, popularly known as *Thakurbari*. He recalls the realities of his life on the estate with and without his family in Selidah, and he typically uses in almost his every third sentence the Bangla word *sukh* (happiness) and *dukh* (sadness). These are frequent words in his writings, and the concordant and rhythmic compound *sukhe-dukhe* (in happiness and sadness) often trips off his tongue in poems and songs.

Critics charged him of 'poeticised stories' and no wonder he was stung! In May 1941, in a conversation with Buddhadeva Bose, one of the leading Bangla critics of the 1930s, he stressed with some pain that his stories were true to life:

> I have written innumerable short lyrics—maybe no other poet in the world has written so many—but I feel surprised when you say that my stories are over poetical. At one time I used to rove down Bengal's rivers, and I observed the wonderful way of life of Bengal's villages. I would say there is no lack of realism in my stories. I wrote from what I saw, what I felt in my heart—my direct experience. Those who say that my stories are fanciful are wrong. Maybe one could say that in stories such as '*Skeleton*' or 'The Hungry Stones' imagination predominates, but not completely even in those. (ibid. 312)

Defenders of Tagore have taken pains to point out the close observation that does indeed lie behind many of the characters, scenes and situations in his stories—the vivid picture of Bengal that is found in them. Buddhadeva Bose himself, for example, in a fine essay on Tagore's short stories, wrote:

> All of Bengal can be found here. Not only facts, but her living soul: we feel her pulse as we turn the pages of *Galpoguchcha.* Her changing seasons, the vital flow of her rivers, her plains, her bamboo-grooves, her festival canopies and chariots; her cool, moist, richly fertile fragrance; her mischievous, noisy, lively boys and girls; her kind, skilled, intelligent women...

Other critics have pointed to the accuracy of the stories as social documents. For Tagore the spirit has two facets. On one hand it is enormously rich ever-changing; it is powerful, frightening and awesome as well as beautiful; and it manifests itself in the abundance and creativity of Nature and the endless variety and complexity of human life. On the other hand, Spirit is something very still, quiet and simple. In his poems written during the 1890s we find both the dimensions; the elaborate poems such as *Basundhara* (Earth) or *Urbasi* or *Manasundari* (Lady of the Mind), in which the *jiban-debata* (Life-God) is identified with the Spirit of Poetry and is given the female form that he always preferred. His book *Ksanika* (The Flitting One, 1900) is devoted throughout to the uncatchable and transient nature of the Spirit. But the other quieter side is conveyed in a poem *Achal Smriti* (Unmoving Memory) in *Sonar Tari* (The Golden Boat, 1894) in which he speaks of a 'still silence'. In a letter the refreshing beauty of the weather after rain gives him the same feeling:

> All my work and all my dealings with people feel very easy. Actually, everything is simple. There is one straight road—if you open your eyes you can go along it. I don't see the need to search for all sorts of clever short cuts. Happiness and sadness are both on the road—there is no road that avoids them—but peace is found only on this road, nowhere else.

Tagore expresses in his stories the deep spiritual bond that he felt with rural Bengal. His realism rather than naturalism, his idealism at the level of style and expression and content operated at the level of feeling. Even if there had been a mature tradition of short story writing in Bangla, and even if the great French and Russian masters had been available to him as models, his stories would probably still have been vulnerable, would still have the mixed perceptive and ingenuous, the realistic with the idealised, the rhetorical with the plain, and the sophisticated with the jejune. His nature demanded it. He was never a writer who could learn from others: his own Life-God (*jiban-debata*) had a relentless grip on him. His stories—not only in their content but in their overall character and 'feel'—belong not wholly to the prosaic real, not wholly to the poetic ideal either, but to the Ghat (cemented steps on the banks of a river or pond) where the two meet: sometimes happily (for the ghat is a place of welcome and homecoming as well as parting) sometimes more uneasily. He may be looked upon as the eternal child who constructs and then breaks, and derives pleasure out of this off-track game of creativity.

The novel, at its peak as a form, is one that deals primarily with society, usually in prose, and studies on a vast and wide canvas the minds of individuals, interpersonal relationships, settings, themes, moods, atmosphere, milieu, characters, and the inseparable twins, plot and story. The modern novel recognises and records the rapid changes brought about in the human psyche and society by historical happenings since the Enlightenment. The novel is defined by its length, primarily, and has the elements of style, characterisation and conflict. It is larger in canvas than the short story, the novella etc. It is descriptive and expands the narrative. Traditional novels have plots that supposedly follow the Freytag's pyramid of exposition, initial incident, rising action, climax, falling action and resolution, in some manner or the other. Antecedents include the roman a clef, the epistolary novel, Pamela, the picaresque narrative, Don Quixote, the serialised one, Oliver Twist, and even Tristram Shandy by Sterne for experimentation in language etc. One cannot forget women novelists like Austen or the Bronte sisters or the great realists like Stendhal, Balzac, Hugo, Hardy and Flaubert followed by Woolf, James Joyce, Faulkner, Hemingway and Steinbeck et al. In India defintely the impetus for writing great novels came from Russia as much as from Britian or America or Europe and there is no doubt that the first major novels came out of Bengal, particularly ones like *Ananda Math* by Bankim Chandra Chatterjee and *Gora* by Tagore. What is amazing about these novels is that the ferment of the times; meaning the fight against colonialism and for independence and for India's formation as a new state led, as is usual in history, to some of the best literature in the world. These were produced in India in the regional tongues, especially Bengali, because of the suffering the times inflicted on one and despite it, against the grain and against all odds. Colossal things were attempted and carried out successfully, in panoramic novels, with the influence of Romanticism evident in them and not just of contemporary history or of ancient learning. India even had women novelists like Swarnakumari Devi, Krupabai Sathianadhan. But Tagore's novels ruled the roost, another example of which would be his creation of novels like *Noukadubi* (Wreck).

The novella is presumably slightly more French, modern and American in origin or formation; its primary indicator being again length; shorter than a novel and longer than a short story. But the most important aspect is the limited canvas here, the delineation has to be finely done by reducing the number of characters, yet not sticking only to the two or three a classic short story requires, not playing around too much with plural points of view or themes or settings or trying to have more than one plot, not having too much of description or psychological analysis of motives and intentions etc, though conflict should not be avoided. The best examples of the novella are, according to many, Hemingway's classic *Old Man and the Sea*, Henry James's *Turn of the Screw*, Steinbeck's *Of Mice and Men*, Dostoevsky's *The Double*, Andre Gide's *Immoralist*, and Hermann Hesse's *Siddhartha* etc. Here too, Tagore with his *Nastaneer* (The Broken Nest), *Dui Bon* (Two Sisters) and *Malancha* (The Garden and the Gardener) could rival the best in his own inimitable manner as did V.M. Basheer in Kerala, later.

Works Cited

Basu, Sankar: *Chekhov and Tagore: A Comparative Study of their Short Stories*. New Delhi: Sterling Publications Private Limited, 1985, p.100.

Buddhadeva, Bose: *Prabandha Samkalan*, Calcutta, 1966, p.60.

Chaliha, Jaya: "Tales from Tagoreana." *India Today*, 10 July 2000. Print.

Collected Short Stories of O. Henry: Rupa & Co. 2000.

Collin, A.S.: *English Literature of the Twentieth Century*.

Dutta, Krishna and Robinson, Andrew: *The Myriad-minded Man: Rabindranath Tagore*, Rupa & Co., 2003, p.102.

Ghosh, J.C.: *Bengali Vocabulary*, p.4.

Iyengar, K. R. Srinivasa: *Indian Writing in English*, Asia Publishing House, 1973, p.34.

____ : *Indian Writing in English*, New Delhi: Sterling Publishers Private Limited, 2001. Print.

Radice, William: *Rabindranath Tagore: Selected Short Stories*, Penguin Books, 1994, p.10.

Sidhanta, Nirmalkumar: "Rabindranath's Short Stories." *Rabindranath Tagore: 1861-1961: A Centenary Volume*. New Delhi: Sahitya Akademi, 1961.p.290.

Tagore, Rabindranath: *Chinnapatrabali* (*The Torn Leaves*), Letter No. 57, 21 June 1892.

____ : *Galpaguchcha*, Vol.IV, *Granthaparichaya*, p.306.

The interview was published in *Forward Magazine*, 23 February 1935.

3

The Female Protagonists and the Social Taboos

The manor house in which Gurudev was born consisted of two main houses. Debendranath and descendants occupied number 6, his younger brother Girindranath and his family occupied number 5. There was another three-storeyed building which was basically built by Prince Dwarkanath to entertain guests. Later, after the death of the younger brother in 1854, it was occupied by his two grandsons, the renowned artists Gaganendranath and Abanindranath. The younger brother of Debendranath performed the idolatrous funeral ceremony for Prince Dwarkanath when Debendranath refused. It was Girindranath who took charge of the household deity brought to Jorasanko. Number 5 was thus more traditional and orthodox in religious matters and the occupants were idol-worshippers, contrasted to the Brahmos in number 6.

The house members lived affably and Tagore's memoirs belong almost as much to number 5 as they do in number 6. In his *Chelebela* (My Boyhood Days, 1940), he draws no distinctions between the two houses. There was a great influence of the families (of number 5 and 6) on his mind. He exercised extreme reserve relating to any tensions of 'joint family' life in his writing. His short stories, novels and poems revolve around family life and teem with people from all over humanity.

Tagore's short stories give an incomplete idea of his genius as a story-teller. He is basically a lyric poet and his stories have remarkable consciousness of this lyrical mysticism. His stories are a combination of rich emotionalism with lyrics, mysticism with elements of surprise and shock. Sometimes there is 'twist in the tail' too.

Tagore never referred to his wife in *My Reminiscences*. "I was married",: was all that he wrote and avoided private and personal references. Moreover, he never candidly dedicated any book to her, only wrote a very few poems explicitly about her. He wrote in *My Reminiscences* about the emptiness in his life:

> Emptiness is a thing man cannot bring himself to believe in: that which is not, is untrue, that which is untrue, is not.

In fact, there is no record of when Tagore's family's hunt for Tagore's bride began. But in early September 1883, Tagore was beckoned by his father Debendranath from the hills—and there is no confirmation what transpired but Tagore's wedding was fixed within three weeks and the girl was a 10-year-old child of an employee on the Tagore Estates. Tagore agreed without even meeting her.

The unadorned and plain wedding in a Brahmo manner was carried out and he wrote to Priyonath Sen, one of his close friends, in his invitation: "his intimate relative Rabindranath Tagore is to be married"—implying that the real Rabindranath was detached from the event of his marriage. He got married to Bhabataini (later named Mrinalini) on 9 December 1883. Soon after his marriage, his poems dedicated to Kadambari Devi (written earlier) were published in 1884 as *Chabi O Gaan* (Picture and Songs). One poem entitled *Rahur Prem* (The Love of Rahu) concerned *Rahu*, a popular demon in Hindu mythology. *Rahu* is a bodiless planet in love with the moon. *Rahu* always hounds her and occasionally gulps her in an eclipse.

Two months after the publication, Kadambari Devi committed suicide, with an overdose of opium. The news of her death was suppressed on the orders of Debendranath to avoid scandal. For Tagore there could be no suppression. Kadambari's death was the first of a person he had deeply cared for. Her death became his constant companion—as at the age of 23, the experience was world-crushing.

Tagore's works intensified in depth and enhanced in quality by Kadambari's death. Later almost all his woman protagonists carried the impression of Kadambari. They were modelled on her extroversion, and even most of his heroines are childless like her. Kadambari was childless, unlike her sisters-in-law but like Charulatha of *Nastaneer* (The Broken Nest), Mrinal of *Streer Patro* (The Wife's Letter) like Harasundari of *Madhyabartini* (The In-Between Girl), Anila of *Poila Number* (The Number One), Giribala of *Maanbhajan* (Breaking of Ice), Chandra of *Shasthi* (The Punishment), Kumudini of *Drishtidaan* (Restoring the Eyesight) and the list goes on or probably Tagore wanted to arouse pity in the reader's mind by making his heroines childless or probably it was unintentional. Even in the *Old Testament*, Abrahams's wife Sarah remained barren into old age. Sarah gave her Egyptian maidservant, Hagar, as concubine to Abraham. Hagar became pregnant and Ishmael was born. This can even be seen as one of the patriarchal superiority and advantages that the male-dominated society likes to have over the fair sex and motherhood is seen as fulfillment of womanhood.

Anila in *Poila Number* (The Number One) breaks away from the confines of home into the uncharted and unknown future. Adwaitacharan's (Anila's husband) continued indifference to her psycho-physical needs leads to the tragedy of husband-wife rupture. The final offer of assistance, which is platonic in its essence, by Sitangshumouli, is slighted because the offer is hardly recuperative of the waste of whole span of a conjugal bliss. Similarly, the final ill-orchestrated re-union between Bhupati and Charu cannot ensure unalloyed happiness.

The indifference of Gopinath to the budding youth of his wife, Giribala, in *Manbhanjan* (The Breaking of Ice) results in Giribala's exit into the free world of theatre. First she waits for her husband's return but later she realises that his infatuation for the theatre artiste Labanga is more and there is no other way to attract him towards her. Therefore she leaps into the world of theatre. In order to take revenge on her uncaring husband she joins the same theatrical group which is the centre of Gopinath's attraction.

This is no sedating solution for distanced/estranged wives. In those days theatres were not respectable centres for women's refuge. But Tagore opts for this solution on the 'pay-you-back-in-your-own-coin' formula, for Gopinath's chief intoxication lies in Labanga of Gandharva Theatre. Giribala's emancipation is the first step of Tagore's experimentation with women's empowerment. He was bold enough to show women going out of the household barricades either to relaise their dreams or teach their men a lesson or just simply to be with the men they love. Charu is the precursor of Mrinal of *Streer Patro* and women of her ilk. Anila of *Poila Number*, Kalyani of *Aparichita*—are the products of Tagore's rationalistic thinking that upholds itself in his '*Sabujpatra*' phase.

Tagore's socio-familial concept took a new turn as he began to probe the husband-wife relationship within the joint family set-up. He was evasive about family life. He was devoted to his wife and children, but he saw them less as individuals and entities than as part of the greater cause to which he felt dedicated. Mrinalini was 11 years his junior; moreover she did not live long enough for him to fully understand that it is not fair for a poet to expect his wife to be his soul-mate. He wrote a letter to her in December 1900:

> If you and I could be comrades in all our work and in all our thoughts it would be splendid, but we cannot attain all that we desire.

The period of late 1898 to mid 1901 was the only one period in which Tagore, his wife and all the children lived as a family. Before that, he lived in Selidah, they in Calcutta. Later his elder daughter Bela was married and moved away to Bihar. The following year, in 1902, Mrinalini died. She spent long periods in Jorasanko; she did not share Tagore's love for villages, particularly Selidah, and the rivers of East Bengal. She was only relieved to have escaped it as she had grown up in a village.

There were other factors that weakened his ties with Selidah. Three grandsons of Debendranath's brother Girindranath were of age now and were entitled to a share of Dwarkanath's bequest. After the court-case in 1897, the Shahzadpur estate and some other lands were transferred to them, and Debendranath's final will of 1899 laid down further divisions. Tagore kept the Birahimpur (Selidah) estate until 1921, then it passed to Satyendranath's son Surendranath; but long before then his interests had shifted to Santiniketan, where his unique experiment in education and community living was inaugurated by the foundation of the Santiniketan Ashram in 1901. His visits to the region he had loved so much became more and more infrequent. In a letter to his wife written towards the end of 1901, we witness the closing of a chapter it is interesting to note the sense of desolation in the following poetic lines:

> I find it very poignant to be back here at Selidah. Its human nature always to find what we are about to leave more beautiful. I associate Selidah with both happy and sad memories—but more of them happy than sad. This is not, though, the best time to be here. Everything is soaked in dew, there is mist until eight o'clock in the morning, and in the evening there is fog. The water is very low in the well and the pond-malaria is widespread. We were right to leave Selidah: the children would have fallen ill if we had stayed. Bolpur is much purer and healthier. But what masses of roses are in bloom! Huge, beautiful roses! And there's a lovely smell of acacia-flowers all around. Your old friend Selidah sends you a few acacia-flowers with this letter.

Undoubtedly, there was a void, a blankness formed in the heart of Tagore which finally gave vent to his feelings in the following account:

> When clouds gather in your heart, their shadow falls on your writing. Your innermost words fall like a shower in *Shraban* (the monsoon month). But nobody will like a piece of rainy-season writing. Whatever may be in my mind, I don't want it to block my readers' sunshine.

In "Haimanti", Tagore has shown the tiresome drudgery, travails and tribulations of a girl who has not brought sufficient dowry to her husband's home. The girl ultimately dies without any medical care. Haimanti dies a slow death by making a firm protest. Most notable thing is the inaction of the husband who flies the coop and fails to fend in front of the mercurial obduracy and obstinacy of his father when the latter refuses to send the daughter-in-law with her father. Her husband is a spineless and weak-kneed young man whocan show no resistance to his parent's will. Men of such ilk are found in every society irrespective of education and civilisation. When his father-in-law is humiliated by his own father and Haimanti's mind turns into a stone, he pleads only feebly with his father to permit him to take Haima to her father's house. Though he knew that his parents were unfair and cruel to his wife but he could not utter a word of protest; could not stand beside his wife. Tagore has said somewhere, "Anyay je kare ar anyay je sahe, tábo ghrina jaeno tare trinosamo dahe" and in English it goes like this, "Those who mete out or tolerate cruelty done unto others, your hatred should incinerate them like drygrass." Haimanti's husband, by failing to stand by his wife, becomes an equal partner in the crime.

Haima's father goes back without his daughter this time being made sure that he would not have to return to fetch his daughter home. Haima dies a slow death and compensates for her father's lack of wealth with her own life.

Tagore's mind was exercised over one of the major evils of the society; the question of dowry and its tragic consequences—the torture, distress and suffering inflicted on the daughters of the indigent and insolvent fathers in their in-laws' houses often result in their deaths. He wrote in *Probashi*: "I have seen… the unredeemed animosity of the mother against the daughter-in-law… .' The picture of the in-laws' house with all control vested in the father-in-law and the sharp-tongued mother-in-law left a deep impression on his mind. *Sasurbari* (the in-law's house) is synonymous with prison. Hence he draws very shocking picture of torture and death in the in-law's house of a girl whose impoverished father fails to provide sufficient dowry for the daughter. *Denapowna* (Dowry) is not an account of Nirupama's woes alone but of the thousands of such hapless and wretched girls whose fathers fail to meet the avid demands of dowry of the in-laws. The following extract from the story indicates the suffering and torment inflicted on Nirupama or such helpless girls through the centuries:

> Nobody cares even for the basic necessities of the daughter-in-law, like food and clothing. If any kind-hearted neighbor mentions some lapse, the mother says, 'This is quite enough!' In other words, if her father paid in full, the daughter would have received cent per cent care. Everybody behaves in a way as if the daughter-in-law has no right here, as if she has entered the household through fraud. (Translated)

But Nirupama's sense of self-respect is aroused when her father brings money by selling his house. Nirupama raises her voice of protest though she dies:

> Niru said, "If you make any payment of money, it amounts to insult (of mine). Do you think your daughter has no dignity? Am I a money-purse only, that as long as there is money, I have value! No father, please don't insult me by giving them the money. Moreover my husband doesn't want it." (Translated)

The irony and sarcasm lies in the last lines of the story where the mother writes to her son about his imminent second marriage which will fetch a dowry of twenty thousand rupees and that too in cash this time!

Tagore's family life too was not free from problems. There were a lot of emotional tides and undertides that flowed within the Jorasanko Mansion. Most of the tension centred on the women. The women themselves were in many cases very intransigent and unbending. A sister-in-law of Tagore remembered in her old age that as a new dark-skinned bride from Jessore, she had been cleansed with a brew by maidservants at the instruction of her mother-in-law (Debendranath's wife, Sharada), in the hope of lightening her skin tone. Another sister-in-law, Tagore's favourite, suffered relentlessly from the unkind and caustic remarks of other women in the household. In general, the women of Tagore household, when evaluated against other relatively well-educated Bengali women of their time, could not be said to have been especially progressive or enlightened. They too were preys of jealousy, smallness and malice like any other womankind.

The Tagore family was conventional and old-fashioned in many matters. Women of the family underwent a lot of tensions and emotional ups and downs which young Rabindranath could feel very well. This must have been another reason for him to stand by Kadambari when the women of the family turned against her.

In *Aparichita* (The Unknown Woman), a rare instance of courage and bravado is shown by Shombhunath Sen, father of a would-be-bride, Kalyani, who teaches the would-be-groom's shameless dowry-hungry guardian the right lesson by refusing to give his daughter in marriage to the groom because his (the groom's) maternal uncle examines the accuracy of the weight of Kalyani's ornaments. But on a strong, disparaging note, Shombhunath Sen, the harried father says:

> I can't give my daughter in marriage to a family which thinks that I have stolen my daughter's ornaments. (Translated)

An adherent of truth and self-righteousness like Mr. Shombhunath Sen, Ramkanai, the old harassed husband and alienated father in *Ramkanaiyer Nirbuddhita* (The Folly of Ramkanai) upholds justice and truth in the forgery case against his own son by giving evidence in favour of his widowed sister-in-law who gets her dead husband's properties, movable and immovable, as decreed in the latter's dying will.

The women depicted in the story are avaricious, acquisitive and they have least respect for their husbands that we encounter in our families. Tagore captures the family feud over a dying will, and Ramkanai pays up for his sin of telling the truth instead of telling the tutored lies in front of the magistrate, and putting his own son behind the bars, with his own life. Tagore successfully pitches women against women in his stories. He shows them as goddesses juxtaposing them against the cruel and merciless one and that is how the storyteller strikes the balance and there lies his uniqueness.

The dowry system with its dreadful offshoots handed down from a feudal past so profoundly intrigued Tagore's mind that in the story like "Aparichita" he untangles the vulnerability of a feudalistic mindset which does not recoil at robbing the sacramental bond of marriage of all decency and dignity. The bridegroom's maternal uncle, weighing and testing the purity of the bride's ornaments, conforms to an ugly piece of the feudalistic marriage system in which the bride is looked upon as nothing more than money-fetching tool. The breakdown of many marriages at the ceremony itself because of non-fulfilment of dowry commitments is not rare even today. But, side by side, with this picture of ugliness Tagore presents another picture—that of self-dignity, first on the part of bride's father, Shombhunath Sen who refuses to give his daughter in marriage to a member of such mean-minded family, and then, Kalyani remains lifelong a spinster by way of protest against such an ugly insult. Here, in the story, Kalyani's role as a daughter who readily agrees and abides by her father's action is rendered in a strong, individualistic image by the author.

If Kalyani's spinster-ship and devotion to social work as the mission of her life is a silent but meaningful protest against the ugliness of the vicious dowry system, Anila's flight from home is a silent but forceful protest against the neglect of her bookworm husband, Adwaitacharan. Haimanti's litany of woes in "Haimanti" does not break the beat of this continuum of a progressive picture of the *Sabujpatra* phase of Tagore's writings, for her individuality is not less pronounced in the story. His vehement rejection of the evils rooted in our social practices and rituals is evident in these stories.

Kusum of *Tyag* (Abandonment) is a lower-caste woman given in marriage to an upper-caste boy Hemanta by her foster-father to settle an old score with Hemanta's father. But, Hemanta who loves his wife dearly, is one of the young men who displays a rare and strong determination and unbending mental strength in standing his ground against the age-old customs and so-called traditions. Hemanta, a dissenter, a young man, a representative of the rising generation refuses to submit to the set patterns of casteism. He becomes a solid bedrock support to his lower-caste wife Kusum because he places love above caste. The author's portraiture of Kusum as a begging, repentant, meek observer is true to life and not fancy-fed. She is helpless and does not have anyone other than Hemanta in the world and she is ready to accept what fate decides for her. In a dramatic way, Tagore writes:

> Again the sound of slippers was heard. Harihar Mukherjee came near the door and called out, Much time has elapsed, I can allow you no more time. Kick out the girl from the room."
>
> As soon as Kusum heard this voice, she pressed Hemanta's both legs with double urgency for a lifetime fulfilment of desire in one single-moment, kissed his feet, took the dust off them on her head and let them go.
>
> Hemanta rose up to his father and said, "I'll not abandon my wife… . I do not observe caste prejudice." "Then you too get out." (Translated)

Hemanta is a member of the upcoming rebel group that goes against the rigid norms of feudalistic father—the protagonist of the story *Tyag* refuses to submit to the parental fatwa of abandoning his wife Kusum because of her lower-caste. Tagore's abhorrence of caste prejudice is not less pronounced in this story.

In some other short stories Tagore touches, sometimes sarcastically, upon some other evils of the society born out of blind customs and unhealthy traditions. The pious concept of the sanctity of the precincts of a Hindu temple is treated, rather satirically, in the story entitled *Anadhikar Prabesh* (The Tresspassing) in which Jaikali, the sanctity-conscious widow owner-custodian of Lord Radhanath temple, gives shelter to a young pig inside the sanctum of the shrine to save it from a rushing group of Doms (lower caste people). The last sentence of the story contains the satirical tone of Tagore:

> The Supreme Lord of living beings was much pleased at this insignificant incident, but the small locality's much smaller god called Society, became very much excited. (Translated)

In this story, Tagore has portrayed Jaikali as an extremely rigid, strict, superstitious and heartless woman who gives severe punishment to one of her orphaned nephews for breaking the fence of the temple. Jaikali loves a pig and saves it from the Doms, but as irony would have it, she locks up a human child in a dark room without any food and water the whole day and night mercilessly. The portraiture of a woman with manly traits who goes to the extreme ends in whatever she does is a very true-to-life characterisation.

A short while before his death Tagore wrote a story called *Musalmanir Galpa* (The Tale of a Muslim Woman) in which he twists the untouchability theme with theme of communal prejudice. Kamala, saved by the old saintly samaritan, Habir Khan, from being waylaid by the notorious bandit, Madhumallar and his men, while on her way to her in-laws' house in her nuptial dress and finery, is accompanied by her newly-married husband and guards. But later as she is refused entry into her uncle's household, she marries Habir's second son and even later saves her uncle's daughter from a similar plight, when she is on her way to her in-laws' house. The story is significant because Kamala, in her changed vision of life, echoes *Gora's* (hero of Tagore's most famous prose fiction *Gora*) view of a casteless society:

> The god who has given me shelter is my god—he is neither Hindu, nor Muslim. I worship him for that honour of love. (Translated)

In *Namanjur Galpa* (Unapproved Story) and *Sanskar* (Reform) expose the self-delusion and false humanism of the so-called patriots and social workers. In the first story the social worker/ patriot Anil's love for Amiya, the college girl-turned worker of the non-cooperation movement evaporates when he is apprised of her birth story and in the second, Kalika refuses to give a lift in her car to a sweeper because of his calling.

Although these stories have a message against casteism and untouchability, there is depiction of women characters who are strong individuals with élan and impulsiveness.

In *Protihingsha* (The Revenge) the strong portraiture of Indrani, a strong-willed woman who does not have property matching her husband's master (where he works as accounts manager), takes revenge with her audacity and determination.

Indrani is always conscious of her high caste, and around her there is such import that when she refuses to have food at her husband's employer's house, the insult becomes inevitable. The lady of the house ill-treats her by making her conscious that her husband is one of their employees. An insulted Indrani comes back and vows to take revenge at the appropriate time.

The wheel of the fortune turns away. Ambikacharan (Indrani's husband) is dismissed from service by the lady of the house. But when Ambikacharan's absence causes problems and moreover, the *Zamindar* Binodbihari takes loans on handnotes and becomes almost a bankrupt, Ambikacharan and Indrani become their saviours. Binodbihari's wife Nayantara refuses to give her jewels to save her husband and just then Indrani offers her heap of jewels to save their master from disgrace and bankruptcy. She rises at once above the masters—in a subtle way she takes revenge, thereby regaining their pristine glory and old prestige by establishing their superiority.

This story shows up woman in another aspect where she is leading the spouse, saving him from the distress and, above all, is ready to sacrifice the most precious things for him. Here, in this story two female characters are pitched against each other, and the master craftsman with his brilliance is able to contrast by juxtaposing them where one creates and another destroys.

Ghater Katha (The River Stairs) is one of the earliest stories of Tagore. Here the speaker is a 'river-stair' which has heard the footfalls of ages and been a silent spectator of the intimate workings and exchanges of the hearts of men and women on the steps of the river. The river-stair is a mute spectator and custodian of emotions, unfulfilled yearnings of numerous men and women since ages.

The story is about a girl widow pining away her life, unknown and uncared for. The river stair knew her when she was a child; it missed her light footsteps when she got married and left for her husband's home, and it recognises her footsteps as she returns now as a widow at eight.

Her soul is stirred when years after a 'sanyasi' comes there and people whisper that this indeed is Kusum's husband who was reported dead. Kusum becomes mentally restless at the appearance of this sanyasi, and seeks peace and joy through daily service of him. Her mind becomes disturbed again, for she has a dream that her religious worship is only the offering of a woman to her lover. Her worship is tainted with carnal desire. But there is platonic angle also to the whole affair. Then she has a short interview with the sanyasi, although the rest of the world has no knowledge of this tense moment on the life of Kusum and the sanyasi. To Kusum, who narrates her experience with sobs and tears, the sanyasi says, "Now that I am a sanyasi, not belonging to this world. You must forget me." The stress on 'you' makes one wonder if the sanyasi has recognised Kusum as his forsaken wife or is speaking to a new devotee.

As Kusum relates her dream with sobs and tears, the sanyasi feels much more agitated and presses the stone surface firmly with his right foot to suppress his weakness for her but not from the river-stair.

Gently and with a hint that the feelings between them are mutual, the 'sanyasi' tells her he must go, and she must forget him. After he has gone, Kusum descends the steps slowly saying, "He has told me to forget him" and drowns herself.

Kusum's story can be interpreted in another way which the author might not have intended—a girl widow emptied of all her feelings, emotions meets a man (probably her own husband) but cannot express her love because her subconscious warns her. She accepts her fate. Tagore has not made any deliberate attempt to say anything but through Kusum he has successfully shown the plight of the young widows who were made to suffer inner torment because of social restrictions imposed on widow re-marriage. The desire remains suppressed; the emotions remain trapped in the lonely hearts.

In *Chinnapatra* (The Torn Leaves: Bunch of Tagore's Letters) there is a letter describing a young bride standing at the Ghat and trying to bring herself to leave:

> At last when it was time to leave I saw them trying to coax that girl, with her cropped hair and big round armlets and bright innocent beauty, to get on to the boat; but she didn't want to go. Eventually they managed, with great difficulty, to pull her abroad. I realised that the poor girl was probably going from her father's house to her husband's. When the boat set sail, the other women stood watching from the bank; one or two of them were gently wiping tears away from their noses with the ends of their saris...

Nothing could escape Tagore's gaze. Everything was imbibed and stored until the moment was ripe for a poem or story or play or song to express it afresh. Moods of nature influenced him constantly. He wrote from the headquarters at Shahzadpur:

> Here I am sole monarch of these rooms and have thrown open all the doors and windows. I feel the mood and the will to write here as nowhere else. The living essence of the outside world floats in freely in verdurous waves of light and air and sound and scent that mingle with my bewitched mind and mould it into story after story after story. The intoxication is especially strong in the afternoons. Heat, hush, solitude, birdsong—particularly the cawing of crows—and languid, limitless leisure together remove me from reality. I believe, though I have no proof that the '*Arabian Nights*' came into being upon such sun-baked afternoons, in Damascus, Samarkand and Bokhara... Such a prodigiously grand and mysterious setting in such a far-away country was bound to lead to a thousand tales—credible and incredible—of the deepest hopes and fears of mankind. Noontime in Shahzadpur is high noon for story writing. It was at this time, I recall, that my story 'The Postmaster' took over my thoughts. The light, the breeze and the movement of leaves on all sides combined and entered my daily writing.

Postmaster (The Postmaster), written in 1891, was among Tagore's earliest stories. Its main character is a bored, desperate Calcutta boy, posted to Shahzadpur—to run a post office. As Tagore made clear in a letter, a real postmaster existed who used to tell him "the most improbable things in the gravest possible fashions". Tagore was gracious and friendly with the local postmaster. A post office was actually situated in a ground floor room of the family house. The real postmaster after reading the story recognised himself and timidly referred to the fact. But the real master does not seem to match the postmaster in Tagore's story. Though he was not from Calcultta he liked the man, probably he identified himself with him. Tagore wrote in a comical anecdote in the story:

> Yesterday he told me that the local people so revered the Ganges that if a relative died they would grind his bones into powder and keep it; then, if anyone came who had drunk the waters of the Ganges, they would mix the bone-powder with pan and, by so doing, imagine that part of their dead relative had mingled with the Ganges. I laughed and said, "You're making it up." He thought soberly for a while and then confessed, "Could be Sir, could be."

The storyline goes like this: a stranger finds himself cantoned as a postmaster in a village in a inaccessible corner in Bengal. He is a bachelor and ill-paid. He cannot set up a costly establishment and maintain his own people in the village where he is posted. He therefore cooks his own food in a thatched hut in which he lives and employs Ratan, a low-caste orphan girl, to assist in doing the household chores. There is little room for the development of any emotional relationship unless one imagines the postmaster falling in love with the servant girl. Such a conception would, indeed, be very cheap, but the author's portraiture of the postmaster and the girl is full of freshness and subtlety.

The postmaster, who hails from Calcutta, feels very lonely in the far-away village (in North Bengal) in which he has no relations and friends, and in which he hardly ever gets a man to talk to. It is the rainy season, and his heart becomes wistful; he wants just someone whom he may call his own and with whom he can exchange confidences in a god-forsaken place. In the absence of a companion, he talks to the servant-girl about his own people and proceeds to teach her letters of the alphabet.

The postmaster from Calcutta is a fish out of water and his village maidservant Ratan, a wispy little orphan girl, not yet a woman. She cooks and cleans for her master, fetches his water, stokes his hookah, and nurses him when malaria strikes. She becomes a key factor to his survival in the village. This one touch of nature wins the heart of Ratan, a poor orphan girl who has nobody in this whole world to feel warmly for her. She waits in keen anticipation for the postmaster's every beck and call and works assiduously at her lessons not so much because she is interested in them but because this is one of the avenues by means of which she can come closer to the postmaster. On an impulse he begins teaching to read and write and she responds very eagerly. Soon she lives for his call. To him, however, she is a pastime, an amusement.

Here is an undefined and indefinable relationship that is subtler than the feeling which one ordinarily calls love. A small, helpless girl has found someone who, she feels, cares for her and to whom she wants to belong without being sure in what exact way she may become connected with this exile from Calcutta. "Anything to thee,'—that is the attitude of the orphan girl who has not learnt to understand the mazy ways of life. The postmaster leaves the place for good, is anxious to make arrangements for the girl and even offers her in charity a large slice of what ready money he has. The girl yearns for much warmer relationship than mere charity and suitable employment. What she looks forward to get from the postmaster she herself does not know, and when she is left disconsolate, her sorrowing face seems to represent the 'great unspoken pervading grief of Mother Earth herself." What

Tagore reveals in this casual acquaintance of a village postmaster is the primeval poignant yearning of human nature which is too deep and mysterious to fit into the coarser arrangement of human society.

The time comes to depart. It is a tragic and touching finale. The postmaster boards the boat and it casts off. The author ends the story on a very moving note but leaves a very deep hurt in the readers' mind about the orphan girl Ratan:

> But Ratan had no such philosophy to console her. All she could do was wander near the post office, weeping copiously. Maybe a faint hope lingered in her mind that Dadababu might return; and this was enough to tie her to the spot, prevent her from going far. O poor, unthinking human heart! Error will not go away, logic and reason are slow to penetrate. We cling with both arms to false hope, refusing to believe the weightiest proofs against it, embracing it with all our strength. In the end, it escapes, ripping our veins and draining our heart's blood; until, regaining consciousness, we rush to fall into snares of delusion all over again. (Translated)

This is the mood of the closing paragraphs of the "The Postmaster", was also the mood of what are perhaps Tagore's most famous poems of Selidah period: *Sonar Tari* (The Golden Boat) and *Jete Nahi Dibo* (I'm Not Letting You Go).

Most of his time on the estates Tagore was alone, except for his retinue of tenants, boatmen and servants. One of the servants prompted a poem from him in 1896, *Karma* (The Worker) that gave a sharp picture of his lonely existence:

> No sign of my servant this morning
> The door stood unlatched my bath-water was unfetched
> The rascal didn't turn up last night.
> Where my clean clothes were I had no clue
> Nor where my meal was coming from

Time passed, the clock ticking I sat, irritation pricking-
I would really tell him off, I would.
At last quite late he came greeted me in the same way
As usual, palms pressed meekly together
I was seized by a fit I cried, "Go, get out,
I don't want to see your face!"
He heard me like dunce as if stunned for once,
He searched my face in surprise.
Then he said, "Last night" he choked, "at midnight
My little girl, she died."
So saying, in haste cloth on shoulder he went to face
his daily chores alone.
And, as on any other day, he cleaned, polished, scrubbed away,
left not a single task undone.

In the story "The Postmaster", Tagore took a similar situation and expanded it, deepening its significance. Like all his village stories, it has the same mixture of detached observation and emotional empathy as in the poem, infused with melancholy and touches of fantasy. Instead of the poem's *zamindar* and his bereaved male servant, the small girl Ratan arouses pity in the readers' mind and Tagore has depicted her as a child growing up into a woman only to be left back into her world of loneliness silently waiting for her master's return.

The sensual attraction of a Guru for the body of *Bostomi* (The Vaishnava Woman) forces her to leave her husband but not as a victim, but to cleanse her corrupt mind and seek spiritual elevation. The woman portrayed here is also quite individualistic, and she is absolutely confident and aware of what she does.

The fortitude of Rajib's love for the widowed Mahamaya in the story *Mahamaya* (Mahamaya) who returns to life and Rajib from the funeral pyre of her dead husband is proved when he takes her to the safety of a distant place. But here Rabindranath takes the couple away not as husband-wife but as live-in couple. His Westernised thinking on women's liberation and emancipation is quite evident here. The resumed love relationship is cut short as Mahamaya sets out into the unknown like Anila of "Poila Number" and to an uncertain future when Rajib pries into her burnt face behind her careful but once removed veil.

Tagore could have ended the story on a happy note but he restrained probably to surprise the reader or he was not ready to untangle the issue of widow remarriage and then discreetly avoids it.

In *Subha* (Subha), which is a story with a thin plot, the author emphasises the affinity that binds the human world to the natural. Banikantha's daughter Subha is dumb like Nature and like Nature, she too is majestic. She is companionless amongst men and women; she is not without friends in the animal world—amongst the goats and cows, who too, have not learnt to distort their emotions by expressing through language.

When she is married off, the husband forsakes her for physical debility and marries a second wife without caring for the emotions of this helpless, mute girl and leaves her in an unmitigable state of lifelong suffering.

In most of the short stories of Tagore the point of interest lies in the surprise turn of events. Kantichandra in *Subhadrishti* (The Auspicious Vision) is fascinated by a beautiful girl who seems to respond to the name of Sudha. He makes a proposal of marriage before the master of the house where he meets her. On inquiry it is found that indeed there is a girl by the name of Sudha in that house. He marries the girl without further inquiry and is painfully surprised to find that his bride is not the girl by whom he was enchanted. But he has a greater surprise in store when he comes to know that the girl, who startled him by her beauty, is dumb and deaf and idiotic. She did not really respond to the name Sudha, being half-wit, she actually had only nodded her head when this name was called. Surprise leads to more surprise, and what might have been a curse becomes a blessing.

Though Kantichandra is saved by the author from a disastrous marriage yet it pains to learn that the half-wit, with whom he almost falls in love with, leaves no impression whatsoever, in his heart, the moment the truth about her is known. Poetic 'injustice' is done to the deaf and dumb girl by the author that could have easily been avoided.

Khata (The Exercise Book) is a story where a girl, Uma, learns how to write and thenceforth she goes on writing wherever she finds place. Her brother gifts a beautifully gilded, ruled exercise-book so that she practises writing. The notebook becomes the soul companion of this seven-year-old girl. First she starts copywriting and then she goes ahead with her own creatively written pieces in it. The exercise book becomes an inseparable possession of this small girl.

At the age of 10 years, she is married off to one Pyarimohan who happens to be a writer like her own brother. While going to her in-laws' house, her maid 'Yashi' carries Uma's most favourite exercise book with them. Uma takes time out of her routine and one fine afternoon, she takes out the 'exercise book' from the tin-box. She scribbles with tears in her eyes, "Yashi has gone back—I will also go to my mother." She starts jotting down her heart out in the notebook in the solitariness of her room. But one day her act of writing gets discovered by her sisters-in-law and soon it becomes a 'news' item in the entire household.

Pyarimohan is told about this, and he at once rails at his wife and stabs her with his gibes and taunts. The little woman's verses get mocked at by her writer-husband and amid laughter of her sisters-in-law, Uma sits covering her face with her hands as her sobs go unheard in the world of her in-laws:

> Uma never got the exercise-book back again. Pyarimohan also had an exercise-book full of various subtly barbed essays, but no one was philanthropic enough to snatch his book away and destroy it. (Translated)

Anathbandhu's irresponsible behavior and selfish life-style in *Prayashchitta* (Penance) brings untold misery and suffering to the life of his self-effacing wife Bindhyabasini. Though overshadowed by the tale the shameless self-seeker who rides roughshod over his innocent wife by playing false with her, Anathbandhu deceives his wife by marrying an English woman during his stay in England for study. The custom of doing penance for crossing the *Kalapaani* is satirised in the story as a secondary theme.

The configuration of sensual lovers is broken by instances of idealism and steadfastness in men in stories like *Rabibar* (Sunday) in which the protagonist Abhikkumar writes to his fiancée Biva from England promising to come back to her with an attitude of surrender:

> As I come far away from you, the unthinkability of love looms with all brightness in my mind; it has enabled me to cross the thorny barrier of reason and arguments—I can visualise you with a supra-terrestrial grace. So far I sought to understand (you) with my reason, now I want to have (you) with my whole of my heart. (Translated)

In this story the woman is portrayed as a calm and serene individual who establishes a strong influence on her partner, and he realises this when he goes away from her.

There are a host of female characters in Tagore's short stories that are as varied and heterogeneous as the stories in which they appear. He shows how a revivalist father's (Bhabanicharan's) over-anxiety for recovering the lost ancestral glory in *Rasmonir Chhele* (Rashmoni's Son) leads to the premature death of his son. Tagore never referred to his ancestral split (between the Pathuriaghat

Tagores and the Jorasanko Tagores) in his memoirs. But it surfaced instead in this moving story which he wrote in 1911—though there are parallels in the pathos of the underlying situation, not in the plot.

> A missing will, obviously removed from a safe by one branch of a wealthy 'joint family' living in the country, is the instrument that divides the family. Eventually the shrewd branch abandons the family seat and goes to live in the town, where it flourishes. The other branch of the family remains in the village and steadily declines in prosperity. Many years later two descendants, one from each branch, unknown to each other, now students in the big city of Calcutta, are reunited by the power of natural affection triumphing over the gulf of difference in wealth. But Tagore did not write happy ending: the indigent scion dies of illness contracted in grinding poverty. The missing will is mysteriously returned to his grieving parents—but it arrives much too late to heal the breach.

But Rashmoni in the story has been very strict with her son, so that he does not get spoilt. She, under the veil of a strict mother dreams of her son's bright future and does tremendous hard work herself to bring him up.

The sensuality of Motimohan in *Bicharak* (The Judge) drags Hemashashi to the hell of prostitution by deceit and a fake profession of love. Motimohan repents but then it is too late. Hemashashi's life has been wasted away because of him and here the author ends the story on "The Scarlet Letter" note but without the penance on the part of Motimohan. Hemashashi also is not allowed to rediscover herself and she is not rehabilitated by the storyteller.

The description of the boys playing at the beginning of *Chuti* (The Homecoming) is taken straight from observation, though the girl who sits on the fallen mast becomes a boy in the story:

> There was large mast lying on the mud by the river. A bunch of naked little boys had, after much debate, realised that if they heaved and puffed and shouted they would be able to roll it along, and that this would be an exciting new game. They set to work to carry out this plan: 'Heave ho! Watch her go! Heave ho!' Each time they managed to roll it over they all cheered. But there were a couple of girls among the boys, and their feelings were different. They were forced, because they had no friends of their own, to join in with the boys, but were obviously not enjoying such a violent, physical game. One of the girls, solemnly and coolly and without speaking, firmly sat herself down on the mast....

This is just an indication as to what extent Tagore's stories were influenced by real-life situation. But his creative genius, seeing the boys playing by the side of the river, could contemplate a story altogether differently hued. Pathik is sent off to his maternal uncle's house by his mother because he troubles his younger brother and moreover, the city promises better education (as advocated by his maternal uncle). In the story there is maladjustment caused by affection colliding with self-interest. It is not a rare incident that the mother taking the side and sheltering her youngest born and in the bargain, the elder ones suffer the brunt. Here in the story also the widowed mother feels relieved when Pathik starts jumping up and down at the proposal of going to Calcutta:

> His mother did not object to seeing her son off, because she always lived in dread that Makhan might be pushed into the river by him or might split his head open in some terrible accident; but she was a little cast down by the eagerness with which Pathik seized the idea of going. (Translated)

Pathik Charavorti is a village lad of 14 or 15, undistinguished in everyday life, but his exile to Calcutta and the harsh treatment meted out by an unsympathetic aunt help to awaken the deeper emotions which lay dormant in this neglected urchin. Indeed, so deep the agony Pathik feels that he becomes very sensitive and miserable. His misery is rendered more acute, because he is an exile from his village, and in the arid surroundings of Calcutta, he misses not only his human mother but also the great Mother Nature who embraced him with a mother's warmth in the glorious meadows, the broad river-banks and the narrow brook of his village:

> A kind of physical love like that of animals; a longing to be in the presence of the one who is beloved; an inexpressible wistfulness during absence; a silent cry of the inmost heart for the mother, like the lowing of a calf in the twilight—this love, which was almost an animal instinct, agitated the shy, nervous, lean, uncouth and ugly boy. It is like the unspoken love of the mother Earth; It is the primal instinct with which she endows her children. It is worth noting that this love of which the boy would have remained unconscious in his village home is awakened by the cramping surroundings of Calcutta and the ill-treatment he receives from his aunt. (Translated)

The women in the story—the biological mother of Pathik, and the cruel aunt—all desert the innocent boy who pays up with his life to make a final reunion with Mother Earth, probably, now in the form of ashes, and goes to the eternal abode.

The story-teller's deep insight into the human nature, the minutest study of every detail of human characters have rendered the women in this story in hateful roles—both as mother and aunt.

Works Cited

Arnold, Edward: *The Poetry of Judith Wright by Shirley Walker*, Australia, Pty. Ltd., 1980, p.91.

Bharathi, Shraban: 1291 (1884), p.154, in Paul, 2, p.278. This is the uncut version of the account published in *Rabindra Rachanabali* (Achalita Shangraha).

Boumella, Penny: *Thomas Hardy and Women*, 1982, pp.59-60.

Tagore, Rabindranath: *Chinnapatra*, No. 17, February, 1891.

____ *: Chinnapatrabali (A Bunch of Torn Leaves)*, Letter No. 24, June 1891.

____ : December 1900, Letters to His Wife, *Vishwa Bharathi Quarterly*, Summer 1953, p.12 (translated by Lila Majumdar), *Chithipatra* 1, p.43.

____ "Karma Chaitali", *Rabindra Rachanabali*, Vol.v, p.16, 1896.

____ "My Reminiscences", *Rabindrarachanabali*, p.179.

Devi, Jnanadanandini: *Smriti Katha*, Sharadiya Ekashan, 1990, p.12.

Dutta & Lago: *Selected Short Stories*, trans., pp.200-38. *Rabindra Rachanabali*, 22, pp.371-407.

Dutta, Krishna and Robinson, Andrew: *The Myriad-minded Man, Rabindranath Tagore*, Rupa & Co., 2003, p. 84.

Dwivedi, A.N.: *The Conflagaration: Kamala Das and Her Poetry*, Doaba House, Delhi, 1983, p.91.

Krishna, Dutt & Andrew, Robinson: *The Myriad-minded Man, Rabindranath Tagore*, Rupa & Co., 2003, p.86.

Mukhopadhyay, Prabhat Kumar: *Rabindrajibani*, Vol.3, 1961, p.339.

Radice, William: *Rabindranath Tagore: Selected Short Stories*, Penguin Books, 1994, p.10.

4

Powerlessness of Chandara in *Shashti*

In *Shasti* (The Punishment) Chidam loves his wife, but it is vegetative love, and this too gets ruptured beyond repair. He names his innocent wife Chandara as the killer of his sister-in-law in order to save his elder brother from the scaffold. Out of a tremendous shock and vehement pique over the unexpected behaviour of her husband, Chandara refuses to utter the tutored language of the defence counsel to save her life, falsely confesses to her crime and goes to the gallows to do penance for her brother-in-law's sin and her husband's biased sense of priority. She is one of her ilk who would never break but would prefer to die and punish others for their sins with her silence. Tagore has used silence as a tool, as a technique to heighten drama and invoke pity in the readers' heart for Chandara.

Dukhiram and Chidam are the brothers of poor Kuri caste who make their living by working as labourers in the fields of other farmers. Radha and Chandara are the wives of both the brothers respectively. The women are very cantankerous and truculent and the brothers are very hot tempered and petulant. The tragic story begins with the disaster of the brutal killing of Radha by her hungry and irritated husband Dukhiram who plunges his farm knife cruelly into her head when he is denied food by his wife impudently. Profusely bleeding Radha collapses and dies in Chandara's arms. It is a very sudden and shocking incident. Chandara squeals loudly but Chidam silences her. At the same time Ramlochan, the most intelligent and respected person of the village enters the house to collect the pending amount of his rent from the brothers. He is a little uncomfortable due to the unusual quiet of the house. When he enquires about the reason, a confused and nervous Chidam, in order to save his brother Dukhiram, tells him a lie that the routine quarrel of both the women this time has turned out gory and Chandara has killed Radha by striking her head with a farm knife. He pretends to be a good husband by seeking his advice about how to save his wife from the claws of the police and law. Ramlochan advises him to shift the blame on Dukhiram, that he killed his wife Radha because she had not prepared the food for him and had insulted him. Chidam dismisses his idea by saying that if he loses his wife he could get another one but if his brother is hanged how he can be replaced by anyone.

This is a complicated story of very complex human relationships and their behaviour. Chidam and Chandara like each other very much but at the same time they strongly disapprove of the traits of their counterparts. Unlike Dukhiram and Radha who are most messy, disorderly and unkempt, Chidam and Chandara are images of physical grace and elegant mannerism. The teen-aged Chandara is quite frisky, lively and a happy-go-lucky kind of person. Chidam too eyes the beauty of other village women with great interest and also likes to be appreciated by them. This flirtation always enrages Chandara and to take offence she takes pride in narrating false stories about Kashi Majumdar's middle son. Chidam feels that a wife as nimble and sharp as Chandara cannot be trusted wholly. Chandara too feels that her husband has roving eyes so he needs to be kept on a tight rein so he does not go astray. Chidam tries hard to keep her stay at home under the strict vigilance of his sister-in-law while Chandara never lets any chance go to move around the village and liberate herself from the undue restraints imposed upon her by Chidam. This intricate love and hate relationship of the husband and wife is the central plot of the story.

Chidam persuades Chandara to take the charge of murdering Radha upon herself. This unwarranted and baseless suggestion breaks her heart and pushes her into a complete shock. Although Chidam assuress her that he would do everything to save her yet it is no solace for a deeply hurt Chandara. Every word Chidam says falls into deaf ears. She accepts the charge of murdering Radha before the police inspector. She is arrested and sent to jail. Now anticipating the repercussions of the whole episode Chidam is very much upset and repentant. He does not want to lose her. He suggests her to tell before the magistrate in court that it was Radha who hit her first and she accidentally killed her in self defence. But his suggestions make no sense to her. She sticks firmly to her stand in the court. Chidam's pleadings that his wife is innocent does not impress the magistrate either as Ramlochan, the most worthy man of the village, stands witness against Chandara. Her case is referred to a session court where both Chidam and Dukhiram's confessions to the crime are treated as their desperate efforts to save the young girl from capital punishment. Chandara does not budge an inch from her stand and is repeatedly telling the same story right from the police investigation to the session's trial. Chandara is sentenced to death. Although throughout the trial Chandara acknowledges and confirms Chidam's undeterred love for her, she strongly refuses to see him just before the hanging. Instead she prefers to see her mother.

The story is exclusive in its plot and treatment. Where it talks about the complex audacities of human behaviour it also reveals the unjust social set-up of those times where a woman carried no status and significance in a family. She was wronged with all kinds of insults, humiliation, physical assault, discrimination and inhumanity. Chidam's words that "a wife can be replaced but a brother cannot be replaced", clearly point out that the women are treated in the meanest manner in that society and were quite vulnerable to all kinds of atrocities meted out to them. Chandara is the strongest character of the story. The writer has left the readers to imagine whether it is Chandra who punishes Chidam or it is court who punishes Chandara.

Chandara, a powerless woman, refuses to take the alibi that Chidam, her husband, offers her, by remaining silent, which ultimately leads to her death, but in the end, she becomes a hero, and Chidam receives the true and actual punishment. Chandara chooses to be found guilty and dies for a crime she did not commit because she does not want to participate in the lies and injustice that is tolerated in the corrupt unjust system that surrounds her; or may be that she just wants to punish Chidam, her husband, who does not love her more than his own blood brother. She chooses silence as her most potent weapon to kill Chidam with the guilt of her own death.

Chandara is powerless because she is both poor and a woman, which supports the premise that in her position, silence is her only power to do what she sees is right. In "The Punishment," the setting is such that women are not equal to men in their freedom and nature. "Chidam felt that a wife as nimble and as sharp as Chandara could not be wholly trusted". Chandara is a contradiction of the average woman because she is just as bendable and as bright as Chidam testing her at every turn. Tagore writes that "Chidam respects Chandara as she respects him though neither one of them win an argument". Chandara is also weak due to her poor socioeconomic status. She lives with Chidam, Dukhiram, and Radha in one house, which is located in an area prone to flooding. "Weeds and scrub round the house had shot up after the rain: the heavy scent of damp vegetation from these and from waterlogged jute-fields formed a solid wall all around". As an obvious indication that Chandara lives in a poor home, Tagore writes that Chidam and Dukhiram are "not paid normal labourers' wages' too. Chandara lives in a family with such a meagre income that the members, she included, are most of the times, starving. Tagore mentions that Chidam and Dukhiram go home hungry, but enter a house that is empty of foodgrains. In all the circumstances, Chandara is too powerless to change any of it, but her powerless position in society is what leads up to her final choice to remain silent. She is expected to be silent, she is expected not to complain but bear the hunger pangs silently like the other three members of the family. In the end, she chooses to get herself killed by keeping silent. Her silence speaks louder than anything she could have done or said.

Chidam offers Chandara an alibi, but she refuses it choosing silence over a reasonable answer to her own rescue. Her resolution to keep silent is the only way she can stand up for herself and what she believes is right. Though she is bold and challenges all parameters of being a wife and a woman, she is always held down by the limitations of the requirements of those parameters. She has to respond to Chidam, who feels she is too wild. Tagore writes that after Chidam finds out Chandara has been hanging out at the ghat, he threatens her, but even after locking her in a room, she finds a way out and leaves. She constantly tries to stand up for her own wants and desires, but she is free in using her silence as her weapon against her husband who wronged her. She also refuses the alibi because it is just another lie and another way to further cover up the truth, even more than it has been covered up by the initial lie, and she would rather die than take part in lying again to add to the cover up. Tagore exposes the corrupt justice system that exists in our country. Ramlochan prompts a false alibi from Chandara, but when she refuses to take the alibi, he feels she must want to die and refuses to assist her any longer than he already has assisted her for fear of what trouble it might cause him to do so. "Ramlochan had previously prepared lots of stories that would save Chandara, but when he found that she herself is bending her neck to receive the noose, he decided, 'Why take the risk of giving false evidence now? I'd better say what little I know.'" Chandara knows no other way to stand up against injustice than to keep her silence, but due to the corrupt nature of the justice system, she is found guilty based on a lie, and she is not willing to lie again even if it would save her life.

Ultimately, though Chandara is the one who dies for the crime, she is not the one who is actually punished. Chidam is the one who is punished, and Chandara, though it may not be the reason why she keeps her silence, does punish him by her actions. She knows that she is going to die for a crime she did not commit, and she would rather do so than stay with Chidam. "In her thoughts, Chandara is saying to her husband, 'I shall give my youth to the gallows instead of you.'" Ironically, Tagore states that Chidam had wondered if his life would be better if she is dead. However, it is he who is tormented and punished by her condemnation and death. He tries to continually say that Chandara is innocent. He also confesses to the crime. All his attempts to save his wife are in vain. "The judge concluded that the brothers had confessed to the crime in order to save the younger wife from the shame of the noose". Right before she dies, he requests to see her, to which she replies, "To hell with him". She is satisfied with her decision, and he takes the punishment. Ironically, he is tormented by her admonition. She is done with him and prefers death over being with a man who has asked her to take the blame for such a hideous crime, knowing the risk to her well-being.

Though faced with death, Chandara realises that she can only stand up for herself and stand for her opposition to injustice by remaining silent. She refuses a reasonable alibi and remains silent at the cost of her own life, but in the end, she is only a hero for her actions. Chidam is more punished by her actions than she is punished by her actions.

This aspect of Indian culture is evident in this story and can be read on the following premises. The patriarchal assignment of the gender roles is also unmistakable in the story. First, the wives both stay home and clean the house like most other women in the village, and Radha looks after her son, and they cook the food. They are also treated as inferior by their husbands. An example of this is when Dukhiram comes home demanding and expecting food from his wife. She treats him as if he were the boss or more important than her. Lastly, Chandara's subaltern identity is proved when she willingly accepts her husband's plea to confess to the crime.

Women have secondary status in society and marriage. Their lack of power or powerlessness is shown in Henrik Ibsen's play *Hedda Gabler*, Anton Chekov's story *The Lady with the Dog* and Tagore's story "The Punishment", and each story has its uniqueness in handling different ways in which each female protagonist copes with her marital situation. How each woman affirms her own value and autonomy after a profound struggle with self and situation is noteworthy. The susceptibility and defencelessness of women in *Hedda Gabler*, *The Lady with the Dog* and "The Punishment", the powerlessness of women within male-dominated societies occupy a central part of each story. Women's inferior status in society and within marriage and their lack of authority or control over their own destinies are emphasised by Henrik Ibsen, Anton Chekov and Tagore. Though these stories are set in considerably different cultures and social systems, each of the female protagonists shares the identification of her vulnerability, and she copes with this issue in significantly different ways. In Ibsen's *Hedda Gabler*, Hedda is described as a beautiful woman who is always surrounded by admirers and who has to do things in style.

Hedda Gabler is a play first published in 1890 by Norwegian playwright Henrik Ibsen. The play's first show was in 1891 in Germany to unenthusiastic and indifferent reviews, but has subsequently gained appreciation as a classic of realism and truths of our societies and nineteenth century theatre, and world drama. The character of Hedda is judged by some critics as one of the great dramatic roles in theatre, the "female Hamlet", and some portrayals have been very controversial. Depending on the interpretation, Hedda may be portrayed as an idealistic heroine fighting society, a victim of circumstance, a prototypical feminist, or a manipulative villain.

Hedda's married name is Hedda Tesman; Gabler is her maiden name. On the subject of the title, Ibsen wrote: "My intention in giving it this name is to indicate that Hedda as a personality is to be regarded rather as her father's daughter than her husband's wife".

Hedda Gabler, daughter of an upper-class General, has just come back to her villa in Kristiania (now Oslo) from her honeymoon. Her husband is Jorgen Tesman, a wannabe, young, dependable (but not brilliant) academic who has pooled research with their honeymoon. It becomes obvious in the course of the play that she has never loved him but has married him for reasons pertaining to the dull nature of her life. It is also suggested that she may be pregnant.

The revisit of Tesman's scholarly rival, Ejlert Lovborg, throws their lives into disorder. Lovborg, a writer, is also a recovered alcoholic who has isted his talent until now. Thanks to a liaison with Hedda's old schoolmate, Thea Elvsted (who has left her husband for him), Lovborg shows signs of healing and has just completed a bestseller in the same field as Tesman.

The critical success of his recently published work transforms Lovborg into a danger to Tesman, as Lovborg becomes a competitor for the university professorship Tesman had been counting on. Tesman and Gabler are financially overstretched, and he tells her that he will not be able to fund the regular pleasurable or lavish maintenance that she has been expecting. Upon meeting Lovborg, however, the couple discover that he has no intention of competing for the professorship, but rather has spent the last few years labouring with Mrs. Elvsted over what he considers to be his masterpiece, the "sequel" to his recently published work.

Apparently jealous of Mrs. Elvsted's influence over Lovborg, Gabler plans to come between them. She goads Lovborg to get drunk and go to a party. Tesman returns home from the party and divulges that he found the manuscript of Lovborg's great work, which the latter lost while he was drunk. When Gabler next sees Lovborg, he confesses to her, desperately, that he has lost the manuscript. Instead of telling him that the manuscript has been found, she pushes him to commit suicide, giving him a pistol. She then burns the manuscript and tells Tesman she has destroyed it to secure their future.

When the news comes that Lovborg has indeed killed himself, Tesman and Mrs. Elvsted are determined to try to rebuild his book from Lovborg's notes, which she has kept. Gabler is shocked to learn from Judge Brack (a friend of Tesman's) that Lovborg's death, in a brothel, is muddled and probably accidental (this "ridiculous and vile" death contrasts with the "beautiful and free" one that Gabler had imagined for him). Worse, Brack knows the origins of the pistol. He tells Gabler that if he reveals what he knows, a scandal will likely occur due to her role in giving Lovborg the pistol. Gabler realises that this places Brack in a position of power over her. Leaving the others, she goes into her smaller room and shoots herself in the head. The others in the room assume that Gabler is simply firing shots, and they follow the sound to inspect. The play ends with Tesman, Brack, and Mrs. Elvsted discovering her body.

Joseph Wood Krutch makes a connection between Hedda Gabler and Freud, whose first work on psychoanalysis is published almost a decade later. In Krutch's analysis, Gabler is one of the first fully built-up neurotic female protagonists of literature. By that Krutch means that Hedda is neither sensible nor insane in the old sense of being random and unaccountable. Her aims and her motives have a secret personal logic of their own. She gets what she wants, but what she wants is not anything that the normal usually admit, publicly at least, to be desirable. One of the significant things that such a character implies is the premise that there is a secret, sometimes unconscious, world of aims and methods—one might almost say a secret system of values—that is often much more important than the rational one. And in this theory, Chandara too fits well. She listens to her own mind and brings justice unto herself by going to the gallows.

For Hedda, the encounter with Brack makes it clear that if she continues to live she will have to be a subservient woman since he will not stop blackmailing her. Her choice in the face of her powerlessness is "to have the courage and the will to rise from the feast of life" (Ibsen). "My final ties in this life will be with them" (Tagore). In each case, the author has created a female character whose power is eventually limited and whose place in society is very much that of a subservient individuals. Chekov's Gurov, in contrast, is an older, married man for whom extramarital affairs are routine. In Tagore's "The Punishment" though assured that her husband will save her from the gallows, Chandara says, "I shall give my youth to the gallows instead of to you". The beautiful and free young wife Chandara becomes the victim of her husband's ploy and is sentenced to death for a crime she did not commit. She is sacrificed because of her husband's desire to save his brother, but finally (like Hedda), gains control over her fate by choosing to submit to death. Hedda heartens Loevborg, a man with whom she is involved, to take his own life and in the end kills herself rather than yield to Brack. However, she is a woman whose predilection for deception leads her to act in a way that leaves her exposed to the blackmail of Brack, a man who comes to gain a great deal of control over her because of her financial faults, her association with another man, and her role in that man's suicide.

In *The Lady with the Dog*, alone and bored in Yalta, Anna enters into a sexual affair and accepts the fact that she has become "a wicked, fallen woman" who has deceived both her husband and herself". Dmitri Gurov is a Moscow banker, married with a daughter and two sons. Unhappy in his marriage, he is frequently unfaithful, and considers women to be of "a lower race". While holidaying in Yalta, he sees a young lady walking along the seafront with her small dog, and endeavours to make her acquaintance. The lady, Anna Sergeyevna, is also vacationing while her husband remains at home in an anonymous local town. They soon are engaged in an affair and spending most of their time together, walking and taking drives to nearby Oreanda.

Though she is expecting her husband to come to Yalta, he eventually sends for her to come home, saying something is wrong with his eyes. Gurov sees her off at the station.

Returning to Moscow and his daily schedule, working by day and clubbing by night, Gurov expects to soon forget young Anna but finds he is obsessed with her memory. On the pretext of going to St. Petersburg to take care of some business, he sets off to her town to find her. Learning the location of the family's residence from a hotel porter, he finds her house, only to realise it would be futile to encroach. In desolation, he reasons that Anna has probably forgotten him and found someone else, and heads back to his hotel for a long nap.

In the evening, he remembers having seen a sign earlier promoting a show of *The Geisha*. Thinking that Anna and her husband may attend the first performance, he goes to the theatre. The couple enters and he watches them intently. When the husband goes out for a smoke during the first interval, Gurov greets Anna, who is dazed and runs from him. After following her through the theatre, he brazens out with her and she confides that she has been thinking of him constantly. Terrified, she begs him to leave and promises to come to see him in Moscow.

She makes excuses to come to Moscow, telling her husband she is going there to see a doctor, which he "believes and does not believe". Gurov realises that for the first time in his life he has actually fallen in love, and wonders how they can continue. While they talk of finding a plan, the story ends without a resolution.

Anton Chekhov considers himself an artist (Chekhov on Writing) and his masterpiece, *The Lady with the Dog* is created with words that capture a place and time, the movement between two people, and the emotion of love discovered and contained in secrecy.

Chekhov in a letter to Alexei Suvorin on October 27, 1888 said, "You are right in demanding that an artist approach his work consciously, but you are confusing two concepts: the solution of a problem and the correct formulation of a problem. Only the second is required of the artist" (Chekhov on Writing). He is true to his word in the story *The Lady with a Dog*. He does not seek a moral solution but suspends the lovers in a timelessness that allows their unveiling to speak of what is real. He shows us the path Gurov and Anna take and how it is their one chance to live above the mundane. He writes in a way that brings life to Gurov and Anna, the main characters in his short story.

Broken into four parts the story portrays the change brought about in Gurov's heart as he encounters the lady with the dog, and begins an affair that he describes in the end as only just beginning. "For Gurov, Anna brings a softening of the heart that allows him to love for the first time in his life. How does love come about and find its unfolding? Chekhov does not answer except to illustrate the mystery that begins with a strange light on the sea: the water ... a soft warm lilac hue ... a golden streak from the moon upon it".

The unasked question Chekhov frames is best read when you examine other works by the author. *About Love* and *The Betrothed* are two short stories written during the same period of time at the end of his life when he lived in Yalta shortly before his death of tuberculosis in 1904 (Coulehan, "Betrothed Annotated"). All are works that explore the crisis caused by the culture of late nineteenth century Russia where arranged marriages are the norm and couples live loveless lives. The result of these arrangements is a monotony of life that the main characters in *The Lady with a Dog*, Gurov and Anna, seek to overcome.

Entering into midlife, Gurov is jaded by what he described as "truly bitter experience". His view on women is unflattering.

Although he cannot live without them and women find something "attractive and elusive which allured" them to him, he soon becomes troubled by relationships that begin light-hearted. He is "eager for life", so he is unfaithful to his wife in spite of his bitter disregard for women. His conclusion on love is that "every intimacy, which at first so agreeably diversifies life and appears a light and charming adventure, inevitably grows into a regular problem of extreme intricacy, and in the long run the situation becomes unbearable".

These thoughts prefigure the affair he begins with the new woman he meets on one sultry evening in Yalta, Anna Sergeyevna Von Diderits. For Gurov, Anna proves to be different. They face the unbearable when it comes, after falling deeply in love. Anna appears to Gurov as young, innocent and ill at ease. He doesn't portray her as good-looking but "recalled her slender delicate neck, her lovely gray eyes". He then states, "There's something pathetic about her, anyway".

Anna's exposure to her own need for love and romance (and perhaps even suffering) leads her to behave in a way that she knows to be wrong. She gives in to love in the full knowledge that she will suffer greatly for her actions. This woman's short life is ultimately ended because her husband "forgot that a lie can be even more terrible" than the truth. Only by radical decisions such as those undertaken by Hedda and Chandara are women able to regain control of their destinies and exercise a degree of power over the men who have placed them in a difficult position. Each of the women is married and despite their marriage, each seeks some means of affirming her own value and autonomy. Though these women's stories are set in fundamentally different cultures and social systems, each of the female protagonists shares the recognition of her vulnerability though they all cope with this issue in much different ways. When Hedda learns that Loevborg did not shoot himself, but is instead killed by another woman, she elects to take her own life.

> Anna's own reaction is positive and though she continues to believe that her association with Gurov is wrong, she cannot help remaining his mistress. She considers herself to have been captured by the Devil and though she recognises that her marriage is an empty shell, she also feels that her attraction to Gurov is so powerful that it cannot be resisted.

For Gurov, a lengthy affair with Anna becomes a need. Hedda's love for her husband, Tesman, is a powerful source of her motivation and of her refusal to submit to Brack. The stories suggest that the power of married women is inherently limited, and that regardless of society or culture, the options available to women are few. Women's inferior status in society and within marriage and their lack of power or control over their own destinies are emphasised by, respectively, Henrik Ibsen, Anton Chekov and Tagore. Having married a man she regards as little more than a tool, she has agreed to be the mistress of a man whose life is lived in secret and whose fidelity to any woman has never been of long duration.

In essence, Chandara, though loving her husband greatly, accepts death at a young age because she realises that her husband considers her less valuable than his brother, and is prepared to place her life in peril in order to save her husband's brother. Like Hedda, she elects to take control of her own destiny and to accept a fate she does not deserve because of the treatment she has received from the men who matter in her life. Chekov's central female character, Anna Sergeyevna, is seen in *The Lady with the Dog* as a sensitive married woman who is all too easily led into an affair with Dmitri Gurov. In loving Gurov and agreeing to be his mistress, Anna simply exchanges one set of fetters for another.

In Hedda Gabler, Hedda is described as a beautiful woman "always so surrounded by admirers" who "has to do things in style." Married to Tesman, she is an amazing woman with a huge sex appeal and cerebral superiority. Finally, he comes to believe that "this little woman, lost in the provincial crowd in no way remarkable..." Her vulnerability is extreme as is Hedda Gabler's and becomes the mechanism that allows an unscrupulous man (Judge Brack) to blackmail her. At least initially, Gurov regards Anna as little more than a diversion enjoyed during a brief vacation. Rather than achieving freedom in her affair, she simply adds to the ties and shackles that limit her life and her options. In "The Punishment", when Chandara is asked to admit to the murder she did not commit she "shrank back". She turns her heart and soul away from him. Chekov's Anna, on the other hand, does not take control of her life and allows herself to become the mistress of an unreliable man rather than be in the power of Brack and "dependent on your will and your demands." Although Chidam loves his wife, he "felt that a wife as nimble and sharp as Chandara could not be wholly trusted."

Chandara is more akin to Hedda than to Anna. But all these three women appear suicidal. Anna in her straying, Hedda in her manipulations (and later her suicide) and Chandara's decision to stick to the untruth to teach her erring husband a lesson, fall in the same category of powerless women and those who later turn hapless.

In the work, *The Madwoman in the Attic*, Gilbert and Gubar examine the concept that women writers like Jane Austen, Mary Shelley, Charlotte and Emily Brontë, George Eliot, Elizabeth Barrett Browning, Christina Rossetti and Emily Dickinson of the nineteenth century have held back in their writings to make their female characters either symbolise the "angel" or the "monster". This struggle stems from male writers' tendencies to categorise female characters as either pure, unadulterated, angelic women or else mutinous, scruffy madwomen. In their argument, Gilbert and Gubar point to Virginia Woolf, who says, women writers must kill the artistic superlative, the aesthetic ideal, through which they themselves have been "killed into art". While it may be easy to interpret that feminist writers embody the "madwoman" or "monster", Gilbert and Gubar stress the implication of killing off both figures because neither are accurate depictions of women nor the images of women writers. Instead, Gilbert and Gubar claim that female writers should try hard for designations beyond this dichotomy, whose options are limited by a patriarchal point of view. Tagore, Ibsen, Tennessee Williams and Chekov's subtle handling of the women characters has made them appear in flesh and blood and not some of those we find only in the mythologies or in the sacred scriptures.

Works Cited

Chekhov, Anton: *The Lady with the Dog, Making Literature Matter: An Anthology For Readers and Writers,* 2nd ed. Eds.John Schilb and John Clifford. Boston: Bedford/St.Martin's, 2003. 871-882

Krutch, Joseph Wood: *Modernism in Modern Drama: A Definition and an Estimate.* Ithaca: Cornell University Press. p. 11

Sanders, Tracy: *Lecture Notes: Hedda Gabler—Fiend or Heroine,* Australian Catholic University, Retrieved 2008

Tagore, Rabindranath: "The Punishment", *The Norton Anthology of World Literature, The Twentieth Century Volume* F. Ed. Sarah Lawall and Maynard Mack. New York: Norton, 2002, Billington, Michael, 2005.

5

Charulata of *Nastaneer*

The story is set in the late nineteenth century Bengal. Bhupati, a well-meaning member of the nationalist aristocracy, uses most of his time on the political magazine he brings out in English. His youthful wife Charulata, following the tradition, is shut into the interior billet of the house, spends lonely hours reading novels and doing needlework. She finds a companion in Bhupati's cousin Amal, a student of an academe of her age. They exchange interest of novels, share keenness for literary journals, and help each other develop into creative writers. All this happens with support from Bhupati.

For Amal, the insight will come too late that the bond has grown into love; and he will be in a situation to break away from the relationship, where he will have to leave the house. For Charu, this crude aspect of growing up, of expressing herself in the world, will not be as easy to reject. She builds a new furtive interior within the interior she inhabits as she finds out, to survive the new reality and the new emotional upsurge. Bhupati comes to know about all this after Charu has built that secret cubicle, after she returns to him as a wife, so to speak. This sighting of the truth also comes for Bhupati after his public endeavour, the magazine fails, when he comes back to the private quarters seeking his wife's companionship for the first time.

In *Nastaneer* (The Broken Nest), the story, is set in 1879, when the renaissance in Bengal was at its climax. Western thoughts of liberty and uniqueness were about to disturb the calm fluff of a feudal society. Women's liberation was being talked about, but not beyond a few cases of widow-remarriage and some education.

Intelligent, sensitive, graceful and serene, Charu is a traditional woman, whose mindset slowly and steadily absorbs the waves from the world beyond. The emotional lattice-work between Amal, Bhupati's cousin who pursues higher studies at the latter's house, and Charulatha, Bhuptai's young wife who becomes a grown woman behind his knowledge because he remains terribly preoccupied with his editorial duties for his self-owned English journal. Tagore probes into the human relationships within the context of 'Joint-family-set-up'. Amal becomes Charu's surrogate companion who fills Bhupati's place in the emotional life of a budding young girl, and the love-relationship develops between them which ruins Bhupati's home. The husband's stolid neglect gives Charu a chance to find unrestraint in love and emotional bond outside marriage.

Nastaneer (The Broken Nest) is the most contentious novella that Tagore wrote and was serialised in *Bharathi*. This is the story that is supposed to be his own relationship with Kadambari and Jyotirindronath 20 years before. The story breaks a new argument, for it explores the depth of the socially unendorsed, adulterous love. But this was the time when he set out to apply his psyche to the taboo subject—women's liberation.

Tagore dedicated four books to Kadambari, his brother Jyotirindronath's wife while she lived. After her death he dedicated two more. In 1901 he modelled Charu in *Nastaneer* on Kadambari. He wrote about her in his poems. In his paintings, a mysterious woman's face appeared again and again which he admitted to one of his artist friends that the woman might well be Kadambari whose "glowing eyes present before my sight not unoften" when painting. Her presence was felt in his songs too.

In *Nastaneer* (The Broken Nest) the entry of Amal into the heart of a love-starved Charu takes place as her editor husband Bhupati remains ignorant about his wife's youth:

> In this way by the time he was engrossed in his newspaper obligations, his girl bride Charulatha slowly stepped into youth. This great news item remained outside the ken of the newspaper Editor's knowledge. (Translated)

Charulatha resents the idea of Amal marrying, because it will take him away from her. She begins to crumple under force of her passion for Amal, her handsome poet-brother-in-law. Though in reality, Kadambari tried to help her husband Jyotirindronath to find a wife for Tagore in reality yet she failed to find him a bride in Jessore. It is believed that she did not want him to marry, and that she committed suicide within a few months of Tagore's marriage was surely not a coincidence.

Bankim's *Women Old and New* was published in 1879 (1879, as we know from the date on the copy of the magazine that Bhupati shows Amal) where he argues for a new woman who would be modern in the traditional way. She would embody the pronouncement of the clash between custom and contemporaneity by finding her place in a re-conceived patriarchy. She would learn to be the 'new old woman'. Satyajit Ray in his film 'Charulata' broke all barriers and took Tagore's story onto a historical framework, the political drama that is brought out into the open. The backdrop was set firmly against the freedom struggle that had led to the search for identity. The story tells us of the formation of the colonial subjects, male and female, and of the foreseeable irony and pain that attend the process. Tagore begins his story by an ironic account of the domains his characters occupy. The idealistic, English-educated Bhupati is worried about the expansion of the British territories beyond the Afghan borders, but hasn't had the time to notice how his child-bride has bloomed into womanhood; Charu's idleness is of a different kind, reminding one of a fruitless tree. As she develops an expressive selfhood, through her love and through her writing, the challenge of the demarcation of domains comes to face her, it demands a heavy price. Tagore, writing more or less from within the social reality that he portrays, was not in a position to uncover the historical dynamics of this matrix. He casts a historical gaze at the story at this level too; he creates a design with characters and spaces and distributes the story along discursive lines of divide. The dichotomy of literature and politics suggested in the story is developed into a strong motif in the story. The first is associated with the woman; the second belongs to the man. Bhupati entrusts Amal with Charu's literary education, admitting that he has no taste for such things, busy as he is with the 'real world' of politics.

Bhupati writes politics in English, Amal and Charu write literature in Bengali. And then we come to a further division: Amal writes for public distribution, in an ornate register, Charu would like to write for a strictly private exchange, in an unembellished style through which she can suggest personal experiences. Towards the end, after Amal has left the house and Bhupati's magazine has failed, Charu and Bhupati go on a vacation to the seaside and plan a poignantly deceptive reunion between the two poles of conflict—between the public and the private, home and the world, politics and culture. Why not bring out another magazine, they propose, which will have politics in English and literature in Bengali!

One can see Charu never believing in this. She is coming face to face with the impracticability of the whole thing; she has had to grow up paying a terrible price. The story brings out this irony of growing up in its most acute historical-political dimensions. Growing into modernity, into citizenship, into prejudice of a nameable kind—all these, marked indelibly with the reality of living through colonialism, would not have been so strongly cramped without the grand design of splits that the story is marked with. In devising his language Tagore moves in and out of the field of literature, it would be difficult to recognise this aspect of his craft if we consider of literature in their pure sovereignty.

Works Cited

Dutta, Krishna & Robinson, Andrew: *The Myriad-minded Man, Rabindranath Tagore*, Rupa & Co., 2003, p.90.

Ray, Satyajit: *Bishay Chalachchitra*. Calcutta: Ananda Publishers Private Limited, 1982.

Tagore, Rabindranath: "The Broken Nest", in *Selected Short Stories*, Translated by Dutta Krishna and Lago Mary. Calcutta: Rupa & Co. 1992.

6

Kumudini of *Jogajog*

Tagore's *Jogajog* (Communication) portrays a clash between two antipodal concepts of marital love and sex as represented by an affluent merchant, Madhusudan and a very sophisticated, refined and sensitive 19-year-old-woman, Kumudini; reared on the Hindu ideals of womanhood and traditional concept of wifehood. In his perception of marital relation with his wife there is nothing as love, fine sense and sensitivity, for he understands sex only realizable by force. The wife is the symbol of captive sex which can be exacted by authority and force. She is nothing but another item in the inventory of his chattels. His idea of the woman has been moulded from a very mean commercial vision:

> Madhusudan has seen women very briefly among the daughters-in-law of the house. They perform the daily chores of the household, engage in quarrels, whisper family secrets to each other, and even shed tears over trifles. In Madhusudan's life there is little contact with them. He never thought of anything better than an insignificant slot of this world for his wife, but rather thought that she would lead a *zenana* life under the silent command of the menfolk's eyes behind the boundary wall shadowed by the littleness of the daily household routine. It did not occupy the slightest space of his account-sharp careful brain that there might crop up a difficult problem gaining or losing something in it. (Translated)

This approach towards women in general and wife in particular explicates the series of his uncouth behaviour with Kumudini starting from his marriage with her. This also explains his perception of procreation:

> There is only one way to tie Kumudini to his own life in tight knot, and that is the way of making her the mother of his child. He finds consolation from the imagination. (Translated)

The trouble of having sex with his newly-wedded wife and her cautiously calibrated distance and disaffection from him from the very first night of their union force him to consider the meanest and basest of the ways for forging control over her body.

In Madhusudan's commercial concept, love is non-existent wife is a commodity for sex-gratification and child is a means of punishing a wilfully disobedient woman named wife. This is a far cry from the blessed husband-wife-child trinity as regarded by Judith Wright of which the child is the result of sex-love between the husband and wife. However, at the end of the story, when Kumudini is reported to be pregnant, he takes her to his home with a show of pomp and power, possibly on the twin goals of subjugating a wayward wife and giving stability to his pedigree.

If Madhusudan's businessman-mindset is the product of an unfaltering and stanch pursuit of wealth, Kumudini's romantic approach is the product of her childhood solitude, her eldest brother Bipradas's influence and her close contact with the classical tradition of India:

> Bipradas has deep devotion to the Sanskrit literature; Kumudini has learnt from him grammar with undivided attention. Ever since she studied *Kumarsambhab* she visualised Lord Siva in her worship of the deity as the hermit of hermits who was the most desired object of Uma's *tapasya*. In the meditated image of the maid her future husband appeared with the blazing glory of divine sacredness. (Translated)

Before her marriage with Madhusudan she had nurtured an idea of a 'loving husband' whom she would admire with devotion and love, and that the entity named husband becomes an impersonal idea to her and, irrespective of any lacuna that may be found in Madhusudan, the individual, and her yield to the idolised husband-image remains unquestioned. But the ground reality after her marriage throws everything out of gear, and a process of cynicism sets in that leads to sex repugnance and disgust for the man himself.

A number of incidents bring about a traumatised transformation in Kumudini. The brusqueness with which Madhusudan proposes that the *Kushandika* ceremony (the ceremony where the husband puts the vermilion in the parting of the hair on the bride's head by performing *yagna*) will be held at the bridegroom's house contrary to the custom is an important eye-opener for her. His conduct just before and at the time of marriage, especially his deliberate intention to dishonour and lower the prestige of Bipradas to settle an old rivalry and quarrel between the two families, does not augur well for a happy wedded life for her. The episode of the sapphire ring in which he forcibly takes away the most prized ring from her establishes his authority and right over his new acquisition, a new possession that his wife. All these instances of his rudeness created ripples of discontent, disgruntlement and raptures that result in the most unusual incident for a bride about to have consummation, and she faints. Madhusudan resorts to lower the dignity and prestige of Bipradas. He hurls abuses and insults at him which at the first instance itself repulse Kumudini of having any physical connection with her husband. It is, however, in the next morning's discovery of the loss of her ring that makes her realise her subservient status in her husband's home as she despondently asks Moti's mother: "Let me ask you one question, will there be nothing to call my own from today?" It is servility that she has been taught and now she cannot take away all that has seeped into her blood through her reading of the Sanskrit classics and epics that had told her the equality of status for the wife. The process of sex-repulsion has started when she feels targeted by a bird of prey:

> Kumudini's heart went shivering just like the female pigeon's seeing the shadow of the hawk from the sky. Her cold hands were sweating, pallid was her face. Immediately after coming out of the room she held the hands of Moti's mother and said, "Take me to a secluded place for some time. Let me be alone for ten minutes." (Translated)

The night of consummation of her marriage teaches her some hard truths in respect of her husband's meanness and the incompatibility of their marital relation. In another incident in the story, to Madhusudan's call to Kumudini to come to his bed, her reply is: "I am not yet mentally prepared. I crave for some time." But ultimately she has to submit to his sex-hunger and invite him to bed and, this amply shows the powerlessness of a woman in our society where she even cannot stay away from appeasing the sexual lust of the partner. Actually, the women do not have any say regarding this. The world seems to move on with the pleasure principles where women's body is just a pleasure site. This is a tragedy for her from which even her God cannot save her. This surrender to the sex-hunger of a loveless, unfeeling husband is nothing but molestation of her womanhood. It is a victory for Madhusudan, but what a victory! Tagore here makes the aberrant authorial comment on Kumudini's defeat and Madhusudan's triumph: "But can it be called a triumph?", thus giving Kumudini's tragic tale a monologue character. The intermittent cry of a dog coming from outside stabbing the silence of the night against which this tragedy is being enacted only focuses on the agony of a molested wife.

This sham reality of loveless sex has close resemblance to the real-life tragedy of a similar kind of latter-day Indian feminist poet Kamala Das for whom marital love was a much-craved-for but elusive reality. The love that she received from her husband was nothing but "an empty gift", "a gilded/empty container, good for show" (Captive). She, therefore, asks her woman-persona as under:

> Woman,
> is this happiness,
> this lying buried Beneath a man?

Kumudini realises the impossibility of establishing a love relationship (which is foremost sexual) with Madhusudan but then considering that it is a great sin to fail to surrender her mind and life to her husband she should at least make a recuperative attempt to behave as *Sati* and *Savitri.* But this attempt of her also fails and finally, when she goes to her sick brother's house, she comes to know of Madhusudan's infidelity. Madhusudan's makes advances to Shyamasundari, his widowed sister-in-law at this point of husband-wife rupture when Kumudini goes to her brother's house. For after Kumudini's departure from his house, he engages in blatant and unabashed acts of adultery with Shyama. Here the great story-teller has subtly pointed to the helplessness of a young widow in a joint-family set-up where she has to succumb to the sexual urges of the members of her dead-husband's family for her own survival. She is powerless, susceptible but then, she too has to survive since there is nothing called financial security for such young widows in our society.

The story ends with Madhusudan's triumph over a recalcitrant wife by posting her with great fanfare to his Mirjapur palace. Before leaving for her husband's house, bowing to social conventions, Kumudini for once burns with anger of protest:

> But one day I will free them, make myself free too; come back I will, you will see. I cannot live in falsehood being false. I am the senior most mistress of their house, what meaning does the position have if I fail to become Kumudini? (Translated)

In the following extract from "Woman to Man" Judith Wright, the famous Australian feminist poet, scripts the history of the birth of child as the product of love-sublimated sex:

> This is no child with a child's face;
> This has no name to name it by
> Yet you and I have known it well.
> This is our hunter and our chase,
> This third who lay in our embrace

The poem gives utmost importance to the woman in the act of creation but Kumudini cannot say of the child born out of such loveless lust, "This is our hunter and our chase, the third who lay in our embrace" like the speaker of the above-mentioned poem.

Confessional writing is a vital part of the literature of the post-modern times. The ones who have left their marks in this genre of writing are Sylvia Plath of the Western literary world and Kamala Das in the East. Their commitment to frank expressions is honest. Tagore's writing, though not confessional, but always gave voice to the muted women of our society. He has almost lent voice to the women who are gagged either by the patriarchal society or by its conventions and rules.

The enigmatic man-woman relationship had baffled these two poetic minds. While Sylvia Plath's women resort to rebellion against their fate, Kamala's sulk and find solace in the extra-marital search for happiness, and Tagore makes them strong and mighty. The monstrous ego of men denigrates women's quest for love.

Plath and Das are sensational for their brutal frankness and virtuosity, and Tagore for his "show and tell". Their dealing with the female psyche becomes immensely successful since both of them created bravura images of women. They all have attacked the male's attitude toward women, they have questioned the underlying malice in men for considering women as commodified sex objects. They have given voice to all the women.

In Sylvia's poems the father-figure looms large and in this story Bipradas's image looms large in front of Kumudini. Sylvia is under the shade of her father's bean tree and Kumudini under Bipradas's care and affection. In her childhood wonder and fancy she tries to see the frightening adult-world as a sad child, a world of make-believe:

> Once I was ordinary:
> Sat by my father's bean tree
> Eating the fingers of wisdom
> The birds made milk
> When it thundered I hid under a flat stone...
> I must swallow it all.

Kumudini shivers like a child and faints when Madhusudan approaches him on the night of consummation. When ultimately Kumudini comes into Madhusudan's room the latter greets her with another bout of spiteful attack upon her and Bipradas that causes deep umbrage in her. The night of consummation of her marriage teaches her some hard truths in respect of her husband's meanness, inferiority complex vis-a-vis Bipradas and the incompatibility of their marital relation.

Fear of sex arises out of absence and unavailability of sex-education in our homes and society. Kumudini was trained to nurture love for the opposite sex as a husband and a lover; but she was not having any idea of her own sexual-needs or the needs of her partner and the result was that she was left unaware of having sex in the manner Madhusudan desired. He too lacked this education. He only knew how to appease his sex-lust through force and physical power. The quixotic essence of love and sex was missing from his charter and that made him appear cruel and heartless to Kumudini.

The defeat of women and the doubtful moral code seemingly baffled Tagore and Plath too and perhaps her being a woman was never considered a virtue by her. Many a time she felt jealous of man's privileges, and expressed fury over the lack of preferences for her. She felt that woman was always at the receiving end and suppressed although out, whereas Tagore's woman goes through turmoil and torture. Sometime there is a win-win situation but most of the time it's she who faces the brutal end.

Kunudini's silent revolt against the authoritarian hegemony of her husband and the subversion of her independent identity and rightful status of equality takes the form of self-ostracism. She takes refuge in the small room for storing oil-lamps adjoining the main store-room. Madhusudan oscillates between command and entreaty for the sole purpose of sex-gratification. In order to win her over so that she submits to him he allows Nabin and Moti's mother to stay on in the house. He is not painted as all-villainous; he too attempts to win over Kumudini's heart so that she consents to his sexual demands and needs happily and he does not have to extract it with pressure. Madhusudan makes some slushy attempts to please Kumudini by giving the sapphire ring back to her, and gifts of pearl necklace and *esraj*. These bribes and lollipop inducements are poor reparation for the space of harm already inflicted and can make little dent in her world of disjuncture.

Kumudini is akin to Tennessee Williams's Stella from *A Streetcar Named Desire*, an American play. Stella in *A Streetcar Named Desire* (1947) is a typical homemaker, socially and financially dependent on Stanley—crude and gauche, a dominating husband who frequently assaults his wife when his temper is out of control. But here Kumudini differs from Stella because the latter is deeply in love with her husband Stanley but the former cannot even find her husband worthy enough of her love; but then both know that in society, they belong to nowhere without their husbands. Stella is very practical when she tries to make her sister Blanche understand that she is physically and economically dependent on Stanley and it is her fervent love for her husband that she ignores his faults. The society Kumudini, Blanche and Stella inhabit is one wherein women are socially, economically and physically reliant on their male counterparts and as a result they are the sufferers of all types of wrongs as we observe in the case of Kumudini, Blanche and Stella. When Stanley seduces Blanche in Scene 10, Stella remains totally unmoved after knowing this; she even does not want to investigate the truth. Also, she does not stop Stanley in sending away her sister in the lobotomy only because her non-compliance of Stanley's wish would debase her position as a loving as well as subservient wife. The agonising irony lies in the ending scene of this play when Blanche is by force taken to the lobotomy, and Stella, incapable of raising any protest, allows her husband to make love to her:

> Stella: Please, Blanche
>
> Blanche: Why are you looking at me like that? Is something wrong with you?
>
> Eunice: You look wonderful, Blanche. Don't she look wonderful?
>
> Stella: Yes
>
> Eunice: I understand you are going on a trip.

> Stella: Yes, Blanche is. She's going on a vacation.
>
> Eunice: I'm green with envy.
>
> Blanche: Help me, help me get dressed!
>
> Stella [handing her dress]: Is this what you?
>
> Blanche: Yes, it will do! I'm anxious to get out of here—this place is a trap!

Madhusudan too has his sexual perversions towards the maids and widowed sister-in-law and has sex with them too. When Kumudini comes to know she says to Moti's mother:

> "See, sister, I came to give myself up to him, but he did not allow me any way. Let him remain with the maid-servant. He will not get me."

The feminist schema of the story is kept up throughout except at the end when Tagore seems to move away bowing to social doctrines and mores. The nature of the conclusion of the story dilutes the feminist agenda, for it is abrupt and goes against the plot. The woman who wages a relentless silent war against the erosion of her honour and an assault on individually has to surrender to an uncalled-for motherhood. Madhusudan takes home the pregnant woman because the question of continuing his lineage is involved with it, thus giving the story an end which is depleting in strength to fight the ills of our society. The story starts with a strong anti-establishment note but dilutes into a conversational one, and consigns the woman to her familiar psychological stress under which she passes the best moments of her married life. The hapless Kumudini is trapped in gestation and childbirth which do not result from sex-love but from a forced-sex that almost amounts to rape. At the end of the novel when Madhusudan takes Kumudini to his Mirjapur Palace with great pomp and show, it signals, once again, the triumph of patriarchy. But this picture of triumph seems to be a staunch sarcastic commentary of Tagore of patriarchy itself.

Recent feminist studies focus on the importance of "women's mothering" and the effect it has, especially its social implications, on producing "a fundamental structure of expectations in women and men concerning mothers' lack of separate interests from their infants' welfare." But in the novel Kumudini and her mothering remain the shade.

It is interesting to note what Tagore himself wrote in a letter to Radharani Devi:

> Such a huge humiliation is equal to adultery—it is as it were an insult to the god—submerging in mire what is best in you.

Another biographer of Tagore, Prabhat Kumar Mukhopadhyay, writes in *Rabindrajibani*.

> The situation in which Kumudini became pregnant is in a way 'legalised rape' by another name.

Works Cited

Arnold, Edward: *The Poetry of Judith Wright by Shirley Walker*, Australia, Pty. Ltd., 1980, p. 91.

Dwivedi, A.N.: *The Conflagaration: Kamala Das and Her Poetry*, Doaba House, Delhi, 1983, p. 91.

Hughes, Ted (Ed.) : *The Collected of Poems*, New York: Harper and Row Publishers, 1981.

Mukhopadhyay, Prabhat Kumar: *Rabindrajibani*, Vol.3, 1961, p. 339.

Tennesse Williams: *Complete Plays*: Penugin, 1984. p.84

7

Sohini of *Laboratory* and Damini of *Chaturanga*

Tagore in the twilight years of his life created the true modern woman—in fact, the Indian version of the new woman in Sohini in the short story, *Laboratory*, by uniting paradoxical forces. She is independent-minded, believes in women's empowerment and is not averse to sexual plurality by virtue of her sexual freedom and yet can stake her life for saving her husband's laboratory. That is, by uniting idealism and individualism Sohini is Tagore's ideal woman. In *Laboratory* his feminist attitude seems to take the most meaningful shape.

Thomas Hardy too indicates a similarly uneven attitude on the gender question. The feminist stance noticed in *The Return of the Native* (1878) takes an about-turn in *The Mayor in Casterbridge* in which Hardy seems to be blatantly patriarchal. Even in the heroine of *Far From the Madding Crowd* (1874) there is an expression of self-beguiling and spontaneous sexual fervour which has given her personality an effulgent glow. Sue Bridehead, the heroine of *Jude the Obscure* is a representative of the class of the 'New Woman' that heralds the New Age. It is possible to consider the characteristics of the 'New Woman' in the heroine of "Laboratory", Sohini. The storyline briefly goes as follows:

> Nandakishore, a Bengali scientist, marries a young Punjabi woman, Sohini. A daughter of a poor, deprived family, Sohini lived with her elderly grandmother. Nandakishore loved her personality, married her and in exchange received her plentiful

> regard and respect. Nandakishore had a laboratory which he set up by himself. It became his place of dedicated work, almost a fixation with him. After his death, Sohini devoted herself to protecting and developing the laboratory, and in this she took the help of their friend and her aficionado Manmatha Chaudhury. She decided to put Rebati Bhattacharya, a praiseworthy student of Nandakishore in charge of the laboratory. Earlier, she had some plan to get her daughter, Nila, married to Rebati, but Nila had neither any depth of character, nor did she have any respect for the laboratory. Her aim was on the one hand to marry Rebati, a good soul, and on the other hand to continue with her wayward and wanton life with Nandakishpore's money. Sohini saw through her daughter's motives. Instead of being blinded by mother's love, she with all her might made Nila's plans flop. The laboratory was saved.

This, in a nutshell, is the tale of *Laboratory*. Sohini, Nila and Rebati's *pishi* (aunt) are the three principal female characters of this woman-centric story. *Pishi* is a mother figure in the story for Rebati. A woman with a powerful personality, she is averse to see Rebati go out of her control. Rabindranath had scant regard for a character like her. His sympathy lay with the sort of mother who is a fountain of love, compassion and self-sacrifice. Such mothers were portrayed, as has been mentioned earlier, in the story *Rasmonir Chhele*: Bhabanicharan's mother Brajasundari looked upon her stepson as her own and his wife Rasmoni single-handedly assumed the responsibility for an encumbered and wretched, poverty-stricken home. In the story *Shesher Ratri* (The Last Night), Jatin's loving *mashi* (aunt) has been immortalised. Rebati's *pishi* is not like them. Nevertheless, she is also a very affectionate aunt in the role of a mother, a mother power. She is the one who wins at the end of the story. Just when Rebati was getting ready to marry Nila, Pishima comes in and calls:

> "Come with me, Rebati." And Rebati, like an obedient boy, followed her out. He did not look back for once. (*Rabindra Rachanabali*, Vol 7: 1010)

Thus Nila's marriage with Rebati breaks off at the last moment, and Sohini's laboratory is saved. The other two women, Nila and Sohini, are poles apart from each other in their nature. Nila is exceptionally beautiful:

> "Nila is very fair complexioned… her skin glows like the white lotus of Kashmir with a hint of the blue lotus in her eyes" (*Rabindra Rachanabali*, Vol 7: 980).

She is well aware of her good looks, rightly skilled in deceit and guiles. She belongs to the clan of lovers. When Rebati is absorbed in his work in the laboratory deep into the night, Nila walks in her night clothes; and brazenly sits on his lap, putting her arms round his neck. In public, she rests her head on his shoulder and tells him, "You do not know how much I want you." In reality, she has no love for Rebati. All that she wants is money and to live life like a free bird. Her aim is to marry this naive man and then do what she is delighted to do. She seeks advice from lawyers who are fascinated by her and with their help she tries to access Nandakishore's money. She cannot compete with her mother, but still has her own strengths. The source of her power is her heady youth. Sohini is the *New Woman*—with her razor-sharp, dazzling eyes, and a lasting smile on her lips like a polished knife. She has a mesmeric persona. She walks in a sari with a knife hidden at her waist. Yet she uses her feminine charm and intrigues when necessary. She asserts astutely, "Deceptions need strategies, just as wars do" (*Rabindra Rachanabali*, Vol. 7: 984).

Interestingly, Rabindranath had no strong disapproval of the tricks sometimes employed by women. In *Swadesh O Samaj*, he wrote:

> Of course women do resort to deception that is also another aspect of women's strength. The demands of men when they exceed the women's resources; are often met by ruses and

> machinations. It is we men who have dubbed women as enchantresses. Indeed we wanted them to so. If they come short, we give them a bad name, when they are useful, we sing their praise. (*Rabindra Rachanabali*, Vol. 13: 21)

His Sohini not only uses these "feminine arsenal" whenever she needs to, but more appreciably, she applies her sharp logical mind and her razor-sharp brain. In her first meeting with Nandakishore, she tells him what the local trading community thought of him—that too, he being a Bengali, has no sense of business, and would be a sitting duck for them.

> "Well, I found," Sohini, the shrewd woman continues, "that none of their intrigues worked. Rather they have fallen into your traps; but they still have not realised this, which I have" (*Rabindra Rachanabali*, Vol. 7: 979).

> Nandakishore is taken aback, "Some girl she is!" he exclaims. Her assessment was perfect. "The spirit of her character comes shining from inside her. It is clear that she knows her worth." (*Rabindra Rachanabali*, Vol. 7: 979-80).

Sohini is fully aware of her merits, so she can neither be ignored nor be defied. In Rabindranath's works there are few characters of such sharp women as Sohini. Her love is that of a strong woman. It may be noted here that Rabindranath believed:

> By natural instinct women are creative and graceful. It is women who make the home, which is no way less valuable or easier than running a business. The motivating force that shapes a home is a womans love. Love is not merely an emotion of the heart. It is a force like the force of gravitation. (*Rabindra Rachanabali*, Vol. 10: 546)

That love is exemplified in Sohini's character. Nandakishore has trained her in his own branch of discipline. He says,

> An engineer husband and the wife, only a homemaker minding the kitchen, are not acceptable. The knots that bind them

> are not the same. I will make them uniform. (*Rabindra Rachanabali*, Vol. 7: 980).

If a man looks for a suitable wife, then they both must have similar assignments in life. Equal status for men and women in a marriage is the message that Tagore conveys through Nandakishore. Although a parallel concept of love is found in *Chitrangada*, an earlier writing of Rabindranath, where Chitrangada, a woman, claims a place beside her husband (*Rabindra Rachanabali*, Vol. 5: 470), this modern concept of love comes out much more forcefully in *Laboratory*. Sohini and Nandkishore's love is not limited to a mere corporeal relation between husband and wife. A bond of respect and thankfulness takes their wedded love to a higher plane. Sohini explains, "He won me over by his steadfast mission of educating me" (*Rabindra Rachanabali*, Vol 7: 986). Brimming with confidence in her own merit as well as of gratitude to her husband, she maintains:

> In relation to the qualities that he found in me, he regarded my shortcomings as insignificant. He reposed his complete trust in a non-descript woman like me, and I have never betrayed this trust.... My smallness he ignored, but gave me unstinted respect where he found I was worthy. Who knows to what level I would have sunk, had he not valued my good qualities? (*Rabindra Rachanabali*, Vol 7: 997)

After Nandakishore's demise, Sohini takes over the mantle of Nandakishore's Laboratory, from a deep sense of love and respect; and moves his mission forward as her own with firm resolution:

> This laboratory was my husband's sacred place of meditation. If I can find a suitable person to occupy the place beneath his altar and keep the lamp burning, then my husband wherever he is, will be at peace. (*Rabindra Rachanabali*, Vol. 7: 982).

Nandakishore has left behind sufficient money, but Sohini does not want it for herself. Every rupee of the legacy is to be spent on the laboratory. Finding a person deserving of the laboratory has become her sole aim in life. Through her dedication to her mission, Tagore portrays the strong bond and loyalty of an exceptional lover.

Sohini is full of warmth. She loves her aged grandmother, who has raised her. She manages to save the about-to-be-sold home of her grandmother with the money of Nandakishore, her would-be husband at the time, and when the grandmother falls ill, she runs to far away Ambala to look after her, leaving behind her precious laboratory. She is very kind also towards animals. She picks up a stray dog and saves its life; she dreams of setting up a hospital for the immobilised dogs and cats and rabbits who suffered from experiments in the laboratory. Without such tenderness of heart Sohini would have been seen as one with a deficient disposition.

Sohini is kind-hearted but not frail. A firm person, she does not allow any barrier to frustrate her mission. If Nila marries Rebati, scientific researches would be affected, "She will destroy whatever comes in her hands" (*Rabindra Rachanabali*, Vol. 7: 992). This fear makes her change her mind about Nila's marriage to Rebati. Her labours now are directed towards keeping them separate:

> She warned Nila; "No way must you ever go near Rebati. Let me tell you that there is just no possibility of your marriage to Rebati.

When Sohini returns from Ambala, she learns that Nila is about to get married to Rebati, and is at the same time consulting lawyers on how to get her share of Nandakishore's money. Sohini then declares explicitly in public that Nila is not his daughter,

> Who do you think your father is? Whose money are you trying to grab? How do you have the impudence to claim shamelessly that you are the daughter of such a noble man?" Sohini has no inhibition in admitting her infidelity. She says that Nandakishore was aware of it: "He received everything from me that he wanted… he was not bothered about anything else". (*Rabindra Rachanabali*, Vol. 7: 1009).

Not only publicly, Sohini had earlier disclosed her infidelity to Manmatha Chaudhury in private:

> I feel ashamed to confess that I had been wanton. The very thought that I have been close to a number of men still ruffles me…. Our temptations lie hidden under our flesh and bones, but flares up at the slightest provocation. It does not inhibit me to tell the truth that very early in my life I went to the bed. We women are not chaste all our life; pretensions are constantly killing us. Even women like Draupudi and Kunti* have to behave like Sita and Savitri. Let me tell you I had no clear perceptions between what was right and what was wrong. I had no teacher to guide me. So I plunged into evil ways as I have been able to come out of it. Yes, my body has been tainted, but not my mind. (*Rabindra Rachanabali*, Vol. 7: 986-87) 2

* Draupadi and Kunti are characters in the *Mahabharata*. Draupadi had five husbands and five different men were fathers of Kunti's five sons. Interestingly, because of their other eminent qualities, they are highly regarded in Indian mythology.

** Sita, the wife of Rama in the *Ramayana*, is an epitome of chastity. Savitri, says a story in the *Purana*, brought back her dead husband alive by defeating the King of Death in an interesting debate.

It is certainly a daring statement not only about her, but about womankind in general. It is society which has forced women to suppress their physical desires and pretend indifference to the temptations of the flesh. In their hearts, however, the flame of desire has existed as strong as that of any man. And since Sohini had not suppressed her desires earlier in life, she had given birth to Nila, an illegitimate child.

Sohini's character is unique and almost matchless in Tagore's works as well as in modern-day literature. Written at the end of the 1930s, Sohini's straightforward admittance of adultery and unfaithfulness was indeed shocking and radical. None of the critics of Tagore, not even the "modernist" *Kallol* writers, had created such a character. A child out of wedlock is a shame for a mother—this was the ingrained view at the time as it is even today. For an Indian woman to admit her "sin" in public is a challenge to the institution. Tagore perhaps intended to do that through Sohini.

Sohini, the "new woman," often says, "I am not a Bengali woman." A question comes in our mind. Why did Tagore show Sohini as a Punjabi woman? Could it be that he did not believe that Bengali women could be so feisty and bold? Unquestionably, Pritilata Waddedar and Kalpana Dutta (Joshi) and other Bengali women carried weapons during the *Biplabi* (revolutionary) movement in our freedom struggle (Mandal 88-100). Tagore's own niece Sarala Ghosal (Devi Chaudhurani) was a image of courage. Possibly he did not wish to shut in Sohini to Bengal, rather chose to present her as a role model for women of India.

In this context, it is important to take note of Tagore's story *Badnaam*. It was published in the journal *Prabasi* in June 1941, a few months after the publication of *Laboratory*. Saudamini of *Badnaam* is also a amazing character. In her daring, in intelligence, in subterfuges, she is no less than Sohini. Sohini's goal in life is to save the laboratory; Saudamini's is to support the struggle for freedom movement. Sohini loves her husband and assumes his responsibility to sustain his life's work. Saudamini loves her husband and yet betrays him in order to continue her life's work. She tells her husband:

> I love you and have looked after you to the best of my ability, and I hoodwinked you for the sake of what I consider my duty.

> The arduous mission that we have accepted leaves no room for love; it asks only to sacrifice oneself.

It has been the conventional Indian belief that a husband is the highest spiritual lord and the most trustworthy person, a saviour too for a wife; Saudamini vehemently attacks this tradition and Tagore takes refuge in her to tell the readers his own mind. Can we then conclude that towards the end of his life, characters like Saudamini and Sohini came crowding in his thoughts? Depiction of these characters only shows how far ahead of his time Tagore was in visualising the "new woman."

Tagore's early perception judgement about women was probably the result of romanticism. In his thirties when he became involved in looking after the family estates, he became conscious of the day-to-day life of the common people as well as the unfair social coercion of women (Bishi, *Rabindra Sarani* 9-10). During the last period of his life, his sensitivity and percept relating to women became fully developed. He discovered that:

> A woman's identity is no longer limited to the role of a mother or a wife. We have arrived at a stage when women are demanding their right as human beings. They want to be counted unreservedly in their identity as individuals. (*Rabindra Rachanabali*, Vol. 13: 28)

He could see that a new age was replacing the existing one:

> I can feel that a new age has dawned in the world.... Women are coming forward to build the new civilisation. The purdah over their faces has vanished, and along with it has gone the purdah that kept their mind away from exposure to the outer world. (*Rabindra Rachanabali*, Vol. 13: 380)

Tagore gave us some very strong women characters befitting the new age. With that he has modestly crushed the traditional and time-honoured social systems and notions antagonistic to the progress of women. His "new woman" for the new age is depicted most forcefully in his story *Laboratory*. "Sohini, undoubtedly, is a woman who in her commitment, in her achievement, in her honest observance of truth is a bold construct of Tagore."

Damini is a widow but an image of a young woman blazing with the passion of physical desires and eager to enjoy life. According to the narrator of the novel, Sribilas, Damini is "the lightning hidden within the folds of Sravan clouds. Outside, youth has brimmed over her physical features; within, flickers of flame are burning scintillatingly."

In Sachish's exact judgement as noted in his diary "she is image of hedonism, one who refuses to deny the pull of her youth, denies death, yearns to enjoy life to its dregs", an antipodal warp to the ways of widowhood.

Connotational device for naming a character is as old as literature itself. The same semantic formulation tells Tagore's naming of characters like Nandini, Damini, Sohini et al. 'Damini' in Bengali means 'lightning' which she irrefutably is, as she exudes glow and warmth of the lightning-flash. It was first serialised in four consecutive issues of *Sabujpatra*, as four different stories under four different names, *Chaturanga*. Though *Damini* is the name of the third part of the novel, which deals with her evolution and development, Damini, the heroine of the novel, makes her appearance in the sixth section of the second part.

Damini of *Chaturanga* is a rebel. A young widow, she is:

> As it were lightning within the fold of Sravan clouds. Externally dollops of youth make up her body; internally moving fire is burning with flashes.... That woman is stranger to death; she drinks deep in the fount of life. Like the flower bower of spring she always fills herself with grace, fragrance and gaiety; she does

> not want to throw away anything, she does not like to entertain a sanyasi in her home; she has pledged not to pay any rent to the north wind. (Translated)

She is a rebel since the death of her husband; in the thin thread of her conjugal life there was no love, only her life had become subjected to untold misery by the 'tyranny of her devotion.' So the unsatiated desire of her body and mind has taken the form of rebellion after the death of her husband. In Lilanandaswami's 'ashram' the women devotees were stuck dumb by seeing Damini's activities:

> On one hand her dress was not like a widow's, on the other she cared a fig for the sage sermon of the guru. Moreover, there was no sign in her of the enlightened state of the mind and body through restraint and purity which spontaneously envelop anybody if he lived close to such a great enlightened personality. (Translated)

But a short while after the appearance of Sachish in the 'ashram', she undergoes a change which is nothing but the expression of her passion of love. In this way Tagore has sketched the story of Sachish-Damini relationship through the skein of attraction and repulsion, and has shown how in spite of the kick/rejection from the object of her love, a slight show of kindness could bring about a change in the mind and demeanour of the love-hungry woman. Considering Damini as an obstruction to his devotional pursuits and asceticism he has asked her to leave the 'ashram'. But Damini has raised her passion for Sachish to the level of reverence-oriented love through process of mental evolution. A sequel to this evolutionary growth is her recognition of Sachish as her guru:

> Damini said, "Be my guru. I shall not accept anybody else. Teach me such a mantra which is far above all these things—so that I can save myself from going astray." (Translated)

Damini's philosophy is an antinomian contrast to the defeatist philosophy of meek passivity projected by Nanibala (the pregnant woman in Jyathamashai chapter, whom Sachish saves, gives shelter and plans to marry against all social calumnies, but fails because she commits suicide) who dies to pay for another man's sin.

Damini is a victim of the specific hegemonistic modes through which patriarchal power operates and castrates female subjectivity. The collapse of her father's jute trade and consequent bankruptcy and poverty destroy the option of her journey back to her father's home. Repression of her bodily needs by an attempt at a vigorous initiation to devotional ways keeps them temporarily subdued, but after her husband's death she refuses to drown herself in the 'wave of devotion' flowing in her house at the cost of her own money. She averts the call of the harassing Guru for giving her counsel, feigning illness. Her repressed desires do not thrust her into destructive behavioural mould; she is love-starved, starved of bodily needs and the possibility of a love-relationship with Sachish, tears off her rebel's mask and assumes a graceful persona of surrender. From the rebel woman she turns a plaint devotee but she wants his love in return. She takes an about turn and mellows down. Sachish, as usual, fails to pierce through the veil of her outward beauty and reach her mind. Here, her disgust with the Guru's devotional ambit and her attraction to come to the fold of Sachish's love are neatly expressed in the form of the broken photograph of the Guru in a meditative posture. There is an apt reference of the imagery of fire and lightning in the phase of Damini's transformation falls in harmony with her inner flame of desire. She is so very actuated by her withdrawn passion that she is seen by Sachish on one calm winter noon after a tiring session of devotional discourse to bang her head on the floor of her bedroom saying, "Stone, O Stone, O Stone, take pity on me, kill me."

Bengali novels before *Chaturanga* depict socially forbidden aberrations of Hindu widowhood and their severe penalty: Matangini for illicit sex relationship with Umashankar in Shibnath Shastri's *Jugantar* and Rohini for her illicit love escapade with Gobindalal and then for betrayal and dual loyalty in Bankim Chandra's *Krishnakanter Will.* They all pay the price of their jaunts with their lives. Damini is not a direct heir of those ill-fated widows, but is a much more urbanised adaptation of a miserable widowhood. She is much improved and vivacious because in between there is Binodini of *Chokher Bali* (The Eye Sore) in this (r) evolutionary route. *Damini* is much braver, more reflective and more resilient. In the hurried quest of her new-found passion for Sachish (though unreciprocated and one-sided) she accompanies the Guru in his travel to some inaccessible terrain because Sachish is a follower (and Sribilas) too. Her vain voyage into the seaside cave where Sachish is resting in solitude, to get only his refusal (in exchange for her deferential love-surrender) and then, her break-down into a tearful retreat, becomes her moments of truth. Though it causes revulsion for Sachish and a temporary umbrage yet it gives her a new illumination about life.

In Sachish's experience in the cave in the dusk of trance and semi-conscious agitation and restiveness, the reality of Damini emerges as a sort of the Jungian shadow; the shadow of the 'mass hunger' that flummoxes his mind. It is the semblance of an *a priori* fear from his devotional path and Damini's behaviour, her banging the head on the floor, is a genuine cause for panic of destabilisation. But to Damini it is the male animus on the part of Sachish that brings indignation and revulsion in its trail. However, it is temporary and contrived towards the object of her love. In her post-cave return to normalcy she feeds her love to distressed animals, gets hold of an injured kite and gives it motherly care and affection, and even nurses an ugly pariah puppy. Her equal care for flowering plants is cognate with this translation and conversion of love. While Adela Questad's hallucinatory experience in the Marabar caves in E.M. Forster's *A Passage to India* shows 'negative refraction', Damini in a worse situation develops a positive attitude to life, her pique notwithstanding.

In the nineteenth century (and also early twentieth century) Bengal, the prevalent social practice was to deprive the widows of all earthly enjoyments. The irony, however, was that the men-folk often forced the widows to have illicit sexual relationship with them. Whenever the illegitimate affair came to light, the entire blame was transferred to the widow, so that she might be chained further (which would even expose her to further sexual torture). The young wives of the old men (a result of the 'kulin' system) also had to face the same kinds of sexual abuse and exploitation. The man who resisted all attempts and endeavours of widow-remarriage was Bankim Chandra Chattopadhyay (he wrote *Bishavriksha* for this purpose). Even before the introduction of Damini, Rabindranath introduces the character of Nanibala in *Chaturanga* to portray the miserable condition of the Hindu Bengali widows and the way they were sexually exploited.

Her attention to Sribilas at this point of her life is tangentially correlated to a sort of 'passivity' in respect of Sachish. Sribilas does her odd jobs and settles towards Damini, but her relationship with him is at best peripheral, for in spite of the bruise on her breast that Sachish has inflicted (by kicking her) in the cave, her passion for the latter still remains undiminished and undeterred. Sribilas' analysis of women's nature in general, "What little I have seen from the surface, from outside has convinced me that women are ready to give their hearts where they are sure to get suffering in return," appears very apposite. It is a kind of masochism and as Helene Deutsch puts it "the attraction of suffering" a prime urge for giving themselves up to men in a force of love-surrender. Helene links it with the 'feminine masochism' and speaks about its genesis thus, "both the outcome of the feminine constitution and of a mechanism of instinctual reversion related to it that turns energies directed towards the outward world inward..." and Damini's submissiveness towards Sachish which is a show of her outer-self may be related to this psychological link with masochism. She demonstrates a pseudo-revulsion for Sachish, yet retains a 'masochistic love bondage' (which is later raised to a spiritual level), with Sachish which is undeniably interwoven with her female psyche. She can neither abandon Sachish nor can foster contempt for him for the pain that he has inflicted on her but above everything else, her internalisation of the male animus causes passivity in her and, she retains her love till the end elevating from passion to a devotional level.

The climax of the story is reached when Damini's rebel mask falls off and she turns into 'Soudamini' (a calm manifestation of Damini) and Sachish's destabilisation starts too; "externally Sachish does not default in meditation, worship and discussions, but a close look at him reveals that within him he is losing grip—his legs are tottering." He makes fervent attempts to bring his mind under control, goes to the seaside solitude to return with a battered body and mind, while Damini lives a puritan, self-imposed life of hardships. It seems to be an uncertain impulse for a woman who has given her heart to an obdurate man, flounders in suffering and yet behaves like a *Khandita Nayika* (offended heroine) of Sanskrit poetry. "Sachish's harshness hurts her, his sweetness soothes." When Sachish comes back and invites her to come and be one with him, the rebel is transformed again, becalmed at the bountiful large-heartedness of the man she worships. Sachish fails to conquer his weakness for Damini, and she becomes an entity of truth that her image, in a tussar (rough silk) sari and just-bathed loosened hair, refuses to go away from his mind and thrusts beyond the boundary of his conscious.

Damini accepts Sachish as her saviour Guru and says, "You become my Guru. I won't accept anyone else. Give me such a *mantra* which is far above all this—by which I can be saved. Don't fix even my god with me." She now accepts love within the parameter of her devotion. Sachish, on the other hand, cannot rise above the dichotomy of his thirst for her flesh and finite beauty and his mad pursuit of the infinite formless. But he finally wins and somehow manages to persuade her to leave the ashram and go away to Calcutta with Sribilas. He says, "Him, I am on the look-out for I need most—to the exclusion of everything else. Damini, have pity on me, do kindly leave me." She consents to Sribilas's offer to marry her. But she dies with unsatiated desires, but with the feeling that "it is not the passion that dogs her like Nemesis to death."

The story has surely achieved a milestone in feminist thinking. Not only did Tagore make a bold and decisive assault on the age-old conservative thinking by bringing about the marriage between Sribilas and widowed Damini, but he has also accorded due importance to the individuality of a woman by prioritising Sachish as the object of true love over Sribilas in the heart of Damini. That Damini rises above Mahamaya, Kusum and Binodini is proved by the fact that the question of society and public libels does not deter her from the path of marriage.

Damini's is not a planar story of a rebel ending up in destruction, but a linear story of transformation and elevation to a status of sublimity and calm brought about by rejection and denial. Her request to Sribilas to take her to the seaside to die with her symbolic 'cardiac pain'—because it is the originating locus of her pain—reminds one of the mountainside death of Wilson in Somerset Maugham's story, *The Lotus Eater* and has the foretaste of peace earned through rebuff.

Tennessee Williams's Stella falls far short if we compare her with Ibsen's Nora and Tagore's Damini, Mrinal and Kumudini. She is completely a submissive but a very practical character. She believes in reality, practicality unlike her sister Blanche who loves to live in a world of dream. Blanche is defeated due to Stanley's wicked scheme but several times she attempted to rebel; she even tries to persuade Stella to leave Stanley but Stella just ignores.

Stella's surrender to Stanley is almost total; she has accepted his world and his values. And that is what we see in our society. We need to be convinced of her fidelity to her husband if we are to accept as credible her collusion in Blanche's committal. Given that Stella cannot imagine life without Stanley, her gameness to sacrifice her sister becomes inevitable. She will carry her guilt as a price to be paid for the preservation of her marriage.

In her paper "Age, Race, Class and Sex: Women Redefining Difference" delivered at the Copeland Colloquium, Amerst College, April 1980, Audre Lorde says:

> But our future survival is predicated upon our ability to relate within equality. As women, we must root out internalised patterns of oppression within ourselves if we are to move beyond the most superficial aspects of social change. Now we must recognise differences among women who are our equals, neither inferior nor superior, and devise ways to use each others' difference to enrich our visions and our joint struggles. The future of our earth may depend upon the ability of all women to identify and develop new definitions of power and new patterns of relating across difference. The old definitions have not served us, nor the earth that supports us. The old patterns,

> no matter how cleverly rearranged to imitate progress, still condemn us to cosmetically altered repetitions of the same old exchanges, the same old guilt, hatred, recrimination, lamentation, and suspicion.

A widespread concept of women is nicely illustrated in Alfred Lord Tennyson's famous poem "Locksley Hall":

> Weakness to be worth with weakness! woman's pleasure, woman's pain,
> Nature made them blinder motions bounded in a shallower brain.
> Woman is the lesser man, and all thy passions, matched with mine,
> Are as moonlight unto sunlight, and as water unto wine.
> (Tennyson, "Locksley Hall" ll.149-153, 1078)

Chaturanga (Four Chapters) fuse to the quartet in the form of a novel as it exists. The first of the chapters "Jyathamosai" is like a foreword and is the sceptical positivity of "Jyathamosai" that Tagore imbibed from the Western culture. *Chaturanga* is mainly a novel of Sachish, Sribilas and Damini. Tagore had written the nationalist novel *Ghare Baire* (Home and the World) the same year, and it is even more stimulating to find him dig into the divine pursuit of humanity in *Chaturanga*. *Ghare Baire* remains a 'period piece' set in the nationalist freedom struggle of British India, *Chaturanga* is timeless.

Tagore's interpretation of Freudian thoughts comments about Kalidas Nag and Tagore's communication on the subject. According to Nag, in reply to his question on the novel *Chaturanga*, Tagore first explained in detail the relationship between Sachish, Damini and Sribilas, three of the central characters, and then proceeded to say the following:

> To the authors of yesteryears life meant desire and frustration, union and separation, birth and death, and certain other similarly imprecise events. Therefore, the play called life had to end either in a cherished and revered union, or with a scene

> devoted to death's vast graveyard. Since a few days now, our impression of our life has been changing—it seems we were so long loitering about the entrance—after a long time we seem to have discovered the way to the inner chambers for the first time. We are awake at the outer side of our consciousness—there we are consciously fighting battles, striking others and are being struck by others. But within these strikes and counter strikes, these ups and downs, something is being created in our ignorance of it. The arena for that gigantic game of creation is our submerged consciousness (*magnachaitanyalok*). (Translated)

It is a new world that has taken birth. This is momentous since in the later part of the novel in an extremely important juncture we find Sachish, Damini and Sribilas spending the night in a cave and Sachish having an erotic libidinal dream. The manipulative use of the cave as a vaginal symbol and fertility—the womb where Sachis and Damini's relationship could have bloomed to a realistic natural consummation—is poised with a Freudian dream sequence of Sachish. An excerpt from Sachish's diary reads:

> After I don't know how long, a thin sheet of numbness spread over my consciousness. At some point in that semi-conscious state I felt the touch of a deep breath close to my feet. That primordial beast! Then something clasped my feet. At first I thought it as a wild animal. But a wild animal is hairy, this creature wasn't. My entire body shrank at the touch. It seemed to be an unknown snakelike creature. I knew nothing of its anatomy—what its head looked like, or its trunk, or its tail—nor could I imagine how it devoured its victims. It was repulsive because of its very softness, its ravenous mass.

That 'primordial beast' curved out to be Damini who possibly comes to Sachish to surrender herself to him. Chaturanga is Tagore's novel with the most overt sexual tensions; and it remains obvious that the references of cave from *Tantrik* mythology and symbol of the hairy animal on Sachish's numb physical identity all are crammed with symbolic eroticism. The author on the one hand copes with with the difference between sane moralising and the pious chase and on the other blends the clash between the fathomless/unformed and the estimable/forms.

This conflict translates to the spiritual and saintly polemics of the 'body' vs the 'soul'. Damini, personifies the 'prakriti' or Nature and the cave as the worldly being, and the main impediment of Sachish is his freedom amidst spiritual arousing. In the long debate between Sachish and Sribilas over this duality where Sachish is forever agitated by the female 'body' and wants Damini to leave the ashram so that he can overcome his passionate desires.

A close fictional sibling of Damini can be Binodini of *Chokher Bali*. Binodini has let herself be a sex toy at the hands of her male counterparts; Damini has unfalteringly been bolshie and at times, wanton—in her sexual liberty and her spiritual access too. In one comprehensive shot she demands explanation where she is treated as a good by her late husband in handing her over to Lilananda Swami. She raises her voice yet again near the end when the wife of one of the disciples of Lilananda Swami commits suicide after finding that her husband has had an affair with her own younger sister.

Our Nora and Damini are supposed to be like this. But their social edifices unfortunately undergo a tsunami change when they refuse to play the archetypal role of femaleness ascribed by the stereotypical gender roles in society by declining to be docile and subservient to their male partners. All these women take on gutsy missions to explore themselves; Nora even forestalls her motherliness. Damini is not a mother and it is to guess what she would do if she had children. Here she stands benefited, as she does not have to consider her surroundings as a mother. Nora deserves more admiration when she tells Helmer that she is no good to play the role of a mother as she is a cheat. Her concluding action is the design of her stirring awareness which further leads her to a long way's drive through life. Tennessee Williams's Stella in the play *A Streetcar Named Desire* chooses to live with Stanley as she plays a docile wife; her agonising love for Stanley outlasts everything. Damini dies at the end of the story with satisfaction and gratitude for Sribilash but why she is not let to live (by the author) remains an unanswered question. If she would not die at the end and if she could live longer, that would somehow give us a positive view that a woman can live happily in conjugal life. At the end, we cannot but admit that Nora, Damini and Stella's are the brutally suffered women in literatures and real life too.

Works Cited

Amrit Sen (Ed.) : *Rupkatha Journal on Interdisciplinary Studies in Humanities*, Vol 2, No 4, 2010 Special Issue on Rabindranath Tagore, ISSN 0975-2935.

Bharati, Ray: *Asiatic*, Vol. 4, No. 2, December 2010.

Bishi, Pramatha Nath: *Rabindranather Chhoto Galpa* (*Rabindranaths Short Stories*). Calcutta: Mitra and Ghosh, 1373 B.E. (C.E 1966-67).

Chaturanga: The Complex Novel, Santanu Biswas's paper, 1916.

Ibsen, H.: *A Doll's House*, trans. James. W. McFarlane, Oxford: Oxford University Press, 1961.

Mandal, Tirtha: *Women Revolutionaries of Bengal*. Calcutta, Minerva, 1991.

Penny, Boumella: *Thomas Hardy and Women*, 1982, p.59-60.

Tagore, Rabindranath: *Rabindra Rachanabali: Birth Centenary Edition*. Vols. 1, 7, 8, 10 &13, Calcutta: Govt. of West Bengal, 1961.

Tennyson, A. L.: "Locksley Hall". 1993. (Ed.). M. H. Abrams. *The Norton Anthology of English Literature* (Vols.2) New York: W. W. Norton & Company.

Williams, T.: *A Streetcar Named Desire*, n.p., Methuen Student Edition, 1984.

8

Mashi, Harasundari of *Madhyabartini*, *Didi*, and Kadambini of *Jibito O Mrito*

Two stories of domestic life—*Mashi* (Aunt) and *Drishtidaan* (Restoring the Eyesight) are remarkable because of the intimate picture which the poet draws of the relationship between the husband and wife and because in both of them there is a touch of abnormality—of psychology in the one and of situation in the other.

Jotin, of *Mashi*, is lying seriously ill, and the story ends with his death. He has tried in vain to win the heart of his wife who cares for nothing so much as idle pleasure and finds it boring to be tied to an ailing husband. An affectionate aunt weaves for the dying patient fantastic stories of his wife's devotion, but the falsity of these stories is easy to see through, and the servant Shambhu pulls down the paradise of lies built by the aunt. Face to face with death, Jotin at first finds it agreeable not press too hard the difference between fact and fiction, and he loves to embrace the hope of Mani clinging to him as a devoted wife, for in the miasmal haziness of the dying man's vision she becomes a less real human being than a world-image with her throne on the altar of the stairs at the confluence of life and death. Indeed, although he waits expectantly for a meeting with her, he is not sorry when she does not really turn up at the expected moment, for his sickly imaginings it seems to him that her physical presence would do violence to this tender vision of her. But there is a sudden and subtle change at the last moment.

Shambhu's exposure tears the image on the ground, and the dying man can no longer afford to dawdle with deceit. He, who has never imposed his claims by violence, has never been a tyrant in his love, wants, before his death, to face the truth above everything else. Not only does he reject the false hopes and the ineffective medicines of the doctor but he also kicks off the shawl which the aunt falsely represented as having been woven by his wife, Mani. This passion for rejecting all false pretences seizes the dying man like frenzy. When death finally closes in upon him and his vision is blurred, and he even cannot see what is at his feet, he exclaims with hectic intensity, "No, Mashi, not that shawl! Not that shawl! That shawl is a fraud!"

In *Drishtidaan* (Restoring the Eyesight) the tragedy is averted in the life of blind Kumudini whose husband returns to the security and confidence after a short fling with Hemangini. This is a story with extraordinary subtlety with which a blind woman's emotions and her penetrating insight are portrayed. There is an atmosphere of feminine delicacy and softness. There is something angelically pure and sweet about Kumo, in her actions even in her shifts and lies. Kumo becomes blind, but her power of perception becomes acute. She easily senses how her husband begins to tire of the attention he has to pay to a blind woman and how gradually he hungers for a new wife. The depiction of the mental chasm that begins to divide the husband and wife relationship is very subtle:

> "The separation caused by the blindness", says she, "is the merest physical trifle. But ah! It suffocates me to find that he is no longer with me where he stood with me in that hour when we both knew that I was blind. That is a separation indeed." (Translated)

The conclusion is both romantic and comical, but unexpected. Kumo's brother gets married to Hemangini and that saves Kumo's husband from embarrassment and, the passion for Hemangini seems like a nightmare which he is even relieved to get rid of. What needs attention in the story is that Kumudini loses her eyesight to treatment given by her amateur doctor husband. She is so overwhelmed by her love for her husband that she becomes suicidal. This portraiture of a tenacious wife who gets herself treated by her doctor husband knowing very well that she is one day going to become blind is quite out of place but probably Tagore wanted to show his women in various hues and tenor, and Kumo is one of them.

In the two stories discussed above—women are contrasted with each other. Mani is true to her ilk of women who do not get bogged down by anything in their life, be it birth or death. But she cannot pretend before her dying husband that she loves him. It has been made obvious in the story that Mani cannot love anybody else other than her own self, whereas, Kumudini prefers to become blind by letting her amateur doctor husband treat her for her blindness. Her blind love for her husband makes her actually blind. The author's deep insight into the human mind and portraiture of the indifferent wife comes out absolutely real and veritable.

The predicament of Nibaran, the husband of Harasundari in *Madhyabartini* (The In-between Girl) is less traumatic but more absurd than that of Jotin's. He is not-so-discontented partner of a charmless conjugal relationship. He agrees to take a second wife under his wife's insistence as she cannot bear him a child. But Nibaran finds charm and novelty in the second wife and Harasundari drifts away from him. But, while giving birth to the child, Sailabala dies and Nibaran makes a hesitant homecoming which leaves disharmony and absurdity between them and now in between them, the dead girl lies:

> Harasundari did not utter a word, nor did Nibaran. They lay on the bed side by side as on the previous nights; but just in the middle lay the dead girl, whom none could cross. (Translated)

Harasundari is yet another tenacious woman who is even ready to sacrifice her conjugal bliss to get her husband a child—unmindful of ruining her own life in the bargain.

Didi (The Elder Sister) records the gradual separation coming in between a husband and a wife, makes use of the technique of the long novel, and the comments of neighbour Tara which seem to serve the purpose of prose chorus. But it is an excellent short story, for in it there are both focus and surprise, the point of the story consisting in the way in which unexpectedly but inevitably the sympathy and the love aroused for an orphan brother cut across the dictates of duty, habit and self-interest. One fascinating feature of the story is the economy of words by means of which, through a few telling strokes, the author portrays this conflict between affection and sense of justice on the one hand and the hostile forces of self-interest on the other. Shashi, the elder sister, pays up with her life (only hinted upon by the author) to save her orphaned brother, Nilmoni, from the clutches of her own husband.

In some stories Nature comes into more cherished contact with human life, and that is why these stories have a lyrical beauty which we do not find in stories that are more investigative. *Shesher Ratri* (The Last Night) is a story of love, but love here receives the ultimate blessing from Nature. The narrator of the story, who is also its hero, does not speak to Surabala who might have been his wife if only he had liked, and has been married to another man; they do not even meet for once in society, and Surabala belongs, for the narrator, to the limbo of unrealised possibilities. But one night when there is a terrible flood, they stand together, facing imminent death; the water has risen to their feet, and if there is just a wave more, it would sweep them both away.

> In our far-off childhood this Surabala had come from some dark primeval realm of mystery, from a life in another orb, and stood my side on this luminous peopled earth; and today, after as wide span of time, she has left the earth, so full of light and human beings, to stand alone by my side amidst this terrible desolate gloom of Nature's death convulsion. (Translated)

This tremendous orgy of Nature seems to give a concrete shape to the unsatisfied and unutterable longings of the speaker, and makes him taste eternal bliss. This experience is so unexpected and yet so all-devouring that it makes all human speech look pitifully small, and that is why not a word is exchanged between him and Surabala; from once at least silence is more expressive than spoken words. Surabala just comes and goes, but she leaves behind her the aroma of the infinite and ineffable. An interesting feature of this story is the socio-comic prelude, giving an account of the hero's ambitions and the frustration. It is the contrast between this comic prelude and the fulfilment of the supreme night that gives the latter its majesty, but the frustration of his hopes shows that the fulfilment is not also without its element of tragedy.

Here in the story, Surabala has accepted her fate. She was once rejected by the hero whom she had loved in her heart. But, now irony would have it that her once craved for man is standing in front of her but they cannot exchange even pleasantries with ease. The very matter-of-fact representation of human mind, and here Tagore does take shelter in his poetic abilities, as in *Ghater*

Katha (The River Stair) to portray the feelings of the frustrated youth.

Kailash Babu has outlived all the pomp and glory of an ancient zamindar, retaining little but the endless witchery of a name. But it is this name that captures his imagination and claimed his loyalty in *Thakurda* (The Babus of Nayanjore). That is why he who is otherwise good-hearted and impeccable would go on weaving impossible yarns about himself and his family with the creative fertility of an artist, and he has also an artist's faith in reality of his own fancies. The old man is a highly attractive person; his yarns do not hurt anyone and they deceive none but the old man himself. There is a touch of pathos, too, because he has little but his pardonable vanity to support him in the hard struggle for existence.

The sequel of "The Babus of Nayanjore" is remarkable in more ways than one. The narrator of the story invents the episode of the Lieutenant Governor in order to befool the old man but his triumph is also his defeat which helps to round off the tale in a very pleasant manner. The double role played by the simple girl Kusum who seemes to be otherwise undistinguished reveals the rich store of human emotion which, under many guises, sustains and sweetens life. The profound affection which the old man entertains for his orphan granddaughter is brought out when, in the height of his joy at her good fortune, he, for the first and last time in his life, admits that he is poor, that the proposal of marriage made by the narrator is for him a boon, thus showing that the deepest emotions of the heart are more powerful than all external attachments, however strong. In the last stage of the story all the characters reveal themselves in an unexpected light—Kusum as well as her grandfather and the narrator who comes to mock and stays to love.

Here in the story Kusum is a strong woman who does understand the intricacies of the human mind and the working of emotions on it.

In *Taraprasanner Kirti* (Taraprasanna's Fame) the wife Dakshayani feels truly great about her writer husband and encourages her like a mother, but as fate would have it, Taraprasanna gets fame but it is not compensated with money. Dakshayani sells off all her assets to finance her writer husband and sends him to Calcutta. She lives in utter penury but keeps her hopes on her husband high. But the irony lies at the end when she is about to give birth to her fifth child (earlier ones all daughters) she realises the need for money. She is about to die during the childbirth and Taraprasanna is unable to fetch a trained midwife. Here the author ends the story showing the fatalistic motherly love of Dakshayani in the following manner:

> Impelled by something, Dakshayani called her husband into her room and said, making him vow to her, "Whenever that pain of your gets bad, don't forget to take your Dream Medicine—and never take off the amulet the Sanyasi gave you." Taking her husband's hands, she secured his promise on countless other minor matters. She also told him not to put trust in Bindubhushan, who had ruined him, so that now there was no question of putting her husband—medicine, amulet, blessings and all—into his hands. She repeatedly warned her husband—her trusting, forgetful, Shiva—like husband—about the heartless and crooked conspirators of this world. Finally, in a whisper, she said, "When my baby daughter is born, if she lives, see that she is called *Vedantaprabha* [The Radiance of Vedanta]" . She took the dust of her husband's feet. In her mind was the thought, "I came into this house to give him nothing but daughters. Perhaps his misfortunes will end now." She dies taking a look at the last born daughter and faintly uttering *Vedantaprabha*.

The motherly love that Dakshayani shows towards her husband is not unnatural. Tagore's keen observation resulted in the making of Dakshayani. A woman taking care of her spouse in a motherly manner is not rare, and where the husbands do not exercise any power to take a decision on their own and are totally dependent on the wives: women like Dakshayani is ready to sacrifice everything, even their life, to protect the spouse.

Kadambini, the widow living with the zamindar Sharadashankar's family, in the story *Jibito O Mrito* (The Living and the Dead) pays up with her life to prove that she was alive. The story goes like this—Kadambini brings up her brother-in-law's son—who is the apple of her eye. She empties all her frustrated widow's love on to this boy, till one night she suddenly dies. To keep the matter quiet, in case the police take notice, her body is taken to the cremation ground on a dark monsoon night. Two of the four Brahmins leave Kadambini's body in the dead of the night at the cremation ground in search of firewood. Suddenly the other two people notice the bed stir a little and the dead body has turned on to its side. They at once run off towards the village. After sometime they return to find the bed empty and the corpse gone.

Kadambini thinks of returning home but then she thinks, "I'm not alive—they won't take me back. It would be curse on them. I am exiled from the land of the living—I am my own ghost." She takes shelter in a distant land in her friend's house. But her mother-heart cries out for the foster son. As the news of her being alive spreads, she returns to Ranihat to see her ailing child. The boy at once recognises his aunt and drinks water from her hands.

The whole household remains stunned to see her as they think her now to be her ghost. Zamindar Sharadashankar, clasping his hands, begs, "Sister-in-law, it is not right of you to do this. Shatish is the only son in the family: why are you casting your eye on him? Are we strangers to you? Ever since you went, he has wasted away day by day; he has been constantly ill, calling out "Kakima, Kakima" day and night. Now that you have bid farewell to the world, please stop attaching yourself to him, please go away—we'll perform your funerary rites."

Kadambini screams out, "I did not die, I did not die, I tell you! How can I make you understand—I did not die! Can't you see; I am alive". She seizes the bell metal bowl which has been dropped on the ground and dashes it against her brow: blood gushes out from the impact. She says, "See here, I am alive!" She goes out running and throws herself into the tank in the courtyard of the house. The author's poetic genius comes alive in the last lines:

> It went on raining all night, and it was still raining the next morning; even in the afternoon there was no let-up. Kadambini had proved, by dying, that she had not died. (Translated)

Tagore in his stories has advocated the cause of women: their problems, their exploitation at the hands of the male-dominated patriarchal society, their sorrows, and their unfulfilled dreams, and finally, he subtly leaves the rest to the reader's imagination. These characters have come alive with his interpretation of their problems. One finds something of the creator in them. He writes about common problems like dowry, poverty, social exploitation of women and their miseries, and in an age when it was met with a lot of criticism from all the corners of the society. Undeterred he went on with his mission and the stories reveal an amazing variety and diersity of their themes.

Works Cited

Bandyopadhyay, Asit: *Rabindranath Tagore: Novelist, Short Story Writer and Essayist, Studies on Rabindranath Tagore.* Vol. I. Ed. Mohit K. Ray. New Delhi: Atlantic Publishers and Distributors, 2004, pp. 47-70.

Iyengar, K. R. Srinivasa: ***Rabindranath Tagore: A Critical Introduction***. New Delhi: Sterling Publications Private Ltd.

Prasad, Hariom.: "Tagore' s Short Stories: A Critical Study." ***Studies on Rabindranath Tagore***.Vol. II. Ed. Mohit K. Ray. New Delhi: Atlantic Publishers and Distributors, 2004. pp. 211-218.

Radice, William: ***Rabindranath Tagore: Selected Short Stories***, Penguin Books, 1994, p.101.

9

Mrinal of *Streer Patro*

Women play the most important role in Tagore's short stories. As the stories revolve around these female characters, they evolve, emancipate in a manner which was unknown to the twentieth century Bengali society during the time when he wrote the stories. The stunning image of Mrinal of *Streer Patro* (The Wife's Letter) opened a new epoch, a new belief.

Streer Patro is a clutter of events happening in a joint family that results in gradual alienation of Mrinal who refuses to be bound to the blood-sapping errands and disgusting household restrictions and to submit to the untrammelled sway of prejudices and superstitions in the family. A meaningful committed relationship might have alleviated her discontent. The suicidal death of Bindu, the orphaned sister of her elder sister-in-law, is the proverbial last straw on the camel's back and she leaves the family and her husband for peace of *Shrikshetra* and the pleasant ambiance of the outside world where she can find her true purport in life. The voice of the rebellion heard from among the lines of her letter to her husband serves as a bolt from the blue on the prejudiced psyche of the patriarchal society:

> You kept me blanketed under the darkness of your habits. Bindu came for a short space of time and surveyed me through an aperture of that cover. That girl through her own death tore that cover as under from end to end. Today on coming outside I know not where to keep my glory. (Translated)

Mrinal's independence, individuality and release in *Streer Patro* opened up new theories of individualism. Her abnegation of the constrictions of man-woman relationship in married life makes her escape from the institutionalised bond of the home (in-laws) to freedom and being. The identity crisis is overcome by her—she refuses to cower down and accept the wrongs being done to Bindu and she goes against the wish of her husband, mother-in-law and all elders of the family to save the girl. She chokes and feels empty from within when she realises that the people around her, in her own household, are so unfeeling and ruthless that to get rid of Bindu (seen as a problematic offshoot of the elder-daughter-in-law), they marry her off to an insane man, which led her to end her life by committing suicide.

Mrinal breaks away from an inert, lifeless relationship with her husband and her sense of freedom and honesty expresses itself in a desire for a free existence. Tagore has rendered her in a bravura image, as an individual who has an identity of her own, a personality which gives jitters to the society and an existence quite distinct and independent from her husband.

Streer Patro (The Wife's Letter) heralded a whole new concept of progressivist thinking together with women's emancipation and feminist stance. This representation of a housewife taking a frantic step, which drew intense censure from the conservative section of the society, is a bold construct that had a lot to do with the discovery in the West of the pride of woman as a woman, irrespective of her value in different roles—mother, daughter, sister and wife.

A patriarchal society is not liberal and progressive in granting its women segment any right, and therefore, women's dignity is an inglorious omission in a traditionalist male-dominated set-up. Any effort at women's progress and improvement or bestowing of equal rights to women quakes the society to its base. Tagore's epoch making story *Streer Patro* invited protest letters and disapproval from the conservative segment of the public after the story was published in *Sabujpataro*. Bipin Chandra Pal's *Mrinaler Patro* and Lalit Chandra Bandopadhaya's *Swamir Patro* published in the monthly journal *Narayan* were not only disdainfully critical of the meliorist writer of *Streer Patro* but predicted bedlam and doom in the family and social life. This progressive and feminist outlook of Tagore championing women's emancipation was not only the result of his personal belief and philosophy; it also assimilated the progressivist thinking of the West:

> It cannot be said that in our society the women had no value; as daughter, wife and mother the woman claimed a romantic outlook and hence love and respect, but outside the family relations the woman had no value as woman; not only in our country, but in any country of the world. The value of the woman is a comparatively recent discovery was first made in the Europe and other Western countries at the beginning of the nineteenth century, but this discovery made its impact in the third and fourth decades of that century and its full-fledged expression was observed after the First World War. *Streer Patro* was the first indication of the impact of that wave on our calm unruffled shores.

Can 'Mrinal : The Untold Story of A New Woman' be a probable sub-title of Tagore's epoch making short story *Streer Patro* (The Wife's Letter)? Tagore had himself acknowledged that this short story was his first endeavour in writing a pro-woman text; the unmistakable agenda of *Streer Patro* is specifically about eliminating the beautiful and submissive wife *Mejo Bou* [the middle-daughter-in-law] to chronicling the birth of Mrinal. This transformation from being a non-entity to a person aware of her uniqueness does not happen all of a sudden. He constructs a very discerning tale in which he gradually traces her rejoinders in her own voice. They become steadily more dense and certain as the text advances and the critical pronouncement not to go back to her husband's house, which could never become a home for her, though she lived there for 15 years:

> But I shall not return to 27, Makhan Baral Lane ever again. I saw what happened to Bindu. I have realised the position women have in this society. I don't want to go through it anymore. (Translated)

Mrinal was 12 years of age when she was married. She was a child bride. This letter is written when she is 27. So the traditionalist debate that a bride identifies with the culture of her marital home more easily if she is married at an early age does not seem convincing and realistic. Mrinal herself is sentient about what sets her apart from the rest of her in-laws' family members. She firmly states that her cerebral mind had been posing a threat to the members of her in-laws' household. So she writes:

> It didn't take you long to forget that I had beauty. But that I was intelligent, that is what you were reminded of at every step... . My mother was always very anxious about this intelligence of mine. For one who has to accept the line of control, if she desires to follow her rational thinking then she is destined to stumble at every step.

Another remarkable feature of this short story is that the clash and shelling comes in the form of a personal letter, the very first letter that the wife writes to her husband in a marriage of 15 years. Mrinal explains that this is her first letter to her husband, since marriage she has been living in her husband's home, so the need for letter writing has never arisen. They both experience lovelessness in their relationship. The politics of daily living make her drift away from her husband is a fact that her husband does not perceive or chooses to disregard taking it to be just another phrase of feminine foible and quirk. Here we are addressing an erudite woman, cultured and educated to the extent to be able to quote from a song of Mirabai. Though the text tells us that Mrinal got married when she was 12 years old, she is not only literate but she even states that she writes poetry:

> I had something that was beyond the precincts of your domestic drill. I used to write poetry secretly. Never mind if it was all nonsense... . That was my freedom. There I could be myself...That I am a poet, that's something you could not discover in the past fifteen years. (Translated)

This proud surrender of Mrinal that she had an undisclosed source of happiness in an environment of endless placations leads us to the tales of many such nineteenth century Bengali women, who found release and relief from the strictness and severity of patriarchy through their ingenuity and creativity.

It may be interesting to review briefly the state of women's education in India, particularly Bengal in this case, during the last part of the nineteenth century and early twentieth century. The report on the State of Education in Bengal in 1836 observed:

> A superstitious feeling is alleged to exist in the majority of Hindu families, principally cherished by the women and not discouraged by the men, that a girl taught to read and write will soon after marriage become a widow. Interestingly, Haimavati Sen's memoir corroborated the official document as she recorded, "But I had no right to education. Though I lived like a boy in every respect, in matters of education I remained a woman. It is a popular superstition in our country that women, if educated, have to suffer widowhood.

In 1849, the first girls' school was founded by Bethune in Calcutta. By 1854, there were 288 girls' schools in Bengal mostly established by missionary societies. Later, the Hunter Commission Report on Indian Education in 1882 stressed the need for higher education for women, and soon enough a few enterprising women educationists set up schools and planned curricula to meet the needs of female schooling in India. The aim of such institutions was to coach women to become "better wives and mothers in a modern world".

It is perhaps quite apt to mention the first lecture tour of America made by a Bengali woman in 1927, a little over a decade after the publication of *Streer Patro*. This woman was introduced in America as the "niece of Tagore." Indeed, Tagore's niece Sushama Mukhopadhyaya, who made this historic tour, was a married woman, a mother of seven children, and her husband was a barrister. However, though she could speak in English and was aware of colonial culture, her personal responses regarding the position of women in India were conventional, conservative or rather drab:

> The supreme, traditional virtues of the Hindu woman are fidelity, sincerity and self sacrificing love. A wife subordinates her wishes to those of her husband.

Also, in a lecture hall in New York, Sushama spoke with strength and arrogance about Hindu culture, marriage and marital relationship:

> Your idea of marriage, companionate marriage and love seems very strange to us. Your divorces startle us. We believe in the holiness of marriage, considering it a sacred and divine union of two souls. Our marriages are regarded as permanent; separation or divorce unspeakable, we stay married.

If this was the response of Rabindranath's educated, cultured, English-speaking married niece in 1927, should Mrinal's letter be regarded as a bromidic sermon? In this context one can remember that in Calcutta, Sushama's friend Lillian Palit created a sensation by becoming the first Bengali woman divorcee. She later remarried a man of her choice. Also, the princesses of Cooch Behar married British husbands and, one Hariprova Takeda married a Japanese man, and left for Japan in 1912. All this happened a little before or after the publication of *Streer Patro.*

Fidelity and sincerity are virtues that are expected everywhere and in every human relationship. So one should not argue about these virtues and true love also demands self-sacrificing, which is natural in almost every love-relation. Sushama speaks of "holiness of marriage" etc, and blasts divorces—is unexpected from a woman whose uncle had written *Streer Patro* or *Manbhanjan*, or married his son to a widow. But, coming from Hemendranath's daughter, it is not very surprising. Sushama Mukhopadhyay may have said this. But she was also an accomplished woman herself and—more importantly, wrote wonderful articles on women's emancipation in many Bengali journals. The fact is that the Adi Brahmo Samaj could not break away from the shackles of some traditional Hindu mores which are at the root of such observations as the one made by Sushama. Especially, Dwijendranath and Hemendranath were too much influenced by conservative Hindu views, which also influenced Hemendranath's children—like Sushama. It was this same Sushama who said to the Americans that "You call God Father, but we call God Mother". This shows that though born as a Brahmo, Sushama was at heart a conservative Hindu, because Brahmos call God "Father", not "Mother". The irony is, Rabindranath's granddaughter (Sushama's niece), Nandini, divorced her husband Ajit Singh Morarji Khatau. This divorce case caused a lot of bitterness, because at that time the Indian divorce laws were heavily loaded against women, and she never got any alimony, though she married for the second time. This puts paid to Sushama's observations against divorce!

Soon after Tagore returned from his second voyage to England, he wrote an essay *Prachyo O Proteechyo* (The East and the West) in 1891, where he noted how in the plays of Henrik Ibsen the women rise up in revolt against patriarchy. He also said that Ibsen showed a society where men would neither allow women to build up homes according to the latter's choice nor would they allow the women to enter the professional world. Hence, there was conflict. This shows that Tagore was well-versed with Ibsen's thoughts. However, one always thinks that even Ibsen would have felt blessed if he could write a story like *Manbhanjan* (Breaking of Ice) (1895) where the victory and revenge of the woman over her husband is so explicitly and graphically shown. Tagore always wrote championing the rights of women. One must not forget that Labonyo or Ela do not depend on their paternal property, and Kumudini openly says that "There are some things one can't give up even for one's son". Even months before his death—on 16 January 1941—Tagore had said that Indian society would not improve unless we learnt to pay respect to women as the West did.

Those who have grown up in a patriarchal social system will find it difficult to appreciate Ibsen's *A Doll's House* or Rabindranath Tagore's *Streer Patro* (The Wife's Letter). India is a country where women are always abused—women are held responsible for attacks against them [blaming their dress, conduct etc], they are harassed in educational institutions or in the professional world, they are looked down upon as commodities, women are forbidden to fall in love, marry according to their own wish or even to talk on mobile phones (Baghpat Khap Panchayat diktat!). In such a social set-up, it is quite natural that most people will find it surprising that Nora walks out of her husband's home, or Mrinal walks out of her husband's home, because most of the Indians are raised to believe that patriarchy is the best.

Tagore's short story drafts the abject cultural taming of three women in their markedly distinct spaces. *Streer Patro* is a story about three women, all represented by the signatory of the explosive letter, Mrinal. As she represents herself, she also represents the disturbing unimportance of Baro Bou, Mrinal's elder sister-in law and her young sister Bindu, she speaks up for all of them. Her close watch, her shrewdness, her free spirit are drafted in each line of this letter of power that questions, destabilises and finally discards the forceful and cruel stronghold of patriarchy. The epistolary storyline possesses a superlative merit, for the insidious voice of the letter-writer establishes a sense of direct familiarity between the reader, and writer and thereby creates a remarkable logic of realism. It is a dialogue held in absentia. The efficacy of this mode is too well known to all who are acquainted with literature representing different cultures, whether of the past or contemporary times.

The delicate but the confident and ironic tone of Mrinal's letter to her husband of 15 years is distinct and powerful. It begins with the customary deferential address *Sricharankamaleshu* (Your Revered Lotus feet) but ends with supreme self assurance as Mrinal signs off with the subscription *Tomader Charantala sroychinno* (Free from the shelter beneath your feet), Mrinal". By signing her own name rather than the explanatory chronological nomenclature attributed to her as *Mejo Bou*, that is, wife of the second son, Mrinal is reborn as herself. The closing celebratory line of Mrinal's letter is a re-scripting of Mirabai's song that is quoted by the wife who has discovered herself and her identity and becomes Mrinal from *Mejo Bou*, "I too will live. I am safe now."

Mrinal's emancipation in a male-authored text indicates that Tagore was able to trumpet and shore up the winds of change. We are not directly aware of his knowledge of and reaction to

Ibsen's feminist play *A Doll's House* published in 1879. But it would be very strange if indeed he had missed reading Ibsen. The critical moment is when Nora rejects the protection and security of her husband's home and closes the door behind her. The decision to step out from a cocoon of satisfied comfort and embarking on the risks for an independent survival has been connected with the emergence of the New Woman in Western culture. It was altogether a new concept in India. Educated Indians were aware of the suffragist movements and the New Woman concepts of the West. As a matter of fact educated women had been scorned, tormented and ostracised by the old school of caste society of the nineteenth century often for imitating the West. But then there was this major distinction. The women of *Thakurbari*, as Tagore's ancestral mansion at Jorasanko is called even to this day, were all educated and many of them were creative writers; many adapted Western lifestyles selectively, and were known for their brilliance in the performing arts. Chitra Deb's significant text *Thakurbarir Andarmahal* is a whole and composite collage of the astounding talents of these women who adorned the Tagore home. However, the women of Tagore's household generally conformed to traditional norms regarding marriage and fitted themselves into the expected roles of homemaker and care giver as wife and daughter.

Other than Mrinal, the two other women in the story are Baro Bou, the eldest daughter-in-law and her orphaned sister Bindu. Baro Bou does not come from a rich family nor is she beautiful. As a result, she withdraws herself and she is always painfully reminded of her parental background. When her unmarried 14-year-old sister comes to stay with her, Baro Bou does not feel happy since she feels more powerless. She is already conscious of herself and her limitations, in this household and on the top of this; Bindu's arrival becomes an added embarrassment. She withdraws herself from any display of affection for her orphaned sister, Bindu. In order to prove that she is not a financial burden on the family, she makes her do the strenuous household works. She tries to project her living in the family as significantly gainful at a minimum investment. Mrinal's own daughter dies soon after birth. Mrinal's longing for a child is somewhat compensated by the arrival of Bindu in the family. She takes upon herself the role of Bindu's proxy mother.

Bindu is so overwhelmed by the compassion shown by Mrinal that she falls hopelessly in love with her. Mrinal writes:

> Bindu began loving me to such an extent that I felt scared. I had never known love like this before. I read about it in books—but that was between men and women...She couldn't take her eyes off my face...The girl became absolutely obsessed with me...the intensity of Bindu's love for me made me restless. Sometimes I would be angry with her for this, but I have to admit that through this love of hers I discovered myself in a way that I never will ever again in my life. That was my free self. (Translated)
>
> Mrinal's sexuality and sexual magnetism has been implicitly quoted in the text. The above example of romantic love between two women is a noteworthy sequence with dominance given to the charm of the female body. Romantic love between siblings, cousins and friends is a recurrent sub-theme of many Bangla novels of the nineteenth and twentieth century. However, erotic love or lesbian relationship, or the possibility of such a relationship between two women have been steadily elided or omitted as a taboo question in women's fiction or fiction representing women. Sometimes those silences and absences boom with an incredible blow. (Translated)

Can we yet afford to appropriate the term 'Queer' for Bangla literature? We need not go into the debate whether subscribing to Western terminologies and identity categories for South Asian local literature is justified or not; actually same-sex love was never really identified in Bengali literature or for that matter in performative arts (dance, dance-drama, yatra, etc) as what we understand as 'queer' today! In fact, to go back to Foucault's 'History of Sexuality Vol. 1', the Greeks would never identify themselves as bisexuals, for erotic desires were organised along different coordinates, not as we define them or try to categorise them today. Therefore, trying to read a Tagore's story using the Queer theory seems epistemologically incorrect reading if not outright anachronistically problematic because, such a Westernised reading completely overlooks the 'local' tradition '*sakhiayani*' where considerable physical intimacy between women was involved. In fact, *Streer Patro* does exactly that! It might not be read in the light of westernised queer theory. Again for that matter, in Bankim Chandra Chattopadhyay's 'Indira', Indira and Subhashini smooch! Do we have to appropriate that in the discourse of Euro-American queer theory? Honestly, it is a kind of homoeroticism which the term 'lesbian' falls short of defining! In fact, in "Devi Chaudhurani", the *sakhyata* (friendship), Prafulla and Sagar Bou share exudes strong undercurrents of homoeroticism, all the more, because at times, their husband Brajeswar appears completely irrelevant to both of them now, is that lesbianism too? In fact, delimiting the myriad possibilities of sexual desires and passions by using terms such as 'queer' or 'lesbian' or 'gay' is absolutely exasperating, and it's high time we gave up such propensity.

The nineteenth century texts and those after that can be read using encounter theory. When two different cultures come face to face both are forced to re-think their own constructed selfhood. We all know that one of the most important aspects of identity is gender. Nineteenth century is such a laboratory where a lot of things were re-thought including gender. We have to say that the Western notion of a queer which comes from their own cultural specificity cannot be ignored altogether while measuring post-colonial Bengali literature. They were contaminated and re-defined as was Europe's own codes of gendering. New myths were born, older identities displaced and supplemented. This is what one can call colonial supplementarity. Now, that we all have a bad habit of abusing colonialism and Western bourgeois enlightenment indiscriminately we try to imagine an uncontaminated real before the encounter. But each encounter initiates a loss of identities—nothing remains the same as before. This loss acts like chemokine—working both ways—positive and negative entangled and in process of production of each other. It is poisor as well as medicine.

Bindu's marriage is arranged. She realises on the very second day of her marriage that husband is mad and aggressive. She is tremendously petrified of him. She run away from his home and Mrinal assures her that she will look after her. But Mrinal's husband and in-laws reject it; Bindu is forced to return to her marital home only to flee again. This time she seeks shelter in her cousin's house but is again forced to return. When Mrinal sends her younger brother Sarat to find out about Bindu's welfare, she gets the news that Bindu has burnt herself to death. Mrinal, on hearing the news of Bindu's death, the author seems to lament through Mrinal's comment

> At last there was peace. The whole country was enraged. They kept on saying, "It's become fashionable for women to commit suicide by setting their saris on fire."
>
> "All of you said: All this is dramatics." May be. But how is it that the fun of drama is enacted on the saris of women and not on the dhotis of the brave Bengali men, that is a fact one needs to think about. (Translated)

In *Streer Patro* Tagore has raised issues that arise out of the system of arranged marriages in our society; and the trapping and enslavement of women as wives. All three women—Mrinal, Baro Bou and Bindu—have loveless marriages. Their husbands provide them with protection, security and sex; Bindu is even denied of that. Adjustment and compromise are the magic words that uphold the fabric of the patriarchal middle class family; there cannot be any potential partnership and camaraderie in this relationship between the powered and the powerless. In the cases of Bindu and Mrinal, there has been resistance to this fraud of their power. Bindu commits suicide while Mrinal leaves in order to breathe and be alive.

Foucault makes a terse scrutiny about such power relations that needs to be quoted in some detail here:

> There cannot be relations of power unless the subjects are free. If one or the other were completely at the disposition of the other and became his thing, an object on which he can exercise an infinite and unlimited violence, there would not be relations of power... Even though the relations of power may be completely unbalanced or when one can truly say that he has "all power" over the other, a power can only be exercised over another to the extent that the latter still has the possibility of committing suicide, of jumping out of the window or killing the other. That means that in the relations of power, there is necessarily the possibility of resistance.

Unaware of Foucault a Bengali Hindu woman Kailashbashini Debi, wrote in 1864:

> In a marital relationship if one person is superior and the other inferior, then the former will, in all probability be contemptuous and brush aside the other...There should be no marriage unless the husband and wife are both equal because there can be no unity unless both are equal and without it love cannot be achieved.

It took another 50 years since *Streer Patra* for a Bengali woman writer to script confrontation and refusal in her path-breaking novel *Pratham Protisruti* published in 1964. In the first novel of Ashapurna Debi's trilogy, Satyabati can be regarded as a true younger sibling of Mrinal, who is educated, confident and has the audacity to stick to her belief. Satyabati decided to leave her husband and home after thirty years of leading a married life. Married as a child bride of eight years of age, Satyabati experienced a rare sense of freedom as she told her husband:

> For thirty years I have been looking at you for everything, now at the fag end I want to look at myself. (Translated)

The kinship between Mrinal and Satyabati is obvious, and both these women in Bengali fiction in 1913 by Tagore and in 1964 by Ashapurna Debi precursored the promise of the surfacing of powerful women as active negotiators of social change.

Interestingly, in 1992, Taslima Nasreen, the renowned Bangladeshi feminist author, wrote in *Nirbachito Column*:

> If you are a woman, you must traverse beyond living death in order to really live. They will teach you fidelity, the virtues of "Sati", they will preach to you about womanhood, they will describe the glory of motherhood. If you step into these evil traps of false education, they will kiss you, lifting you in their arms they will dance with frenzy, they will give you four walls, golden chains, they will offer you food as they do to their pet parrot. If you are a human being then just break off your chains and stand up.

Taslima's trenchant prose is harsh and violent but the essential message of her text is same as the previously discussed texts. There is a strange resemblance in the response in these texts of Tagore, Ashapurna and Taslima. These three texts cover the whole twentieth century, comprising both colonial and postcolonial India. But *Streer Patro* is as much a feminist text as *Pratham Pratisruti* and *Nirbachito Column*.

Henrik Ibsen's Nora, Tagore's Mrinal and Tennessee Williams's Stella are three women characters from three different literary pieces, *The Wife's Letter*, *A Doll's House*, and *A Streetcar Named Desire* from India, Europe and America respectively. Though their lifestyles are not similar and belong to different socio-political contexts, the predicament and misery they have to endure are almost alike as they are the representatives of women in general. Nora's conversion from a doll to a lively human, Mrinal's refusal to continue living in her in-laws' household and Stella's acceptance of the tragedy to be her fate are departure from the stereotype gender roles assigned by the conservative male members of society.

Women are just seen as 'women'—the patriarchal notion of being the better-half of man, the source of warmth, amusement and nursing, some kind of service provider or showpiece to prettify men's house, the mother attributed with motherliness, a home manager of household duties. Stella too is such a typical, tame wife of Stanley in Tennessee Williams's *A Streetcar Named Desire*. Both Nora in *A Doll's House* and Mrinal have played all these roles (except that Mrinal was not a mother) as long as they were acknowledged as Stella as Mrs. Stanley, Mrs. Helmer (Nora as wife of Helmer) or Mrinal as the *mejo bou*. But at a certain point they have to preclude their uniqueness as some gentleman's wife or a daughter-in-law because situations make them do so. The societies wherein they have been living for years are likely to revile them but their final actions have paved the way to view themselves as human beings ascribed with a deep longing for love, free will, self-discovery and self-security.

Nora is the main character in Henrik Ibsen's famous play *A Doll's House*, published in the year 1879. It was the time when even in Europe, the idea of a married woman deciding to go away from her family and refusing to render absolute submission to her husband was somehow weird and appalling. The play had a memorandum to the contemporary European society which sought to rouse a sense of individual responsibility among women.

Nora's accomplishment apparently seems disturbing, impetuous; but it is more beyond gross emotion—it is the revelation of her strong feelings with reference to how she has been disgraced in her husband's house. At the same time we know that Nora and her husband are the products of patriarchal society that teaches men to be superior to women. Nora is the much-loved, adored wife of Helmer, an esteemed man, rigidly candid, of high ethical ideals, and fervently devoted to his wife and children—as she believes him to be. Nora is just the doll wife of Helmer; she is always concerned to avoid things that he dislikes. As he wants Nora should not eat macaroons, Nora dare not take it though her strong craving for macaroons sometimes let her taste it stealthily.

Nora, too, considers herself fortunate. Indeed, she worships her husband, believes in him unconditionally, and is sure that if ever her safety should be menaced, Helmer, her idol, her God, would perform the miracle. When her husband's life is in danger, it is a self-propelling duty for her to forge her father's name on a note and scrounge an amount of money on it, in order to take her sick husband to Italy. She works hard, and saves every penny of her pin-money to pay back the amount she borrowed on the forged cheque. She is light-hearted and cheerful, in fact without complexity, depth of her mind.

In the perception of Nora there clearly lies a dormant persona and character, which could come into full bloom only through a great miracle—not the kind she hopes for, but a miracle just the same. Even when she is confronted with this repulsive threat, she does not fear for herself, only for Helmer, who has such an aversion to debts, and who loves her so devotedly that for her sake he would take the blame upon himself. Nora, who cannot understand why a daughter has no right to spare her dying father's anxiety, or why a wife has no right to save her husband's life, is surely not aware of the true character of her idol. But sequentially the curtain withdraws. And in the last Act, the final blow comes. For 48 hours, Nora combats for her ideal, never apprehending Helmer for a moment. The end comes, and with it the doll's house topples down, and she casts off her doll's dress—she discards her skin, as it were, then she realises how much she has been mistreated, that she is only a game, a doll to Helmer. In her disillusionment:

> Nora: You have never loved me. You only thought it amusing to be in love with me.
>
> Helmer: Why, Nora, what a thing to say!
>
> Nora: Yes, it is so, Torvald. While I was at home with father he used to tell me all his opinions and I held the same opinions. If I had others I concealed them, because he would not have liked it. He used to call me his doll child, and play with me as I played with my dolls. Then I came to live in your house... I mean I passed from father's hands into yours. You settled everything according to your taste; and I got the same tastes as you; or I pretended to—I don't know which—both ways perhaps. When I look back on it now, I seem to have been living here like a beggar, from hand to mouth. I lived by performing tricks for you, Torvald. But you would have it so. You and father have done me a great wrong. It's your fault that my life has been wasted...
>
> Helmer: It's exasperating! Can you forsake your holiest duties in this way?
>
> Nora: What do you call my holiest duties?
>
> Helmer: Do you ask me that? Your duties to your husband and children.
>
> Nora: I have other duties equally sacred.

> Helmer: Impossible! What duties do you mean?
>
> Nora: My duties toward myself.
>
> Helmer: Before all else *you* are a wife and a mother.
>
> Nora: That I no longer believe. I think that before all else I am a human being, just as much as you are—or, at least, I will try to become one. I know that most people agree with you, Torvald, and that they say so in books... I must think things out for myself and try to get clear about them.... I had been living here these eight years with a strange man, and had borne him three children—Oh! I can't bear to think of it—I could tear myself to pieces! I can't spend the night in a strange man's house. (Ibsen)

In real life there is nothing more degrading to a woman than to live with a stranger, and bear him children. She has to conform to the societal notion of duty and she needs being not anything else other than a toy, a doll, a nonentity.

Nora has been living for eight years in Helmer's house but she has no power in deciding on anything, rather, it is Helmer who is the master and decision maker in his house. It is because of her frail persona that she has be converted into a doll in Helmer's hand and in her 'Papa's house' which she realises at the end of the play. With a view to saving her husband's life, she fakes her dead father's signature. On the other hand, her friend Mrs. Linden is a woman of strong personality who gives priority to looking after her sick mother and helpless brothers; she knows what will make her happy and she acts accordingly. At the end of the play, we see Mrs. Linden and Krogstaad are planning to tie the marriage-knot whereas Nora and Helmer are going to be estranged—Nora laughing at her marriage bond. What strong points she lacks are possessed by Mrs. Linden—now it is her turn to know what she indeed needs. When Nora slams behind her the door of her doll's house, she opens wide the entrance of life to be viewed by a woman as a human being, and decrees the stirrer communication that true freedom and unity make a fair bond between man and woman.

Nora, too, exercises her will power but that we do not notice till the end of the play. In her case, we notice a complete makeover in her; she is a passive character in the first place whose eating practice is also guided by Helmer but there is an abrupt high-level of development in her character at the end of the play. Symbolically her 'Tarantella' dance helps her gather her spiritual strength. Now she becomes orally and actually articulated. Her exit is the most critical step to know her, to let her exercise what her heart wants.

Works Cited

Chakraborty, Santosh: *Studies in Tagore*, Atlantic Publishers and Distributors, New Delhi, 2004.

Deb, Chitra: *Thakurbarir Andarmahal*. Calcutta: Ananda Publishers, 1983, p.153.

Debi, Ashapurna: *Pratham Pratisruti*, Calcutta: Mitra O. Ghosh Publishers, 1964, p.433.

Forbes, Geraldine: *Women in Modern India*, Cambridge University Press, India, 1996, p.33.

Karlekar, Malavika: *Voices from Within*, New Delhi, Oxford University Press, 1993. p.59.

Manu Smriti, 3.55. See http://www.scribd.com/doc/7189037/Manu-Smriti-Sanskrit-Text-With-English-Translation.

McNay, Lois: *Foucault and Feminism*, California, Notheastern University 1992, p.173.

Nasreen, Taslima: *Nirbachito Column*,Calcutta: Ananda Publishers, 1992, p.128.

Sarkar, Tanika: "Mrinal Onyo Itihaser Sakhar" *Desh*, 5 August, 2005, p. 35.

Tagore, Rabindranat: *Streer Patro*, *Rabindra Rachanavali*, Vol. 7, Calcutta: Visva-Bharati, 1986. p. 647.

10

The Enigmatic Binodini of *Chokher Bali*

The personality and sexual independence of Binodini in Tagore's *Chokher Bali* (The Eye Sore) are the inevitable results of this twentieth century concept of individualism and liberty.

The presence of child-widows became inevitable in the middle class homes in Indian society because of the custom of unequal marriage between tender aged girls and old men. Then, on the one hand their harsh lifestyle brought them untold misery, and on the other, the natural youthful growth and repressed sexual urges helped develop a socially unacceptable illicit sex relationship with the younger male members of the family. The sex feelings that arise in the mind of Binodini make her jealous of the Mahendra-Asha conjugality. Again, the jealousy that has been created in her seeing the excess of affection in Bihari for Asha is another expression of her repressed sexual feelings (it must be remembered that Binodini is a child-widow). Tagore writes:

> Bihari could not see Binodini's face in the dark, envy flashed on her face. Today seeing Bihari she understood that his heart was tormented with pity for Asha. Binodini herself was none! She was born only to shield Asha, only to remove all the thorns from her path and only to help in the full realisation Asha's happiness. Mahendra would marry Asha, and so under the machinations of fate Binodini would have to live with wild monkeys at Barasat, Bihari cannot bear innocent Asha shedding tears. So Binodini would always have to stand ready with the

> end of her sari. Once Binodini wants to show this Mahendra and this Bihari who is Asha and who is Binodini by lowering them to the dust along with the shadow at her back! She was to show what a great difference exists between them! Because of adverse fate having failed to unobtrusively ensconce her talent in the mind of a man, Binodini assumed the form of destruction by wielding the fiery *shakitshel*. (*Rabindra Upanyas Samagraha*, Viswa Bharati, 1990, 229, translated).

According Freud, moral development coincides with the development of the super ego. The most significant moment in the development of the super ego in boys, in the resolution of the Oedipus complex, arises from the fear of castration. In the case of little girls the question of this fear does not arise and, therefore, in them the resolution of the Oedipus complex is not as complete as in boys with the result that their centre of morality remains underdeveloped. In other words, in Freud's view the sense of morality is less developed in girls than in boys. Though these views of Freud have now come to be contested by recent researchers, Binodini's desire for establishing a covert, illicit relationship with Mahendra seems to have a Freudian perspective. But in real terms what is discreditable in this desire is more of game playing than sincerity. True, she has expressed the hunger of her heart to Mahendra in letters written on behalf of Asha, but she has never capitulated herself in the sex advances of Mahendra. The object of her love is Bihari and Mahendra. This at least is proved by her submission to Bihari after Mahendra proposes to elope with her:

> "Lord of my life, I knew that you are not mine internally, but kindly love me or a moment today. Then I will retire to our forest without demanding anything from anybody. Give me something which I can remember till death." Saying this Binodini advanced her lips towards Bihari closing her eyes. (Translated)

Mahendra's love advances have been rejected umpteen times, and when at last she agrees to leave home with him, it is only to go in search of the fugitive Bihari. Only once does she come close to submitting herself to Mahendra's sexuality, during Asha's sojourn to Beneras. She is drawn to him in the name of nursing him in his illness:

> Sitting near his head when she was mildly massaging his forehead, Binodini's head was slowly being bent under the heavy weight of her confounded with; at last the tips of her locks touched Mahendra's forehead by the shaken slight touch of the wind-wafted hair locks his whole body began to tremble repeatedly, suddenly his breath seemed to get stuck near his breast and found no outlet. (Translated)

It is conjecturable whether this incident shows the attraction for Mahendra or whether it shows the naturally jealous women's attempt at creating fissures in the Mahendra-Asha relationship. Both these assumptions hold up. Mahendra is charmed by Binodini and she, in turn, needs someone to soothe her long-suppressed sexual needs.

Tagore has portrayed two contradictory personas of Binodini. In fact, she personifies two opposite personas of a woman—she is the source of familial and societal good/well being and at the same time, she is destructive. To Bihari her part-overt identity is that she is "a beautiful riddle" and again, like "the planet Saturn" she takes on the incarnation of ruin and damage by destroying "the love of a friend, conjugal love, and peace and sanctity of the home". She is a woman who is wronged by society and she is the one who punishes herself to punish and ruin those who come near her. She becomes sadisitic and masochistic at the same time. She too, is a rebel.

For creating fissures in the Mahendra-Asha conjugal relationship her identity to Rajalakshmi is that of an 'enchantress'.

Yet Binodini is the enchantress whom Rajalakshmi uses to realise her own end:

> Binodini restrained herself from saying something but said, "its true, Auntie, nobody knows anybody. Does anybody know his or her own mind? Did you never want to wean away the mind of your son through this enchantress out of jealousy for your daughter-in-law?" (Translated)

The story of Mahendra-Rajalakshmi relationship has an oedipal perspective. Out of jealousy for her daughter-in-law, Rajalakshmi uses Binodini as Asha's double by. But when the same Binodini decentralises Mahendra, and both enter into a sexual relationship, then Rajalakshmi with her motherly authority seeks to restrict her manoeuvreability and limit her space.

However, Tagore has not lowered Mahendra-Binodini relationship to the level of illicit sexuality and on the other hand, has idealised Bihari-Binodini relationship at the romantic Platonic level. Just as Mahendra reverts to the secured domestic fold of Asha's love, being finally rejected by Binodini at the Allahabad garden-house, so Binodini too accepts Platonic love as the ideal of her life after rejecting Bihari's offer of marriage with due reverence and greedlessnes:

> Binodini: Fie, fie, I am ashamed to think of this. I am a widow, tainted; shall I shame you before the whole society? I can never allow it to happen. Fie, fie, don't utter such things. (Translated)

By not conceding to widow remarriage by spotlighting Binodini's individuality and sexual independence, Tagore has practically accepted the age-old tradition. He could have easily shown Binodini marrying Bihari instead of leaving the novel open ended and banishing her to anonymity!

Chokher Bali is a story of three widows—Rajalakshmi, who has indulged her son to the point of spoiling him; Annapurna, the aunt who observes the proscriptions placed on widows and retreats to Kashi in a time-honoured fashion; and Binodini, rejected by Rajalakshmi's son Mahendra, is married to a much older man, and widowed early. What drives the plot is a string of affection and confusion between Mahendra, his young girl-wife Asha, his friend Bihari, and Binodini, who enters his home as a widowed relative when she could once have entered it as his bride. Binodini is an incredible creation, especially when one considers that this was Tagore's first attempt at fleshing out a character at novel length: passionate, indignant, intelligent, her ideals always at war with an insistence that she should have rights too. Tagore took an easy way out when he ended the novel with a tamed Binodini repairing to Kashi to ponder on the knot she has caused in all their lives.

If there's one aspect of the novel that makes the novel great is the running commentary on the practice of reading and writing. In Tagore's first novel, he chose to use writing and reading as strong motifs for all its characters. Asha is unlettered, and it is Mahendra's insistence that his paternalistic handling of her education supersede her duties as a housewife that draws the wrath of his mother. Binodini is as articulate, in speech and in her writing, as Asha is tongue-tied, unable to put a name to the emotions she experiences. In the village, Binodini leaves volumes of Bankim and Dinabandhu by the bedside of her guests. Much later, when she accompanies Rajalakshmi back from the village to Mahendra's house in Calcutta, a key exchange occurs when Mahendra finds her reading Bankim Chandra's *Bishobriksha* (The Poison Tree). Tagore and his audience knew very well, The "Poison Tree" also deals with the destiny of widows. Its protagonist, Kundanandini, is a young widow who catches the eye of a rich man, Nagendra. He marries her over the protests of his wife, who deserts him; when she returns to the home ultimately, Kundanandini kills herself.

Other works of Bankim have a part to play in *Chokher Bali*—Binodini reads aloud to the household from *Kapalakundala* and *Ananda Math*, for instance—but the significance of "The Poison Tree" is inescapable. "Don't fritter your heart away on fictitious characters," Mahendra reprimands Binodini lightly when he discovers her furtively reading the book, and when he learns what she's reading, he is amused at the secrecy. "The Poison Tree" with its conservative conclusion is a perfectly reputable book—Mahendra misses the echoes that Kundanandini's quandary raises in Binodini's heart. Later, it will be the letters that she ghostwrites for Asha that allow her to declare her interest in Mahendra. Asha's naïveté and illiteracy blind her to the degree that Mahendra reads correctly; he knows that his wife could not have written with such flowing fervour and passion, he guesses rightly that this is Binodini's work, and their affiliation changes, with engaging consequences for everyone involved. It's left to Bihari to voice a different point of view. Mahendra wants to abandon his wife for Binodini; she demands to know why she has no right to a life of her own, why Asha's needs must be placed before a widow's desires. And Bihari responds in this exchange:

> "You've spoken as plainly as possible, now let me speak plainly too. The actions you've engineered today, the words you've spoken are derived from the books you read. Three-fourths are from plays and novels". "Binodini exclaims: Plays! Novels!" Bihari continues: "Yes, plays, novels. And that too not of a very high standard! You believe these are all your own ideas—they're not. They are echoes of the printing press. If you'd been an unperceptive, stupid, simple-minded little girl, the world might still have had some sympathy for you and found a place for you. But the heroine of a play is attractive only under the flood lights she has no place in a family". (Translated)

Bihari's view finds echoes in the novel everywhere. His argument is that none of Binodini's emotions is her own, that she is attempting to make herself the heroine of her own melodrama—in other words, that her reading has pushed her into an illusory world. But the squabble also reflects the unease among many of Tagore's contemporaries, who agreed that a woman should be educated up to a point. A woman's education was supposed to fit her for the duties of the household, not to enable her to question the fixed scheme of things and her place in that scheme.

Binodini never directly disclaims Bihari's charge—she can't, because it is partially true. As per Bihari, reading is not an especially useful activity, and to look to books for instructions about the real world is to waste time. It is also to do authors a disservice—writers are under no obligation to be moral instructors. But reading, or even the business of putting the thoughts into words, as so many of the characters in *Chokher Bali* do in their crisscrossing letters, is dangerous. Binodini has no escape from her thoughts; reading acts as a stimulus on her, forces her to question and re-examine the role she is supposed to play as a young widow. Tagore is ambiguous and unclear; he gives to the readers Bihari's opinion, but never reveals his own thoughts about the effects of literature on an impressionable mind. But then, he was not just a skilful writer—he was an ardent reader, too.

Chokher Bali was published in book form in 1903 and it is truly Tagore's Fin de siècle novel in which an unswerving conflict between "*se kaal and e kaal*" (that time and this time) —is very strongly felt. Rajalakshmi, the doting mother of Mahendra, the hero and, Annapurna, Rajalakshmi's brother-in-law's wife, both elderly widows, belong to the 'bygone' era and Asha, Mahendra's young wife, and Binodini, the youthful 'Western educated' widow are products of the contemporary Bengal. The two eras are split by only one or two decades. Within a very short span, the arrival of colonial modernity has made a sweeping crack in the belief-systems and lifestyles even of women, living inside the closely-guarded confines of antapur ('the inner house'). The chronological setting of the novel is such where two completely separate outlooks to life, of which women of two separate generations are the carriers, clash with great force. Rajalakshmi plays the role of 'the good mother' to Mahendra whom, in his early youth even, she sensitively thinks no more grown-up than a suckling child. The Oedipal nature of the relationship between Rajalakshmi and Mahendra not only influences Mahendra's 'self' and his subsequent course of actions in the novel. It also becomes a clear sign of Rajalakshmi's assuming the role of a mother, over and above everything, thereby, attaining a position of undoubted preeminence and power in the female quarter. This is the role that the 'conservative' patriarchal society assigns to a woman and later, acknowledges her position of power in the family. The motherhood issues make the other elderly widow of the family like Annapurna stay away from any significant role in the family affairs. They are marginalised. Here we see women being marginalised by women of authority and power. Though her love for Mahendra is nothing less than his biological mother, and we have seen that she voluntarily retires herself to the widow-quarters of Benaras.

Ashalata, in the novel, is more a child than a fully-grown up woman. Her education is such that she reads modern novels and believes the incidents in them as nothing but truth. Her husband, the Western-educated Mahendra, a prospective medico, looks for a true companion for 'romance' in her. She only thinks him as God deserving to be worshipped, but cannot have pleasures and bonding of camaraderie. Their 'incompatible' marriage (the incompatibility is as much for the differences in age as for his Western education) soon decays for Mahendra. He has earlier severed the ties of an extremely close friendship with Bihari who was initially chosen as the husband for Asha by Annapurna. "The price that Mahendra pays for winning, over Bihari, the heart of Ashalata seems to be a gross overpayment for him as Ashalata hardly knows how to give her heart away in 'love'".

At this juncture, Binodini enters—young, stunningly beautiful, 'educated' in a more complete sense, the woman with a lethal mixture of mystery and voluptuousness. She is a widow and her marriage to a sick husband was hardly consummated. By a cruel twist of fate and wayward ignorance on the part of Mahendra she has earlier missed out on the occasion to become either Mahendra's wife or Bihari's. Rajalakshmi visits her ancestral village and picks Binodini up who, according to Tagore:

> ...has been surviving like a solitary garden-creeper amidst the jungle, leading a joyless existence in the village.

She is the 'emergent' kind of new woman whom Western education, has transformed into a woman with a mind of her own and unique sense and sensibility. She distances herself away from the mantle of religion and holiness that the society would have to offer her as a widow; instead, she wants acknowledgement and joy from the society. Binodini's ripe sexuality and enigmatic charm attracts Mahendra and she gives in because she wants all those from him what Asha gets as his wife.

> Interestingly enough, it all starts with photography, a technologised art-form that is a gift of colonial modernity to the urban bourgeoisie of nineteenth century Calcutta. Mahendra comes near to Binodini, to the point of touching her body, while clicking her photos. It is the sensitive nature of Bihari, Mahendra's 'dialogic double' in the story (in whom

> Mahendra is negated in order to be renewed) which can identify the real 'womanly' qualities in her, during his conversation with her in a picnic.

She talks at length about her country and her past to him. Up to this point in the novel, she has been nothing but an object of lust, without the social sanction. Bihari notices a sensual young woman in Binodini—that of a devoted lady absorbed in her isolated worship. Tagore's fiction addresses through the portrayal of characters like Binodini, Sohini, Damini, Mrinal et al, who are at a threshold or transitional stage cannot be 'typecast' as either traditional housewives, promiscuous women or any other.

Nirad C. Chowdhuri, in his *A Passage to England*, writes:

> The history of love in Bengali Hindu society is fairly well established. It was introduced from the West… . We in Bengal began to deal with love from the literary end… at first it was transferred to Bengali literature from English literature, and then taken over from literature to life.

One of the paradoxes of Tagore's socio-literary discernment is that he reverted to the groove of tradition and convention after breaking fresh grounds in his fictions on the cupid question and women's emancipation. If in *Chokher Bali* (The Eyesore), serialised in the revamped *Bangadarshan* journal, he retreated to a safe and sound stance of traditionality.

Controversial, extra-marital and unconventional sex problems that seized Tagore's mind in his early years, evolved in concrete shapes with their myriad ramifications in *Nastaneer* (The Broken Nest), first treated as a novel and later included in his collection of short stories. This novella was serialised in the *Bharathi* Journal contemporaneously with *Chokher Bali* or possibly after it, but its importance as a seminal work on the problem of emotive love relations as in *Nastaneer*. It allows free-mixing between a married, young woman and an unmarried young brother-in-law, finding ministration and sustenance from the neglect of an indifferent husband, while in *Chokher Bali* the problem is seen from the angle of free-mixing between a married young and a young widow, springing from lust. By simultaneously serialising a novelette and a full-length novel into different prestigious journals, Tagore sought to weigh the reaction of the greedy reader which was then fed on the rendering of idyllic romance in novels.

A comparison can be made with Bankimchandra's treatment of emotive, extramarital, sexual and the stress and problem developing in the family from it, as noticed in *Krishnakanter Will* (The Will of Krishnakanta) shows how Tagore took portrayal of sexuality to a bold overt level. Bankimchandra is the first novelist to discuss the problems of uncontrolled sexual urge and its inevitable tragic fictions in the domestic front, carefully avoiding the description of overt sexual relation.

At the emerging incohate stage of Gobindalal-Rohini's illicit relationship, when Gobindalal raises the drowned Rohini from the Baruni pond and goes through the process of oral respiration, he is triggered by something more than the simple survivor spirit:

> Finding no alternative, Gobindalal said to him (the gardener), "Then you slowly raise her hands in this way, why I blow air into her mouth. Then slowly lower the hands." The gardener agreed. He raised the hands (of Rohini) slowly—and Gobindalal, placing his red full blossomed flower-like lips upon the red full blossomed flower-like lips (of Rohini) blew air into the mouth of Rohini.

Contrast this with the natural explicit description of the love between husband and wife, where Bankim Chandra does not hesitate at referring to kissing as natural between husband and a wife.

Tagore too refers to kissing as a form of caressing of the wife by the husband and the reference is brief, natural as in this sequence between Mahendra and Asha in *Chokher Bali*: "Then Mahendra drew her (Asha) close and kissed her." But in the passionate account of an illicit love sequence (illicit because of society's firm condemnation of any love relationship with a widow), he is most bold and intrepid and even canonises a taboo subject, and breaks the barriers of conventionalism and primness in literature:

> Slowly the effulgent glow of those listless eyes dimmed; those thirst-dried eyes became moist with tears and softened and gradually overflowed with deep emotions; in a moment that tear-mild form fell near the feet of Bihari and pressed both his legs to her breast with utmost strength—then in a trice growing like an illusory plant on the trellis of Bihari's physique brought up to his lips a kiss-bound face which resembled a just blossomed fragrant flower.

But most original and innovative is the depiction of the frantic insolence and audacity with which Mahendra vows in the presence of his mother to clear off the bonds of domesticity to live with Bindodini:

> Mahendra's distraught eyes were turned for a moment to his mother's face; then turning to Binodini again Mahendra said, "I am going away leaving everything, tell me, will you go with me?"

This professedly shameful admission of extramarital passion and thinking the marital bond with Asha, worth not even a hoot, and declaring the same in the presence of a mother is an aberration which goes verily against the established social mores.

Mahendra's uninhibited and unreserved incontinence has got him into a degenerated indulgence. It is not Asha who lacks love for him, servitude and appeal which can satisfy Mahendra's hunger for psycho-physical needs; but Tagore demarcates the newly-wedded love in terms of adolescent lasciviousness, designates it as 'craziness.' Asha's main weakness as a developing woman is her innocent naivety and huge, almost inexplicable faith in her husband. Even after learning about the illicit relationship between her husband and Binodini from a letter which accidentally falls in her hand on her return from the Benaras, she does not develop any ruinous contempt for Mahendra. On the other hand, she silently suffers humiliation when her mother-in-law reproofs her for failing to hold her son within the bounds of domesticity. She is a 'doll' compared to Binodini's identity as an 'exquisitely beautiful enigma.'

In the Indian society of the yesteryear when child-widows were an inevitable offshoot of child marriage, those helpless creatures had to pass through a rigorous regimen of fasting, observance of religious rights, vegetarianism and myriad social taboos, forcing deprivation of the body and impoverishment of the soul. But such a cruel deprivation and repression had its inevitable and unpalatable, socially intractable problem of illicit sexual relationship between widows and there and close relations.

Having grown up through disregard and deprivation as a child widow, Binodini develops a kind of unappeasable envy at the happy conjugality of Mahendra and Asha. Her flirtatious motive in respect of Mahendra for whom she pours her hearts passion in letters written to him in the name of Asha. This shows her first response to her need for psycho-physical satisfaction. With an easy and malleable Mahendra as the target, to wreck the domestic bond and peace is not a difficult scheme. But her hunger is for love and, hence, possibly realising the preposterous nature of her position in the Mahendra household, she nurtures a sneaking affectation for Bihari ever since he addresses her as 'Goddess', requesting her to save the innocent Asha from the cruel assaults of circumstances. She does not conceal anything but unabashedly shows off her pretentious love for Bihari. Such a generous praise of Binodini sends her swinging with an unspeakable feeling of ecstasy for she never experienced such a unique treatment. In fact, it is a defining moment in Binodini's love realtion. Tagore justifies the recklessness and haste of Binodini's character by attributing it to the permanent 'scar' that she is left with being a child-widow.

Mahendra's humiliating accusation against Bihari that he loves Asha and his smarmy offer to Binodini to go away with him are two important milestones in the steady development of his love. It is passionate, yet sort of abiding fulfilment for she knows the societal constraints against it: "my life's ultimate, I know you are not mine forever but do love me for a moment only. After that I shall disappear into the jungles of ours, and never demand anything from anybody. But give something which I can remember till death." But even with her secret store of love for Bihari, if she carries on with her dalliance with Mahendra and allows him to go to the brink, because of Bihari's concern for Asha, which is unbearable to her, and Mahendra's incontinence. She stretches Mahendra to the point of no-return because she knows the essential weakness of his character. And she is made to appear as villainously scheming. If she is wronged by the society, she too, does not mind ruining the people around her to avenge herself. She does not suffer from any self-pity but enjoys every act that she does by making two most important men in the story fall for her.

However, the story of Mahendra's sexual urge has a three stage development: pretense (initially he is shy of striking an social contact with Binodini), impudence (he wants to enjoy both Asha and Binodini in the same household like 'a planet served by two moons', a kind of captive adultery and sex, which even Gobindalal in *Krishnakanter Will* does not dare engage in) and rampant lust (he wants to go away with his paramour tearing off all familial-marital connections).

In *Chokher Bali*, the 'literary' angle to the theme of romance is presented to a significant extent through the letters that the protagonists write. Letters exchanged between Asha, Mahendra, Binodini and Bihari are an important marker of the element of the noveli ('novel-like') in the life of the newly-educated middle-class youth, a strange kind of transposition of the 'fictional' onto the 'real' life. It is, also, a clear warning of the different degrees of the 'internalisation' of that education as observed in the prejudices and chauvinism of the characters. While Bihari's letters are prosaic and pragmatic and Mahendra criticises himself for composing a letter to Asha with an excess of 'literary fervour' in it, Binodini writes letters on behalf of Asha in which she consciously overplays the novelistic style of writing, made popular in her times through a number of discourses of 'romance'. The three letters that she writes for Asha are cleverly designed 'speech-acts' created by Binodini to highlight the 'incomplete' nature of Asha's education on the one hand (as Mahendra knows Asha's incapablity of showing such a supreme command over Bangla language and recording, in such an exhaustive manner, her feelings) and on the other, these letters become 'her' love-letters to Mahendra, an 'act of seduction', an act only which can offer a substitute for her (a young widow's) cravings for 'romantic love' in such a 'closed' society. 'Fiction', 'real life', 'love', 'lust', 'licentiousness' and 'society'—all these discourses fuse in a breathtakingly heteroglogic manner when during one of the love-games that Mahendra and Binodini play he discovers that she has been reading Bankim Chandra's *Bishabrikkho* (an extremely popular contemporary novel of extra-marital love).

As the affair between Binodini and Mahendra gets going in a full-blown manner the members of inner quarters are at a loss as to what to do with her latent seditious sexuality. Rajalakshmi has so far been providing shelter to Binodini because to her she has been nothing but a figure of loving womanliness, a role which would have full societal sanction. Her new role as Mahendra's lover (and in turn the wrecker of Asha's home) is miles away from the *Grihalakshmi* construct, or even that of a benign mother of the patriarchal discourse. The 'emergent' nature of her subjectivity, thus, seems to be in direct contrast to Annapurna's self, the other childless widows of the text, whose act of dwelling within the discourses of *Iswarbhakti/Swamibhakti* (love for God/ love for the husband) cannot but be the 'residual' strand of the dynamics of Bangali culture. The clash between the 'ideal' and the 'real' reaches a flashpoint when Binodini has a showdown with Rajalakshmi, her provider in Mahendra's home. Binodini, by now, refuses to be tied down to the role of an austere widow and thus she declares:

> "I am not afraid of the society. I obey nobody", tells Rajalakshmi on her face, "Pishima, we are a race of temptresses. I did not know what allurement I had in me, you found that out. You too did not know what trap you were setting up, I found that out. But there was guile, otherwise things would not have come to this...we are by nature devious". (Translated)

This happens when an 'identity; is not allowed to attain full flourish in a society; where women are ascribed certain 'roles' and are expected to 'conform' to it. It is not correct to blame everything on the colonised setting. Downplaying the 'subversive' female sexuality can hardly defy the temptation of illicit enjoyment, doing damage to the subjectivities of both the sexes; cannot be termed as something the society learned from the colonisers. This is a human instinct and the plight of the child-widows was beyond any moral correction. They were used as sex-toys by the sex-hungry relatives or it happened with mutual consent.

In the next drift of the text, we find Binodini, for a temporary phase, retiring to the countryside, searching for anonymity. But, as we know, that the distance between the country and the city has become remarkably less due to the introduction of the railways and news from the city reaches the country in no time. Her acts of unsanctioned sexcapade reach the village and there too, the village community does not accept her 'pervert' behaviour nor does she find quietude and beauty of an 'organic community' which has been destroyed by urban invasion. For anonymity she would have to return to the gas-lit streets of Calcutta. The artistic plan of the text does not allow us to see Binodini as a wicked woman. We see that she possesses 'motherly' instincts like any other woman. This becomes clear when she interacts with Basanta, Bihari's teen-aged step-son. Her 'protest' and Ashalata's 'silence' are the dangers of governing the 'womanhood' discursively. Along with Binodini's motherly self, Tagore shows us, how Ashalata, quite like adolescent Mrinmoyee in the short-story, *Samapti*, attains womanhood and becomes the lady of the house in the end.

Rajalakshmi falls sick, refuses to get treatment and says, "In the older days widows were better off; they were burnt alive. This is simply to tie them up in order to rot and die." Annapurna takes Binodini along to Benaras. Widows are a burden—a 'real' problem which the text fails to resolve. Tagore does not, for a moment, become didactic; he simply shows and tells, leaving the reader to draw conclusions. It is only Bihari who can discover the full magnitude of Binodini's womanliness when in the end he declares his love for Binodini, the 'complete' woman. She refuses to marry Bihari as it seems unlikely to her that Bihari, with such a spotless character, should marry a 'widow.' The Widow Remarriage Act was passed on 26 July 1856.

A translation of a four-line poem, composed after the Act was passed, by Iswarchandra Gupta, a mid nineteenth century poet seems apt to be quoted here:

> Where is the courage, where the conviction?
> Nothing takes place with a mere enunciation
> Pointless all ceremony, pointless bidding time
> Not empty words, only real act will do it fine.

Works Cited

Bandyopadhyay, Asit.: *Tagore: Novelist, Short Story Writer and Essayist, Studies on Tagore, Vol. I.* (Ed.) Mohit K. Ray, New Delhi, Atlantic Publishers and Distributors, 2004.

Iyengar, K. R. Srinivasa: *Rabindranath Tagore: A Critical Introduction.* New Delhi: Sterling Publications Private Limited, 1987. Print.

Prasad, Hariom: *Tagore's Short Stories: A Critical Study, Studies on Tagore. Vol. II.* Ed. Mohit K. Ray. New Delhi: Atlantic Publishers and Distributors, 2004.

Sastri, K. S. Ramaswami. *Sir Tagore: His Life, Personality and Genius.* New Delhi: Akashdeep Publishing House, 1988.

11

Bimala of *Ghare Baire*

In *Ghare Baire* (Home and the World) Tagore is again a traditionalist. Here, in this novel Bimala wants to live the life of a traditional Hindu woman according to the age-old Indian custom. Since her mother is the exemple of conventional Hindu womanhood to her, she expresses a desire at the very outset of the novel to mould herself on her mother's ideal:

> Mother, I remember today the vermillion mark on the parting of your hair, that red bordered sari, those two eyes of yours—calm, mellow, deep. I have seen them as the crimson of the sun at dawn in my mind's sky that started his journey on my day of days with the golden provision. I am not handsome, but I pray to god that I might be given the glory of a chaste woman like my mother. (Translated)

Bimala has been slowly weaned away from Nikhilesh by the twin forces of Sandeep's magnetic power and her own false sense of self-glory:

> Gradually, I had a conviction that Sandeepbabu was at the root of every work that was being done in the whole country, and the guiding force of it all was the simple, innocuous intelligence of an insignificant woman. My mind was filled with glory of a vast responsibility. (Translated)

Sandeep's philosophy is "the teaching of the whole world is that whatever I can snatch away is mine proper." His discussion on sex relationship between man and woman completely outside the scope of Swadeshi matters, addiction to women, his connection with the widowed Kusum and an Anglo-Indian girl, for example, and his feeling of pride thereof, and his irresistible attraction to Bimala et al., have as much unmasked him as it pushed Bimala to the brink. Bimala develops a dichotomial attitude towards Sandeep very soon:

> She knows that she has a false infatuation for Sandeep and yet she cannot get out of it. It is a dichotomy which divides her into two. (Translated)

On the one hand Bimala is thrown off the domestic whole under Sandeep's magnetic pull and on the other, her infatuation for the outside world has rendered Nikhilesh's home abandoned and lifeless. It cannot be contested that this husband-wife rapture is a result of the licence and freedom that Nikhilesh allows her at the first instance. On the other hand, with a low hedonistic mindset Sandeep enjoys personal pleasures at the cost of Bimala when he asked her to give him fifty thousand rupees in the country's cause, caught between a sense of duty and the call of the country, 'a fake call though'. Bimala is forced to steal 'mohurs' from her husband's (that is, her own) iron safe. But when Sandeep rushes forward greedily to take the 'mohurs' from her, she pushes him with all her might so much so that he falls to the ground. This theft is the most crucial point in the Bimala-Sandeep relationship, for her realisation of guilt forces the reverse journey from the world to home, from Sandeep to Nikhilesh. "The moment I handed over the money after committing a theft on my husband's coppers, the very music of our relationship was gone."

The next part of the story teaches a repentant Bimala's surrender and homecoming. In the words of Nikhilesh:

> She began to bow her head down to my feet repeatedly, kneeling after freeing her hands from mine a little a forcibly. As soon as I took away my feet, she clasped both my feet and with an emotion filled voice said, "No, no, no, do not take away your feet. Let me worship you. (Translated)

In this way, Tagore has made a discourse of the traditional Indian way of life in the circular structure of Bimala's story and has registered a triumph of patriarchy by highlighting the pitfalls of Bimala's unsolicited empowerment.

Ghare Baire (Home and the World) is a search for the national perception in the portrayal of Bimala by Tagore. The early years of the twentieth century was a time of change in the socio-cultural and political awareness of Bengali life. It was the time after Raja Rammohan Roy had set ablaze the edifying scruples of Bengal by constantly striving for the betterment of the average Bengali. The expansion of the Arya Samaj and the Brahmo Samaj had particularly brought about massive changes in the attitude of the average Bengali. The *bhadralok samaj* had learnt to tend two dissimilar things at the same point of time. On one, it had wished to lodge the benefits of Western education and thought, and on the other hand, it saw intrinsic dichotomy of such a system because in the long run, the benefits would be washed away by the over-dependence on the English education system. The peril was that the British Raj would be able to find a reason in making the Indians weaker in their cultural perception.

The growth of the Indian National Congress since 1885 was the first authentic as well as the evident step on the part of the Indian intelligentsia to challenge the authority of the British on the political front.

> However, it must be noted that within the Indian National Congress itself sharp contradictions existed on the methodology

> to be followed in challenging the British political authority in India and its very obvious military might, coming as it was at the back of the glorious successes of the British in establishing colonial rule during the rule of Queen Victoria. In India, the British had previously been challenged with limited success by the Indians as was during what we call today as the First War of Independence or what the British historians prefer to call only as the Sepoy Mutiny of 1857. The growth of the Indian National Congress (INC) was, however, different in the sense that a section of the British administration had been willing enough to oversee the setting up of the INC, particularly as they thought that the INC could function as a valid platform for the exchange of ideas between the British intelligentsia and the British administrators. The rather the vocal protests on part of the Congress leaders at times, despite the language being of persuasion on their part, and the increasing awareness that the INC was beginning to represent the aspirations of the common Indian for gaining independence, became a matter of great discomfort to the British.

It is in the background of these socio-political concerns that we need to analyse the Partition of Bengal which was decreed by the Viceroy Lord Curzon in 1905. The details of the official papers available to *Amrit Bazaar Patrika*, a Bengali newspaper point out that Lord Curzon felt that Bengal had become too large a province to be managed administratively with efficiency. The details were made public on 19 July 1905. The official effect of the decree came about on 16 October, 1905. Lord Curzon remarked in the decree that "Bengal was antiquated, illogical and productive of inefficiency". Tagore's reaction to the Partition of Bengal came in the form of writing a novel called *Ghare Baire* which was serialised in the year 1914 and published in the year 1916 in the novel form. The English translation "The Home and the World" was rendered by Tagore's brother, Surendranath. Most critics opine that in many ways *Ghare Baire* evolved from *Nastaneer*, which he had written in 1901, the novel being a product of the personal loss that the novelist had suffered at the suicide of his 'bou-than' or sister-in-law Kadambari Devi, the wife of Tagore's brother, Jyotirindranath. That apart, to return to the point, the writing of *Ghare Baire* was necessary to respond to the Partition of Bengal.

Tagore considered nationalism to be quite contrary to the thoughts of the ordinary Indian mind. Modernism and nationalism were primarily anathema to him. We can prove this point through Bimala of *Ghare Baire*. In the novel, she is the wife of a rich zamindar, Nikhil. Sandip, a nationalist leader of violent intent, who is also the friend of Nikhi, enters into her life. Nikhil is freethinking and hates to be a tyrant for his subjects but at times, he is too strait-jacketed by the failure of his own optimism and the traditions that he has to answer to. Sandip, on the other hand, has no such strings attached. Tagore shows the interface between Sandip and Bimala to be the core of social change. Tagore shows Sandip to be smooth-tongued who weaves his way into the heart of Bimala. He makes her believe that she is his Muse, the re-embodiment of the centre of power from which he derives both his force and his aspiration to liberate his country from the rule of British. At this point of time Nikhil makes one crucial error. He introduces Bimala to Sandip and unshackles her from the confines of fixed survival that the Indian woman was subjected to, in the alcoves of the *andarmahal* (interior billet). He contrasts the two women characters of his novel to show the struggle between tradition and liberation of the soul through the description of Bimala and Bou-Rani.

Bou-Rani is the widowed sister-in-law of Nikhil whose life is dictated not only by her predicament but also by the age-old customs that were imposed on her lot by society. She is shown to be having a mordant tongue and can hardly digest the independence that Bimala enjoys. In some ways, Tagore through the characterisation of Bou-Rani brings about the latent scruples of Bimala as she stands at the moment of apparent truths of her life. The way ahead for Bimala is certainly laden with dangers. Now, if we study the way Sandip goes out for Bimala, then the moment when Nikhil takes her out from the purdah of the *andarmahal* and introduces her to the outside world and makes her speak to Sandip, is in fact, the moment when through her vacillating steps Tagore shows the construct of a nation to be stirring to its new realisation and its example of a liberated soul through Nikhileh. However, the analysis of Prayer then it is indeed difficult to garb Bimala in the glory of a nationalistic symbolisation. Prayer says:

> He was also a critic of modernism. Its mechanical operation and lifelessness, he thought, constrained the free expression of man's spirituality. He contrasted these imports from the West with the richness of Indian civilisation, which he saw as symbolised by the shakti, the divine female energy giving life and sustaining the world. He criticised the nationalist interpretation of shakti and projected the predicament of Indian civilisation through the unhappy story of some of his female characters.

Here lies the two-facedness of the society of the time that was caught between the enlightenment that colonisers' education brought upon us and, the difficult moral obligations that we were wrapped in. The paradox that our society had started to live that leads to the creation these half-baked motives of the 'bhadralok samaj'.

Tagore would have us believe that Bimala in trying to become the Muse of Sandip had actually misread the Sandip's devices and designs. His make of nationalism was more in keeping with the policy of 'restraint and temperance' of the Indian National Congress lead by Surendranath Banerjee and Dadabhai

Naoroji. For him, the intention of the British in giving any form of independence to the Indians was surreptitious, but at the same time, force was not a solution to the partition of India. His ideas on Swadeshi were exclusive from those expressed by Sandip in the novel. In the novel, he shows Sandip meeting a violent death. The vacillations regarding the nationalist movement have been aptly brought out by Tagore through the weave of the three protagonists and the self-analysis that these characters make in this novel. Let us refer to some of the passages that the three characters utter and thus try to understand their respective mental frameworks. When it is Bimala's narrative the prose meanders in confusion:

> Nature has many anodynes in her pharmacy, which she secretly administers when vital relations are being insidiously severed, so that none may know of the operation, till at last one awakes to know what a great rent has been made. When the knife was busy with my life's most intimate tie, my mind was so clouded with fumes of intoxicating gas that I was not in the least aware of what a cruel thing was happening. (Translated)

Nikhil is conscientiously righteous when he says:

> If my heart is breaking-let it break! That will not make the world bankrupt,—nor even me; for man is so much greater than the things he loses in life. The very ocean of tears has its other shore, else no one would have ever wept. (Translated)

Sandip's narrative makes it incredibly pompous:

> My theory of life makes me certain that the great is cruel. To be just is for ordinary men,—it is reserved for the great to be unjust. The surface of earth was even. The volcano butted it with its fiery horn and found its own eminence. Successful injustice and genuine cruelty have been the only forces by which individual or nation have become millionaire or monarch.

When we look at the three passages aforementioned, then, we find that Bimala understands that her actions of falling in love with Sandip is actually wrong and as a symbol of the liberated woman, the archetypal '*Shakti*' as Prayer puts it, it is most unbecoming on her part to use her liberation for wrong ends. Sandip on the other hand, lacks the conscience and ethics to carry out the essence of a national struggle. His selfcenteredness and egotism are the very basis of the abhorrence that Tagore had for the Swadeshi struggle and its apparent political ends. He strongly believed it was the liberation of the soul that was needed at the hour of crisis. Nikhil stands for the patience that Tagore wished for with regard to the Swadeshi movement. Bimala's characterisation, for Tagore, stood for the liberated feminist that he wished for in his own bou-than, Kadamari which unfortunately was lost due to her untimely death. Both for Charulata in *Nastaneer* (The Broken Nest) and Binodini in *Chokher Bali* (The Eye Sore), the liberation of the Indian woman like that of Bimala remained only partially fulfilled. But Mrinal's stands apart as a rebel and a woman of substance.

Amartya Sen questions the various constraints of the theme of patriotism in the thought of Tagore and also points out to its realistic demonstrations, particularly through, the characterisation of Bimala in *Ghare Baire*. Sen writes:

> Tagore's criticism of patriotism is a persistent theme in his writings. As early as 1908, he put his position succinctly in a letter replying to the criticism of Abala Bose, the wife of a great Indian scientist, Jagadish Chandra Bose: "Patriotism cannot be our final spiritual shelter; my refuge is humanity. I will not buy glass for the price of diamonds, and I will never allow patriotism to triumph over humanity as long as I live". His novel *Ghare Baire* (The Home and the World) has much to say about this theme. In the novel, Nikhil, who is keen on social reform, including women's liberation, but cool toward nationalism,

> gradually loses the esteem of his spirited wife, Bimala, because of his failure to be enthusiastic about anti-British agitations, which she sees as a lack of patriotic commitment. Bimala becomes fascinated with Nikhil's nationalist friend Sandip, who speaks brilliantly and acts with patriotic militancy, and she falls in love with him. Nikhil refuses to change his views: "I am willing to serve my country; but my worship I reserve for Right which is far greater than my country. To worship my country as a god is to bring a curse upon it."

Sen argues that the comparable development of national consciousness and the nouveau emancipation of the women that Tagore professes in Bimala is a contradiction in itself. In the end, neither is nationalism achieved nor the feministic platform gets reinforced by the shifting, unsure and often immoral attitude of women like Bimala or Binodini or Charulata, for that matter. Sen is, in particular, "very disillusioned with Tagore for letting an opportunity slip by in making a strong statement on both nationalism, in the context of Swadeshi, and feminism in the context of women like Bimala, Charulata and Binodini". Sen calls Sandip's brand of nationalism as being that of sectarist's. He further goes on to suggest that perhaps the best case would have been made out for both the construct of the nation as well as that of feminism if it had been shown by Tagore that Bimala comes out of the confines of her house to support the unfashionable, yet more consistent and patient version of the capturing of the nation construct by Nikhil. Here, we find Sen to be dogmatic. He is unable to take in the reality and legitimacy of Bimala's actions. He does not endorse Tagore's feminism. Sen seems to belong to the old school where, to talk of radical feminism was banned; uncalled for. He snubs the text by saying that both the aims of nationalism and feminism have not been achieved—then, does he really mean to say that Tagore was swaying with an apparent perplexity and confusion? To this, the anwer will be 'no'.

Tagore was sensitive enough not to add fantasy to reality and take the story to the planes of unreality and futility; where the plot would have fallen in well-preset tight compartments. The charm of suspense, politically speaking, that is so essential to a fiction, would have been lost.

Tagore's make of nationalism is to treat this fear factor and expel it from the hearts and minds of the ordinary Indian in order to realise the true and universal appeal of nationalism. For both Sandip and Bimala, the failure of their relationship lie in the fear that is ever present in the recesses of their heart. Bimal has the fear of breaking of her own nest, where her fear almost becomes her guilt, and Sadnip's fear is his sham nationalistic feeling. Tagore's idea of the nation refers to, "where the mind is without fear". The 'tireless striving' is necessary to nurture both the national construct the feministic idealism. Jennifer Takhar sees Bimala in the avatar of Durga and Parvati, both a continuation of the realisation referred to earlier by Mario Prayer. Takhar writes in her essay on the realisation of Shakti and her thoughts are as follows:

> The devil (or goddess) in India is presented as fulfilling many different roles ... . These feminine figures cannot be truly understood without the attachment of the figure of Shakti... . In a broader sense shakti is the vitalae lan, the animating factor as illustrated in the fiercely anti-colonial Bengali novel Ghare Baire by Tagore, where the tribune, Sandip, asks the self-emancipating woman, Bimala to become the shakti of the nation.

At the same point of time Jasodhara Bagchi states that

> The nation is, in the current post-modernist onslaught on all things that smack of 'modernity', a meta-narrative in which the entire hegemonic establishment is implicated. Assessing the event from a feminist perspective one cannot help noticing the deep collusion between the community at one end of the

> spectrum and the nation on the other. The majoritarian religious ideology turning into natural common sense is thus not just the threat posed by the nation state. It is also the threat of the community and the family that make such naturalisation possible.
>
> As long as Bimala is with Sandip she is within the construct of the majoritarian standpoint of the nation, the centre-point of 'shakti', but when Sandip dies, she returns to Nikhil, as Tagore would want us to understand that she is able to remove the coloured goggles of feminism for she had been told to think of by Sandip, and is disenchanted with the evolving challenges of the national construct within the borders of the British rule. Tagore's thoughts are shown by Bagchi to be an interpretation of the prejudices that are inherent within the confines of neo-nationalism in the garb of Swadeshi. Mohammed Quayum defines Swadeshi as 'of our own country'. He notes that the true flavour of the realisation of the nation construct and its power of 'shakti' was lost on Tagore in the novel partially, in fact, due to the narrative followed by Tagore in the novel. Tagore's biographer Krishna Kripalani mentions that this happened as: Tagore was no Tolstoy or Balzac… [a myriad-minded writer] the poet, the singer and the teacher constantly meddled with the novelist.

Tagore was a realist. He was the first person to lead the *Bongo Bhongo Andolon* in 1905, and he understood the futility of the movement when he found that the capital of the country was shifted to Delhi, while Bihar, Orissa and Assam were separated from Bengal Presidency. He also understood the futility of boycotting the British goods without creating the indigenous manufacturing bases in the country. He, therefore, did not approve the path of Sandip who was basically dishonest with an unknown motive whereas Nikhil was a person who loved human beings and his subjects dearly. There lies the contradiction and maybe the confusion. He depicted Nikhil as a true conscientious man in contrast to Sandip who is selfish, ambitious and an infidel. Nikhil is a builder while Sandip is a destroyer.

"Feministic platform is failed by the immoral attitude"—the term 'immoral attitude' of women is itself a patriarchal construction. Perhaps Amartya Sen, while criticising Tagore's heroines, slips to the androcentric criticism. Tagore's feminism is neither radical nor reformist (in that age especially that was radical indeed in the Indian society, like the French feminism of the 70's but Tagore heralds a new beginning in the feminist thought. Nikhil goes on to construct a new nationalism through a humanitarian approach whereas Bimala fails to cross the boundary of home finally. Her failure is a question to the patriarchal society about the limitation of women's endeavour in the fight for independence. Her immorality is not a question here rather Sen's analysis comes under the feminist observation. Tagore differed with Gandhiji on his call for boycott of classes by the students. He, as a teacher, understood its futility and never allowed his students at Santiniketan to take part in active politics. In fact, his concept of life, his concept of socialism, his concept of humanism may be emulated even today.

Tagore has created many echelons of perceptions through the description of Bimala in *Ghare Baire*. On one hand, he wishes to project her as an icon of the liberated woman who is granted free access to the 'baire' or 'bahir' or the world and on the other, her failed relationship with Sandip signals the re-entry to the 'ghar' or the home. Tagore seems to create the idea that women like Bimala were not yet fully ready for the outside world, the space being beyond them in not its contours but in its magnitude. The liberation of the soul is as much important to Tagore as is the physical self. The stirring of Bimala is a protest against the Partition of Bengal, as much as Sandip is shown to be a messenger of the nationalistic perception of the early twentieth century mind. However, Bimala cannot be said to be the 'shakti' that Sandip yearns for and thus over-fanatical projects through Bimala.

It does not seem to be appropriate to read the text exclusively from the feminist angle. Bimala does not leave her home but just steps outside to taste freedom; she is neither a rebel like Mrinal nor she is a Sohini. She is a woman who retraces her steps after realising the truths about her existence and reality and returns to the home of her husband, Nikhil.

Works Cited

Bagchi, Jasodhara: *Freedom in an Idiom of Loss*, p.3.

Chatterjee, Partha: *The Nation and Its Fragments: Colonial and Postcolonial Histories.* Princeton: Princeton University Press, 1994.

Prayer, Mario: "Shakti and Womanhood in Tagore's Criticism of Nationalism", *Journal of South Asia Women Studies*, International Symposium, 18th October 2004, originally printed in 13th October, 2003, JSAWS, Vol.9, No.1.p. 5.

Quayum, Mohammed: *Review of Tagore: Ghare Baire* (*The Home and the World*). Mukto-Mona, Bengali blog, pp. 2-3, 2007.

Ray, Niharranjan: *Rabindra Sahityer Bhumika*, 1962.

Sen, Amartya: *Development as Freedom*, New Delhi, Oxford University Press, pp.159-203.

____ : *Tagore and His India*, OUP, pp.10-11.

12

The Feminine Personage: Anandomoyi in *Gora*

Tagore's novel *Gora* is the characterisation of the principal women in the novel, Sucharita, the liberated young woman with a strong mind of her own, and equally at ease within and outside 'home', as well as Anandamoyi—'mother' of the protagonist (Gora), confined only to home and yet, with a liberated outlook ready to break the shackles of dogma. The novel, created and serialised at the turn of twentieth century, is regarded as an essential landmark in the history of Indian fiction, and there have been numerous attempts to deduce each move that Tagore has made in the novel.

Gora—should one read the novel from the perspective of Gourmohan, the Irish orphan adopted by a Brahmin family in the midst of the Sepoy mutiny of 1857? Or should one take it as a tale of a victory over colour and caste discriminations? Another alternative attempt is to read the story as the sophisticated 'bhadralok samaj' of Bengal and whole of India, coming to terms with the forces of Westernisation. The reader can gather "Gora's" multiple layers of import as it focuses on the cultural root of Bengal and Bengalis, and the degradation of the society from the assault of the Western mode of thinking that was brought about by the British rule. Incidentally, Tagore, the author of this 500-odd-page novel could have named his work for some reasons—after its central character, Gourmohan, also called Gora by his friends, or called it gora ('the white-skinned') after the complexion of the central character's skin, or called gora which can be translated into foundation, root and essence of a matter. Addressing the novel on these three different podia would spawn confronting and remarkable comparisons about the details of the novel. But the central theme of freedom as well as the yearning for it would not change. Tagore's feminism through the vision of Gourmohan and Binoybhushan is researched here.

Throughout human history, the female person has been portrayed as a symbol of fertility (Venus of Willendorf), a goddess representing the Motherland (Bengal's worship of Goddess Kali as Shakti), or even as a class of people whose best place is in the kitchen and within the home, *ranna gharer pratibha* (the talent of the kitchen). In each of these cases, the woman is not viewed as an individual, but she is a part of a whole, signifying one philosophy or a belief system. Tagore begins his novel with Binoybhushan, an erudite Bengali youngman who debates on the socio-religious facets of education and national concerns and the things that were then considered to be matters to be dealt by women, namely, the woman's relationship within and outside their gender. Binoy, as he is called, is seen looking out of his window in a conciliatory mood. While doing so, he hears a baul singer singing a folk song:

> The unknown bird flies in and out of the cage,
> if I could catch it, I would place
> the chains of my mind on its feet. (Translated)

At that very moment a road mishap gives a jump-start to the novel and Binoy meets Sucharita, face to face, and his world changes forever. Binoy, like most Indian male youths, has not interacted much with women, except for those in his family. He has seen women only as a symbol of maternity (Anandamoyi) or one who spends her entire life at the servitude of the men at home. For the first time, he looks at Sucharita's reflection in the mirror, a face "lowered in loving anxiety glowed with a tenderness" which is to him a "newly manifested wonder of nature." It should be interesting to note that he does not find the fortitude to look at her directly; instead, he opts to look at her reflection. If the reflection of a woman could redefine Nature (considered feminine in its own right), how is she to be viewed when considered as a person? Is she the bird, the baul singer was singing about? "He had never known any woman who was of his own class outside the family circle, and now he was fascinated by the beautiful face he saw reflected in the mirror. His eyes were not adequately trained to examine each line and curve of a countenance..." writes the author to describe Binoy's predicament.

Tagore introduces Sucharita, a central female character, as a reflection of Nature, and as the novel progresses, slowly but indiscernibly, he converts this symbol into a form and a figure, and provides her with a very free and individual mind. Gora is introduced into the plot using an argument with Binoy about the latter's accepting Paresh Babu's invite. Binoy is genuinely eager to connect himself with Paresh Babu's family to learn more about the family, and acquaint himself with this woman who lit up the whole room like Goddess Saraswati. Gora is a staunch Hindu Brahmin boy who had initially associated himself with the Brahmo-Samaj for a short period of time but now fervently abhors this new creed of 'the British bootlicking educated ones reflecting so much like the Christians'. He does not endorse Binoy's resolution to visit this Brahmo neighbour of his. The tall, broad shouldered Brahmin shoots arrows at Binoy's "temptation", as he proclaims that it is best to "worship woman" where "they are installed as Mother." Gora's idea of womanhood is extremely stereotypical and is what is prevalent even now in India. The mother is offered the highest pedestal to a woman under such a scheme. "The Feminine Personage" is not given an individual status. Gora assumes Binoy's approbation to be a vent for his lust. Gora seems to be a voice for the reformist Brahmins rather than that of an enlightened individual. This tragedy of Gora is the fate of Indian women as well, who could at best be the homemaker, or a force like Kali, or Shakti ready to step out of home to destroy all evils, but never as an ordinary woman in the then educated Bengali society. Binoy is a man of the heart but Gourmohan is a man of revivalist Hindu ideology. The fallacy of Gora's dogma is evident when he restricts Binoy from eating the food served by Lachmiya, the Christian maid who saved Gora's life when he was suffering from smallpox in his childhood. Tagore, here, uses food as a weapon used to wield power and control the lives of other subalterns. Even though Gora preaches the ideology of placing women at a mother's mantle, yet he forgets to pay his respects to the woman, Lachmiya who nursed him along with Anandamoyi. As the narrator notes that 'the statement of a concept no longer has the same certainty when applied to a person', Gora is incapable to practise this theory in his own life, and this incapacity is amplified when he interacts with the womenfolk of the novel—particularly, when he is shown as refraining from any communication with Sucharita in several encounters that they have in the novel.

Tagore was not only a prolific artist-philosopher; he was also one of the stalwarts of Indian freedom movement. Unlike Mahatma Gandhi, he did not believe in adopting the path of a *brahmachari* (an ascetic), and this philosophy is projected in the contrast between the characters of Gora and Binoy. In some ways Gora, a loyalist of Hinduism, is fashioned on the lines of Gandhi—a man who gave women the place of a goddess and did not indulge in sexual relation with his wife after the spiritual conversion of his mind and former self, and chose the path of a monk, while Tagore on the other hand, gave women his respect but did not believe in abstaining from loving women or cultivating an intellectual relationship with them. Gandhi lived his visionary life by keeping romance treed. He placed womanhood at a level of religious worship and love, with a total disregard to their needs and desire. Whereas, the "oritental sage" was against any idolisation of womanhood, he preferred them to be treated as a human being first. If Gora is a manipulated form of a Gandhian philosophy then Binoy is the "poised humane" image of himself and his Santiniketan reflection.

Anandamoyi is one of the leading protagonists of *Gora*. She is the foster-mother of Gourmohan, a one-time orthodox Brahmin girl who was married to Krishnadayal, a "forward" thinking Bengali youth who lent his intellect and loyalty to the services of his British masters. Although her transformation into the generous and kindhearted human persona is not dealt detail in the novel, yet, the change is something that the modern-day feminists would praise. Generally, the last name of the woman changes in a marriage, and then, she is mired further in the family issues. She has to gratify herself with the little that men oblige her with. But in *Gora*, Anadamoyi is shown as raising an Irish-British orphan as her own child. Even though she is not his biological mother, she stands strong amidst societal pressures and disdains to raise a gora (fair-skinned) child as a part of her own family. Anandamoyi is portrayed with her feminine and motherly traits along with a strong individualistic personality in this novel. Her individualism is nothing to do with any image of patriarchy.

Anadamoyi is a noble woman who does not want to get into voluble debates on which is the virtuous path, but she is the one who wants to improve and intensify her emergence as 'human being', without which all religions, societies, customs, ideologies—

with all reformist or intransigent ideas—become a dreadful burden and bondage on humanity. All her actions bear evidence to the fact of her being an emancipated one.

Tagore depicted Anandamoyi's womanhood without any disregard or defiance to religion, but shows a philosophical and tacit protest against what most people often make out religions to be. The personality of Anandamoyi has been reflected in many ways in the novel, with broadminded and tolerant attitudes of her manifesting in others who Gora comes to contact with in his life, and from whom he learns lessons of life. She illumines life of those who comes in contact with her. 'It is not only the liberal and humanistic streak in Paresh babu that attracts him and Binoy, where he sees the reflection of the same values that Anandamoyi stood for—the broad humanistic concerns', but even in Gora's leaving home and see the world a little bit. Gora comes to a primarily Muslim village, which happens to be the only one of that kind in that area, where he finds only one Hindu family of a barber taking care of a Muslim boy. This neighbourhood is in trouble because it is the only neighbourhood that has not yielded to the unreasonable nuisances and impositions of the British sahibs. Gora finds in Foru Sardar, the leader of the Muslim village, the fortitude and resolve to stand up and refuse to be conquered and give in. The barber humbly shares his vision with Gora and it is here, that he realises that liberal humanism is more important than sectarian beliefs. He empathises with the victims of injustice:

> What kind of monstrous irreligiosity we are upholding in India by turning purity into an external object. My caste would be saved in the home of those who are persecuting Muslims, and it would be lost in the home of that person who is willing to endure hardship, danger and disaffection to save a Muslim child!

The event of Ghoshpara actuates Gora's heart. After his encounter with the poor barber family does he adopt Binoy's philosophy of applying principles and theories for changing the lives of the people and he understands that the abstract ideas and dogmas are nothing but a quagmire of expressions and statements. Gora reflects on himself in jail, and amusingly enough he is overwhelmed by the same romantic disease of love that he had accused Binoy of. The episodes of 'Nanda's death, the Muslim man and his shopping basket being knocked aside by the Brahmin cab', discrimination and intolerance at Ghoshpara and the inspection of casteism in rural Bengal bring forth a new face of India to him. It ceases to be a dream and comes alive as a land filled with millions of people. In his trance, he sees Sucharita's affectionate face appear in his mind. His bafflement is not a fashion anymore, as Sucharita does not understand her fondness towards Gora, a man she considers to be hard-hitting, rough, loud and outright frightening. This is also the time that Gora has his transformed awareness, wakefulness of India, and the miasma of staunch caste beliefs slowly started moving away from his eyes.

Tagore makes use of the thoughts of Swami Vivekananda, who emphasised the importance of women, by making us realise that the history of India is flawed without taking the trials and tribulations of women into consideration. The great Indian epic the *Mahabharata* documents the social, religious, political, and philosophical dialogues through the plangency of some central characters—in *Gora*, Tagore does the same with Anandamoyi and Sucharita. They can be compared to Kunti for they share their eagerness to bring rightful action into the forefront of matters. There can be similar readings from these two books; as the way Kunti hides the truth of Karna's birth, so does Anandamoyi conceal Gora's roots from him. Sucharita is adopted by the Bhattacharya family just as Kunti was taken into King Bhoja's home. 'Both the characters go through a name change—but their interior cores do not change'. Sucharita is as upright and a frank feminist just as Draupadi was.

Although Draupadi and Sucharita are feminist, yet, Draupadi's frustration is sexual, and she is rancorous of the Kauravas and she craves for sexual freedom; yet Sucharita is not aggressive, nor does she have insolence and pride in her because of Paresh Babu's training, care and concern. In all his heroines, Tagore gives feminism a meaning of his own. Anandamoyi and Sucharita are not the rebel kind but they are evolved and emancipated women and stand calm in ruffled weather. The other heroines cause mighty blows to the society and they show extreme pride which often appears as recklessness. Tagore's heroines are not formidable beings; they either stand for justice for themselves or for the others like them. Sucharita's initial hostility towards Gora is explainable and Anandomoyi's selfless love is quite estimable.

Moral improvement is not the aim for writing *Gora;* rather Tagore takes his characters through a life journey of kindness and compassion. He published Gora in 1924, although it appeared serially even earlier. The story was written fashionable to the times he lived in. 'Lolita's failure is Tagore's instrument to convince the then feminists of Indian society (if only a handful) that the sudden uproar for freedom and dissolution of woman from Hindu society would get them very little—the little Baradasundari got from her Brahmo feminist ideology that let her wear revealing clothes, and converse with men in daylight.' Tagore's heroines and his feminist stance did not bring forth any cultural and social revolution in the society but it successfully stirred the thought process of the elitist soceity.

Indian novels were often platters of "greater-than-thou Eastern philosophy" and had little real-life characters, but in *Gora,*

Tagore successfully meshed life in a unique complete approach. Despite the social collapse, Tagore, generously senesces Lolita into a mature person and in her conversation with Anandamoyi, she tells her that it is not "necessary for him to give up all that in order to establish mutual relations with another human being." Binoy's predicament is clarified with Anandamoyi's help. Binoy is a product the gnawing Tagorean humanism. Tagore's humanism is evident when Binoy says, "If affection cannot put up with differences, then why do differences exist anywhere in the world?"

In *Gora* Tagore effectively combines natural lingusitics of human temperament with the details of everyday life. The reader cannot but value the liberal expression of Hinduism that Anandamoyi stood for. This Gora achieves only after a meaningful journey of life. Against this true demonstration of the great collapse in the moral fibre and human values among Hindus, Anandamoyi stands out as a brilliant woman who tutors Gora to learn and acquire those values that go against sectarianism and unite man with man.

The heroines in the novel—Sucharita and Lolita—are the liberated, unconventional young women with a strong mind of their own. Anandmoyi is the figurative image of Mother India. Gora, in his emotional outburst, finds *Bharatvarsha* in her—"Ma, you are my only mother. The mother for whom I have looked everywhere all this time she was sitting in my house. You have no caste, you do not discriminate against people, you do not hate—you are the image of benediction. You are my Bharatvarsha." Tagore exalts her conviction that people are above religion or caste.

The novel records the odyssey of a young man Gora from the narrowness of the committed religion he believed in, to cynicism and illumination as a 'human being'. The journey is conclusively alleviated by the fact that he was brought up by an open-minded Hindu surrogate mother. She is much ahead of her time and society. In her conduct throughout the novel, she is a noble woman who does not want to get into effusive debates on which is the virtuous path, but one that desires to supplement and deepen our growth as human beings. 'The freedom that she entrusted to Gora, and the ease with which she is able to integrate others who come in his life-story add to her weakness for the dignity and refinement in Binoy's approach all are testimony to this fact. 'In Tagore's delineation of Gora's mother, there is no disregard or defiance of religion, but an intense and tacit protest against what people themselves often make out religions to be.'

Works Cited

Chatterjee, Partha: *The Nation and Its Fragments: Colonial and Postcolonial Histories*. Princeton: Princeton University Press, 1994.

Kripalani, Krishna: *Tagore: A Biography*, Visva-Bharati, Calcutta, 1980.

Sen, Sukumar: *Rabindranath Thakur*, Eastern Publishers, Calcutta, 4th edn, 1969.

13

Stylising the Feminine in Films: Mrinmoyee in *Samapti*

Tagore's short story *Samapti* (The Conclusion) is, perhaps, best known for its cinematic version by Satyajit Ray in *Teen Kanya* (The Three Daughters). Ray's 1961 film strings together three short stories, *Postmaster* (The Postmaster), *Monihara* (The Lost Jewel) and *Samapti* (The Conclusion), written by Tagore in the 1890s. As the title of the film suggests, Ray chose to read these stories as Tagore's fictions of the feminine focusing on the inquiry of the complex 'psychology' of two adolescent girls and a young woman. Among the three, *Samapti* is perhaps the least disconcerting because of its unadventurous and safe 'romantic' wrapping up and the founding of the observance of conjugality.

In *Samapti*, Tagore shows another kind of boldness on the part of a young man which saves the fledgling conjugal life and love of Apurba-Mrinmoyee. Apurba's smartness and bold handling of a wild girl-wife establishes herself to her responsible self and sets her firmly on the threshold of a budding romance. Mrinmoyee is portrayed as the naughtiest possible village girl by Tagore who plays pranks on almost everybody in the village, but the author's craftsmanship lies in making her grow into womanhood slowly and subtly.

The last scene of *Samapti* in which the bedroom door of the couple bangs shut in the face of the bemused and nonplussed mother panting up the staircase provides the comic closure of this carefully orchestrated film; it is an appropriate 'conclusion' to the assorted tales of female yearning. This is the way, however, Tagore's story ends:

> He (Apurba) was about to get into the bed, when suddenly a pair of soft arms accompanied by the tinkling sound of bangles, encircled him in a tight embrace; a pair of petal-soft lips fell upon his own like a bandit, leaving him no scope to express his surprise at the wet tear-stained passionate kiss. Apurba taken aback realised that a venture once interrupted by giggles had finally found its fitting conclusion in tears.

There remains the vexed question of the fidelity and accuracy of Ray's cinematic variation to Tagore's 'original' literary work. Ray's film, particularly the endings, aids a shutout, a deconstructive feminist reading of Tagore's short stories. One cannot find a concerted feminist agenda in *Samapti*, a claim that could be made for Tagore's stories discussed in the preceding chapters; *Poila Namber* (Number One) or *Streer Patro* (The Wife's Letter), in which strong-minded, insightful, moral and liberated women challenge the prevailing patriarchal beliefs of marriage, often posing as sweeping and daring alternates. In fact, nothing could be less true of *Samapti* in terms of its ideological alternates—it is conservative but not in the damning sense in positing marriage as the idyllic and desired option, a realisation that slowly dawns on Mrinmoyee, the adolescent heroine. Her transmutation into a romantic woman is reflected on her attaining hetero-normative, dogmatic and prescriptive femininity apt for a young wife. This creates a carking note in a story which begins by rejoicing the *joie de vivre* of an adolescent village girl whose manner and behaviour openly disobeys norms of gendered demeanour.

The model of an adolescent girl who acts in a hoydenish manner would seem weird, if not odd, in the context of late nineteenth century recommendations of proper feminine behaviour in rural communities. The trace to the genesis of the story is told in a letter in *Chhinapatra* (The Torn Leaves), 1895, an edited selection of noteworthy letters that he wrote to his favourite niece Indira who, discovering the merit of the missives, wrote them down in her notebook and presented it back to her uncle, 'Robikaka' (Tagore).

The letters provide the reader an exciting peek into the very process through which the latticework of imagination works upon the writer's memoirs, and events or encounters that transform into short stories. They were originally published in prestigious literary journals like *Hitabadi*, *Sadhana*, *Bharathi* and *Sabujpatra* and later brought out as collection of short stories or *Galpaguchha*. Here is a selection from a letter which contains the clue to the genesis of the idea of the unconventional adolescent heroine of *Samapti*:

> There is one girl in this group who attracts my attention in particular. She would perhaps be about twelve or thirteen but being rather buxom and healthy she could easily seem around fourteen or fifteen. Her face is winsome, rather dark yet good-looking. Her hair is cut short like a boy's and that becomes her face with its intelligence, its frank and innocent expression .... It is this half-boyish, half-girlish manner that rivets the attention; the boyish lack of self consciousness blends with a feminine charm to create an entirely novel kind of girl. I had never expected to encounter such type among the village folk in Bengal.

Evidently this village belle had left a long-lasting impression on the mind of Tagore; within two years he wrote *Samapti* in which the unknown village belle, sans her haircut, makes her appearance in the avatar of the story's heroine.

> Mrinmoyee had a dark complexion; her short curly hair reached till the middle of her back. The expression on her face was frank

> like a boy's. There wasn't a trace of shame, fear or guile in her large dark eyes. She was strong, well-developed and healthy but it didn't occur to anyone to ask her age. Had they been curious people would have inevitably censured her parents that she was not yet married. (Translated)

It is not merely that Mrinmoyee's looks are not conventional to the notions of the feminine, yet her cheeky 'tomboyish' behaviour is source of great disquiet among the women in the village community:

> She was quite infamous in the village. The men affectionately referred to her as crazy, but the women were worried and petrified of her. She played only with the boys of the village, shunning and treating girls of her own age with contempt. In the children's world this girl was a veritable marauder, a borgi. (Translated)

These two extracts it may be seen as the 'problematic' that Tagore posed in the story about the fate of this atypical adolescent girl:

> Would it be possible to imagine a situation in which this curiously de-gendered young girl would find a groom? How, then would she fit into the conventional codes of the feminine expected of the typical Bengali wife? The first few chapters of *Samapti* may be read as a response to this problematic of the first query: the only possible solution would be through a romantic liaison, to have a young man capable of recognising and responding to what Tagore hypothesised as the "wild undisciplined female nature open and free as the fleeing forest deer' (Translated)

This portrayal is strikingly in the cast of 'romantic' sensibility and philosophy, a fête of the 'natural' as opposed to the 'artificial' social one which was seen as imposing restrictions on the *joie de vivre* that characterises human beings. The series of encounters between Apurbakrishna and Mrinmoyee indicate that Tagore took this typically 'romantic' position, a curiously modern take on what constitutes heterosexual romance:

> Mrinmoyee's aberrant 'unfeminine' behavior is represented as possessing an extraordinary charm to impress especially since it shown to advantage against Apurba's prospective bride, a younger girl, schooled and disciplined by the elder women of the household into becoming docile, dull and domesticated. (Translated)

Mrinmoyee breaks into peals of laughter as Apurba, a newly arrived alien, from Calcutta slips and falls on the muddy banks of the river. The undomesticated girl arrives like a whirlwind in the house where Apurba has come apparently to select a bride for himself and disrupts the social occasion, and this improper behaviour concludes when she steals his new slippers; and then returns them when he is cautiously navigating his way back home along the muddy tracks. It is the last occasion, there is a close physical propinquity between the two as Apurba pins the hands of the miscreant and looks into her eyes which are like the "pure sparkling water of a spring dappled by sunlight."

Throughout these stumble-upons and occurrences the reader along with Apurba are startled by Mrinmoyee's candidness and her lack of reticence that expresses in her swelling, lucid laughter. The English-educated urbane young man is besotted by the appeal of this curious country girl and insists, much to the exasperation of his loving widowed mother, that she is the bride he has selected. This settles the first of the two problematics: that of finding a groom for the adolescent girl who runs wild and refuses to 'grow' up into femininity. The story accentuates Mrinmoyee's battle against societal stereotypes of gendering, both before and after her marriage. When her own mother and the elderly village women try to infuse in her codes of suitable 'feminine' deportment through severe reprimands for her uncontrolled laughter, her bearing, food habits and playing with boys, Mrinmoyee learns to consider marriage as a horror and like a, "naughty pony horse shakes her head and says, 'I shall not get married.'"

Samapti is an amazing story for several reasons. Apurba's longing for Mrinmoyee is clearly not fickle infatuation but a powerful emotion; he is curiously caring and encouraging of his 'crazy' wife and her apparent boisterousness.

Tagore's stereotyping of conjugality in the opus of short stories, particularly those written during this time, in which, we find, scathing satire arraigning male insensitivity and selfishness, a typical husbandly behaviour. For instance, one could cite *Khata* (The Note Book) (already discussed in a preceding chapter) written during the same time. Mrinmoyee's lot is very different from that of nine-year-old Uma in the story. This lonely and depressed child-bride also has an educated husband Pyarimohan who uses his husbandly right and authority to control and chastise young Uma who commits the 'irremissible' act of female noncompliance: she brings to the house of her in-laws her favourite notebook, in which she doodles her thoughts or the lyrics of songs sung by peripatetic female singers. *Khata*, a heartrending account, emphasises what must have been the truth for many young girls: the distress and anguish of marriage to men much older than themselves and the wretchedness and pain of insult in which they would be made to suffer in the hands of the in-laws.

In *Samapti* Tagore chose to symbolise marriage as a condition of a wish fulfilment in numerous ways; not only Mrinmoyee gets a warm and caring husband, she is also not subjected to any repression by her mother-in-law, even when, she takes it upon herself to tame Mrinmoyee into becoming a good housewife by 'taming the shrew'. Domesticity and 'homeliness' are revolting to Mrinmoyee and she attempts to flee from her patrilocation into the freedom of her pre-marital days a number of times. She is a wanderer-child of Nature who cannot be chained within he domestic walls. During one such occasion, she leaves her marital home on a monsoon night to meet her father, Ishan Majumdar, a petty clerk in Kushiganj who has not been granted leave even to attend his daughter's marriage. This particular episode of Tagore's story, missing in Ray's film (this is one of the major departures from the story in the great film), has a strange resemblance with a real-life incident which is worth quoting at length:

> The year was 1888 or 1889. Suradhuni had been married at the tender age of six. Soon after the marriage, her husband went back to Assam, where he worked as a schoolteacher. Suradhuni was left behind with her in-laws. A few months had passed since the marriage. She was lonely and homesick and wanted to visit her parents who lived across the river in Nabadwip. But her in-laws would not hear of it. One day she slipped out of the house, went to the river ghat and asked one of the boatmen to give her a ride across the river to her parent's house. The boatman recognised the unchaperoned girl, and advised her to go back. She pleaded with him, and against his better judgement he escorted Suradhuni to her parent's house. When Suradhuni's parents learned that she had come without her in-laws' permission, they sent her back. But her in-laws would not take her in. Having left the house without permission, Suradhuni had left her kula. Her parents were afraid of the social repercussions of taking back a girl who had received such opprobrium; they had two more daughters to marry off. By taking a kulatyagi daughter they did not want to imperil the chances of marriage for the other daughters. So Suradhuni's father took the little girl to Calcutta and abandoned her there.

This could have been the fate of Mrinmoyee too, especially, since she seems to be remarkably 'unhomely'—her kinship lies with the world outside her home which seems to be her natural home. Yet, not only is she saved by the foresighted Bonomali, an elderly villager who brings her back to her in-laws, she also gets to meet her father. Intensely sensitive to her longings, it is Apurba who furtively arranges to take her to Kushiganj. One perhaps wonders at the lyrical description of the countryside and the bliss in the quotidian that marks the couple's boat-trip. The experience of young Tagore who had enjoyed brief spells of domesticity with his wife Mrinalini and his young children on the boat has been composed beautifully, thus:

> It is in this newly felt romance of domesticity that Apurba longs for a kiss from Mrinmoyee on the eve of his departure toCalcutta: 'I want you', he tells her 'to willingly, lovingly, give me a kiss.' However, not only does Mrinmoyee fail to respond to the romantic yearning of her college educated 'modern' husband but finds this desire patently ridiculous. Indeed, each time she attempts to strike a solemn pose and approaches her husband's lips she breaks into an irrepressible giggle.

Since the genre and ideological reinforcements of this particular story does not leave any room for any coercive social modus operandi of gendering, Mrinmoyee's growth has to be tracked within the paradigm of the natural, which is the second 'problematic': her natural conversion from a hoydenish adolescent into a woman capable of responding to her husband's passionate yearning. Thus unlike the ending scene of Ray's film (which is another departure from the story), the closed doors merely provide a teasing hint of the intimacy between the couple, whereas, Tagore makes his heroine Mrinmoyee taking the initiative to surprise her husband with a passionate kiss. Tagore's *Samapti* situates the ideology of the naturally evolved 'feminisation' through the event of Mrinmoyee's parting from her husband, and here lies the great stroyteller's aritistry. He shows the growth of his heroine gradually, from a child to a woman, and he does not make any haste. Formalised and stylised in Vaishnava poetry as *biraha* (separation), it is the sublime parting from the loved one that suddenly tosses her from her teasing, blithe youth into a mature femininity whose ultimate emotion is pain.

There is in fact an overt metaphorical fairy-tale frame of the import of Mrinmoyee's laughter and her tears in this story tellingly embodies as Apurba's ruminations as he stares at his sleeping wife washed in moonlight:

> He felt that someone had touched the princess with the silver wand and rendered her unconscious. If only one could lay hands on the golden wand it would be possible to awaken this somnolent soul and exchange garlands with her. The silver wand was laughter, the golden one was tears. (Translated)

The last line of this excerpt marks attenuation from Apurba's reflections to an authorial intrusion which may be considered as an interpretive hint. Within the erotic cutback on the fictional connubial bliss it seems apt to what the kiss signifies. The arousing of quiescent female sexuality replaces the laughter with tears of ecstasy and contentment.

It is apparent that the central argument of the story is the "female rite of passage from adolescence to adulthood", a stage marked by the budding of Mrinmoyee's sexuality in which longing is fused into romantic hunger for her absent husband. The worth of the title lies in squeezing this skill into a climactic erotic turn of phrase "Mrinmoyee kissing Apurba with passion". The unsettling element in *Samapti* is Mrinmoyee's 'natural' transformation into a tender wife, capable of having a romantic ache for her absent husband, is founded on her acquirement of a femininity which was earlier alien to her nature and identity.

Works Cited

Chattopadhyay, Swati: *Representing Calcutta: Modernity, Nationalism and the Colonial Uncanny*, London and New York: Routledge, 2005, p.225.

Tagore, Rabindranath: *Samapti, Galpaguccha*, Vol.I, Calcutta Visva-Bharati, 1999.

____ : *Glimpses of Bengal: Selected from the Letters of Sir Tagore 1885-1895*. London: Macmillan, 1921.

____ : "Saturday 4 July 1891" in *Chhinapatrabali*. Calcutta: Visva-Bharati, 2004. p.53.

14

Womanism of Labonyo of *Shesher Kobita*

Tagore resembles Amit Ray in his magnum opus *Shesher Kobita* (The Last Poem). He has apotheosised Amit Ray in his own persona. Almost every artist writes something that somehow represents his personality, style, emotional rejoinder and eon. A creation that draws on the penultimate portraiture in terms of words, expression and technique and here, Tagore has created Amit Ray in his own mirror image.

For Tagore *Shesher Kobita* is close to his life and has autobiographical elements in it. The setting is quaint Shillong. Amit Ray is an Oxford-educated and a high society man from Calcutta who has a way with words. Indeed he writes verses under the pseudonym of Nibaran Chakraborty. Labonyo Dutt comes from an ordinary background and is highly educated. She has a determined will. This novel is about the love between Amit and Labonyo. They are in awe of each other but find their difference in class difficult to overcome. It is a very poetic piece of writing which explores the realities of love as romance and its culmination in marriage as a meeting of two mature minds. It questions the importance of the institution of marriage as the ultimate consequence of a love affair. Love, it claims, happens for the sake of love and not to an impetuous unexciting matrimony. Tagore completed writing *Shesher Kobita* (The Last Poem) in Bangalore on June 25, 1928, presumably around the beginning of an Indian monsoon in that city.

It is hard to visualise a poet, frugal and fastidious with language, having so much pleasure, leaving us stuck in this overflow of lyrical words. It is like inhabiting a 'waking dream'.

So one fateful day, Amit meets the love of his life, Labonyo. A strangely modern accident, considering the time (the late 1920s), the place (a hilly, meandering, desolate Shillong road with old forests sloping down on one side), involving two cars brings about their first meeting, a peculiarly modern accident that sets the tone for an enduring (if not, filmy) love-story.

Amit, of course, has his own views on the magnitude of time and timeliness:

> Only those with time on hand should be punctual. God has infinite time, so the sun rises and sets punctually. We mortals can't be wasteful enough to spend time being punctual. When Amaravati's questioner asks, "What did you do on earth?" can I unblushingly reply, "I was so busy working with one eye on the clock that I let all of life's timeless moments slip by?" (Translated)

Amit's philosophy earns him some 70 days eternally caught in musing. An action-packed, frank man would have rushed home after a chance meeting with a silent, not very exciting woman on a dusty road in Shillong.

Amit is a very prosperous 20-something barrister, educated in Oxford and London, who does next to nothing professionally, in Calcutta, but is at ease to be a social gadfly. Eloquent, argumentative and sophisticated and counters people endlessy with his opposing views. He has inherited wealth, avid reading, individualism and willingness to be urbanely attentive; make him immensely attractive to women, but men tended to be antagonistic.

Labonyo is a few years younger than Amit. She is brought up by her widower father, the principal of a college in western India, to be as well educated and independent as any man. She is also a graceful, good-looking woman with a beautiful voice. On their second meeting, after a very brief, cheerful talk with her, Amit knows why he likes her: more than her physical beauty, it's her calm, firm, meditative intelligence that endears her to him. Now here the author says, "Labonyo, we know, did not exhibit this calm intelligence to the other young man who was smitten with her. A series of events led to Labonyo finding work as a resident tutor. She is spending the summer in Shillong with her employer and the employer's two children, of whom the daughter is Labonyo's pupil."

Labonyo and Amit chance upon each other at points in their lives during which they secretly pass through crises. Amit is wild, vain, having nothing in his life that has any prospect of permanence. He loves to talk but lacks listening skills, and is unable to comprehend the earnestness behind his nonstop vocal showmanship. A listener can even inspire or discover that vein of seriousness of his jugglery of talks. His life lacks meaning and intention. The business of doing nothing except arguing and judging the caprices of his society leaves him with nothing to savour and no cause to pursue.

Labonyo has started her new life after alienating from another man, her other suitor, the withdrawn and cerebral Shovanlal, whom she regards as her competitor, for academic honours, her enigmatic, exasperating punch bag. Shovanlal is so reticent he never mustered up the courage to talk to her, and the author says, "his very timorousness gave Labonyo an unrealistic sense of her own superiority and also, in the odd manner of girls—barely acknowledged even to herself—her future husband". In ignorance or meditative calm she also manoeuvers her father's remarriage and refuses his financial support. Fortunately, she likes her work and her employer, Jogomaya. She fills her leisure with meticulous study of English literature and classical history. The indulgent, garrulous, appealing, intelligent Amit now arrives like a force of nature and innundates the superficial dryness of Labonyo's life.

"I'm now a captive in a world I don't know. Only when I can read this world will I be set free." Amit says during one of the funniest conversations in *Shesher Kobita*. He hasn't disclosed the name "Nibaron Chakrabarty" yet to Labonyo, but acknowledges quoting this "special poet". He offers the quoted line in explanation after the opening lines of a poem he possibly composes extempore. "Nibaron Chakrabarty" is an alias of Amit. Even though the poem turns out to be a pronouncement of love, and Labonyo is recognised with the Unknown who the poet will go to war to unravel, it is also representational of what Amit goes through in those two months in Shillong. He finds in himself longing and pining away. His freedom lies in recognition of new feelings that stir him, and his salvation lies in his wish-fulfilment, at whatever price.

Amit wrecks the anxious calm of Labonyo's life like a force of nature, but it is Labonyo who bedazzles his mind with her unaffectedness and simplicity. In the awful, terrifying incidents of their first meeting it had seemed to "Amit that Labonyo had 'apparated' (to use Potterese) rather than simply got out of the car she had been riding, as if white-hot lightning had etched her against the enormous gloom of the hillside." He, wading through taper, meets the violent waters of a wavy river. Providentially, the meeting is symbolic and he immediately knows its life-changing moment in his life.

Labonyo's education has polished her quintessential personality. There are no conceit and alteration and no pretence. She is now distinctively herself. Amit, for whom all new knowledge takes the form of fascinating detours from his own vaguely defined centre, finds her such, and says so:

> By happy chance we sometimes come across a person who makes us start and say, "This person is uniquely himself/herself, not like anyone else." (Translated)

Amit doesn't hesitate in proposing marriage to Labonyo, but she refuses. She is apprehensive of this being one passing fancy of his, who in fact, considers marriage "vulgar". In response Amit says, "Character evolves too." In other words, Labonyo may have made five precise observations about his disposition, but that hardly proves she knows the whole story—because human character is not an inert thing. He proposes other persuasive arguments, but Labonyo is not ready to award him any firm incentive beyond his articulacy.

Amusingly, Labonyo halts at a turn in her life when she has rejected daft adulation and by rejecting Amit's proposal, she establishes her womanist approach. He quotes Donne's famous lines from 'The Canonisation', "For God's sake hold your tongue, and let me love," cannot hold his own tongue or make her believe so. Labonyo thinks of the memory of Amit's love as one perfect happening in her life that appears like the Taj Mahal to her. He himself questions his purpose—he feels he is conveying his most profoundly-felt emotions very well through words, but then he only has his words but no strong love! As if to strengthen this qualm in our minds he goes into a disappointing judgement of men and women. According to him, men are creators who keep destroying the old, whereas women employ all their might to protect what exists. The latter cannot let things go from their hearts and life. This sort of gender ideas are difficult to match with the men and women of today, but Tagore's steadfast feminism dictated him to state thus.

Amit thinks he knows Labonyo really well but this juxtaposition of a theoretical gender divide on her views makes the reader wonders at whether Tagore was a campaigner of womanism or commenting on the elusiveness or evasiveness of Labonyo as any ordinary woman. Labonyo fears that Amit's fascination about her won't last forever. She is utterly romantic and fails to understand that in all marriages, rountine and humdrum set in at a cetain point of time. Love does not appear new anymore over a period and to reject him purely thinking his love as infatuation, seems to be a little far-flung on her part. Almost all loves start with infatuation and move on from one level to another. Therefore, her belief that Amit needs to continuously move on to remain true to his character, he should not be tied down to one woman. She has merely caught his eye as a new enticement. Sooner or later, he would reject her to keep being himself. Does this show that Labonyo wants to keep her love pristine that she received from him? Or she is just exhibiting her insightful traits? Or may be that she suffers from 'inferiority complex'?

But her rejection of the suitable boy makes her appear emancipated and liberated. The analytical mind that Tagore gave to Labonyo speaks volumes in itself: strong-willed, unmoved and capable of loving and at the same time doesn't sway with passion. She creates and destroys too. She is Tagore's new woman with sense, sensibilities and sensuality. It could well be, but surely this desire to protect what she considers perfect and precious is not a gender spur but a human one.

In a later dialogue with Jogomaya Labonyo spells out her fears: she knows Amit loves her, but the person he loves is not her, an ordinary woman, but someone permeated through with the glamour of his own overgenerous mind. This view also comes across in the poem she writes to him at the end, the last poem. If they are married, she won't long stay unique, and lose her lustre. In order to sustain his love in real life, his nature must change; but she doesn't want to change him in any way for her sake. In this muddle, one thing is sure that in this love entangle, it is difficult to understand whether Amit's love is erroneous (as she makes it out to be) or it is she, who never could love Amit since she weighs and measures their love too much.

With her collection of what Alice Walker herself calls "womanist prose" she affirms her reputation as a black feminist on theoretical grounds, coining the term "Womanism" to refer to black feminism. Tagore, a long while ago, in his poetry, fiction, drama and essays, as in music, dance, painting, and sculpture, worked not only with a new sense of belief and purpose but also with a sense of achievement, perhaps, never before experienced and practised by any artists in the long, troubled history of the peoples all over the world and particulary in India. Labonyo is a unique creation of Tagore after Mrinal, Charulata, Binodini, Bimala et al. Here an attempt is made to study Labonyo against Alice Walker's womanist theory.

Alice Walker invented the term 'womanism' in her anthology of essays entitled *In Search of Our Mothers' Gardens*, published in 1983. In the opening of the collection she gives a definition of this "feminist, Afrocentric, healing, embodied, and spiritual" (Razak, 2006: 100) concept:

> Womanist 1. From womanish. (Opp. of "girlish", i.e., frivolous, irresponsible, not serious.) A black feminist or feminist of colour. From the black folk expression of mothers to female children, "You acting womanish," i.e., like a woman. Usually referring to outrageous, audacious, courageous or wilful behavior. Wanting to know more and in great depth than is considered "good" for one. Interested in grown-up doings. Acting grown up. Being grown up. Interchangeable with another black folk expression: "You are trying to be grown." Responsible. In charge. Serious. 2. Also: A woman who loves other women, sexually and/or non-sexually. Appreciates and prefers women's culture, women's emotional flexibility (values tears as natural counterbalance of laughter), and women's strength. Sometimes loves individual men, sexually and/or non-sexually. Committed to survival and wholeness of entire people, male and female. Not a separatist, except periodically, for health. Traditionally universalist, as in: "Mama, why are we brown, pink, and yellow, and our cousins are white, beige, and black?" Ans.: "Well, you know the coloured race is just like a flower garden, with every colour flower represented." Traditionally capable, as in: "Mama, I'm walking to Canada and I'm taking you and a bunch of other slaves with me." Reply: "It wouldn't be the first time." 3. Loves music. Loves dance. Loves the moon. Loves the Spirit. Loves love and food and roundness. Loves struggle. Loves the Folk. Loves herself. Regardless. 4. Womanist is to feminist as purple to lavender. (Walker, 1984: xi-xii)

This chaotic listing suggests that womanism represents very different things, which makes it difficult to fully grasp what Walker is saying.

At the first ingress Walker defines "womanist" in reference to the origin and the original use and meaning of the term. The only phrase that does not go into these more etymological issues is the one in which she indicates that "womanist" is a synonym for a black feminist, or by extension, a feminist of colour. By adding the generalisation of "colour", Walker makes sure that she is not guilty of the discrimination as the white feminists are. But, as we have seen, the major part of this first entry deals with the origin of the term "womanist". "This noun is derived from the black folk adjective "womanish", which is primarily used in the black folk expression "You are acting womanish." Mothers say to their daughters and which means the same as another folk expression: "You trying to be grown." As Collins argues, by " (t) aking the term from the Southern black folk expression of mothers to female children (…), Walker suggests that black women's concrete history fosters a womanist worldview accessible primarily and perhaps exclusively to black women." (Collins, 1996: 10)

The two folk expressions involve three internally connected meanings. First of all, the expressions indicate "outrageous, audacious, courageous or wilful behavior" (Walker, 1984: xi). These four adjectives all refer to doing/saying something that is not self-evident or easy, yet doing/saying it with strong determination and a lot of motivation. As Saunders argues, "(t)he emphasis is on 'wilfull' because for so long, so many black women have not been considered to be in possession of their own free wills, and no small part of the problem has resided in the psyche of black men" (Saunders, 1988). Secondly, both expressions refer to an attitude that is characterised by " (w) anting to know more and in greater depth than is considered 'good' for one" (Walker, 1984: xi). This again implies the non-self-evident side of womanism. Thirdly, the expressions indicate a mature, grown attitude. As Walker says in the beginning of the entry, "womanish" is the opposite of "girlish", which means "frivolous, irresponsible, not serious," Walker (1984: xi). In opposition, "womanish" means not only acting, but also growing up. It is associated with being responsible and serious. This emphasis on the mature side of womanists may indicate that the zeal for the black woman's case does not derive from a childish passion or a naïve whim. Instead, it is rooted in a feeling of responsibility, of being in charge of the fate of black women.

Tagore, while creating the persona of Labonyo, perhaps might have thought of a strong womanist (a later day feminist term) figure who can easily withdraw her love and settle herself in a world of her own that might hurt her emotions but then she would not care, because she would prefer to live a long married life, if not totally happy yet a fulfilled one.

Labonyo refuses Amit fearing that his love for her has its roots in imaginative infatuation and he has woven a picture image of her in his mind that defies the 'actual/real' Labonyo. She, at no point of time, wants to give him a chance to come in terms with reality in harsh way. She knows her decision will baffle him and, it does so too, but the she is a womanist to her fingertips, and she respects her own self as much she respects his love for her. It is thrust upon here that Alice Walker's womanism puts emphasis on the word 'black', and here it would be safe to emphasise on the 'brown' as in the case of Labonyo and to study women as a race different from men in their want, desires, mind and body. Labonyo does not succumb to her love for Amit but by refusing his love and marrying a much lesser intellectual, Shobhonlal, she and Tagore bring home the points successfully that marriages are not always theory-based, but have to be pragmatic in order for them to run longer.

At the second ingress, Walker defines "womanist" by referring to the different types of relationships that can occur between women. Most importantly, womanists love other women, especially for those things that make them female, like their specific female culture, their emotional life, their strength. Besides just loving these female characteristics, Walker adds that womanists should even prefer them (implying to those of a man).

It seems that Walker not only means that women should love other women, but that, more importantly, they should also adore what is specifically female about them. Labonyo too conforms to this category. She loves her feminine self and her interaction with other women truly shows her liberated view and her love of herself being a 'woman'.

Although Walker refers to lesbian relationships in the first sentence of this entry already, she clearly does not despise heterosexual relationships. This is probably the feature that constitutes the most striking difference between womanism and white feminism. Although she overtly pleads with her audience to love themselves solely because of the fact that they are female, she is not at all hostile towards men. In other words, she specifies that a tolerant attitude is not only needed among sexes, but also among races. In that way, she offers a viewpoint here that is useful not only for black women, but for the whole of mankind. Her definition thus clearly has both a concrete dimension, the rooting of the term in black (female) folk expressions, and a more universal one, the mythical, worldwide image of the garden. As Davis says, Walker's definition illustrates that "individuals are not separate from the survival of the earth, but instead act as extensions of the universe itself."

Walker further refers to one specific relationship between women: the relationship between a mother and her child. The fact that her two examples in this entry involve a mother-child (presumably a daughter) situation suggests that she considers motherhood essential in the experience of being a woman. As Razak claims, Walker focuses on the "sharing and mentorship that are a traditional part of idealised Black mother-daughter relationships." Lastly, she uses a mild form of humour in this entry, for example, when she says that womanists are sometimes separatists "for health" or in the last dialogue between mother and child. Probably, this is to create a positive atmosphere. Tagore's heroines are mostly childless and he cleverly avoids the topics of 'mothering' in his making of these strong new women. In this novel, Tagore has done away with Labonyo's mother and shows a role reversal by showing Labonyo finding a match for her widower father.

At the third ingress, Walker defines "womanist" associatorily. In an inventory which lists things a womanist loves, she mainly considers the irrational side women are traditionally said to have, the moon as a symbol of femininity. In her list, she includes music and dance, love, food and roundness as symbols for the worldly, bodily pleasures in life as well as the moon and the spirit as symbols for the spiritual dimension of our being. Furthermore, she says womanists love struggle, which probably means that they do not give up to easily in their striving. And besides loving their people ("folk") in general, womanists also love themselves. It is not clear whether the italicised "regardless" at the end of the list solely modifies the penultimate phrase, or whether it applies to the whole list. Labonyo copiously and completely falls in this group of women. Her love of herself as a woman and other artistic excellences in her, she knows them well and considers them as her strength.

The fourth and last ingress consists solely of the phrase "Womanist is to feminist as purple to lavender," Walker (1984: xii), which has become famous. With this statement, she indicates those both have things in common, but in the end are undeniably and uniquely different. By ending on this sentence, she moreover closes the circle her definition is, as she began with a similar observation in the first entry, namely, that a womanist is a black feminist. Why she chose purple and lavender as the colours of reference (and not blue and violet), is not clear. It certainly makes one think of *The Color Purple*. Whether this was intended by Walker, we do not know. Labonyo, Mrinal, Charulata, Binodini, Bimala, Mrinmoyee, Anandomoyi, all conform to this colour code. They are neither purple nor lavender but they are mauve.

In her definition of womanism, Walker indicates a number of different things that are not easily figured out. Most importantly, she sketches (black) women as beautiful and strong beings without denouncing men or white people in the process. As Davis puts it:

> Through her four-part definition, (Walker) draws her reader's attention to the importance of women's intellectual, physical, emotional, and spiritual wholeness, and she stresses the need to create a global community where all members of society are encouraged to survive and survive whole. Madhu Dubey argues that Walker's womanist project seeks to "integrate the past and present, individual and community, personal and political change, into a unified whole." (Davis, 2004: 33)

Labonyo declines the proposal of marriage, but Amit doesn't leave Shillong, and ultimately she does the easier thing by accepting him. Amit is to return to Calcutta and Labonyo sets the condition that they wouldn't meet again till their wedding in November-December. But he doesn't leave because his sister Shomita ("CiCi") arrives in Shillong with her friend Ketaki (Katie"). For a few days, he leads a strange dual life: he sleeps at the hotel where his sister has put up, but every afternoon he goes to the dilapidated little house he had first rented and then bought. There he changes his Western wear for the traditional Indian clothing that Labonyo and Jogomaya are used to seeing him in, and presents himself to them at tea-time. Why does he behave in this strange way? Why doesn't he disclose his wedding plans to his sister and Ketaki and introduce them to Labonyo? The secrets he and Labonyo keep from each other spoil their idyll. It is odd that while they talk so freely and so much to each other, they fail to mention, even when the topic arises, times in the past when they may have made or been on the brink of making emotional commitments. In a different context Labonyo once tells Amit, "he exacts the truth to be known; only then people don't dare disregard". But this lucidity she does not show in her own behaviour, not even when Shobhonlal's name comes up. Nor does he tell her about the love of his youth, who still holds a torch for him and wears the ring he gave her. However, Amit still fully anticipates spending the rest of his days with Labonyo. She, on the contrary, never frees herself of doubts about him. "Cocooned in magical words, neither shows the will to cut a clear path for the future by bringing out in the open secrets that are like 'thorns', 'lightning', and 'neuralgia pain'—the very type of flinty, hurtful disclosures that Amit boastfully claimed his avatar 'Nibaron Chakravarty', as opposed to poor old moribund, maudlin "Robi Thakur (Tagore) " had the poetic valour to say."

At last, the day arrives when Ketaki and her ring break the magic charm. Like Kalidasa's Shakuntala, she revives her declining fortunes with the reminiscences restrained by the ring. Unlike Shakuntala, she never lost her ring, but like Dushyant, Amit has lost his memory of her eighteenth summer. He returns her the ring. She urges him to take a trip to Cherrapunji for a few days. When he returns, Jogomaya's Shillong home is empty. In Calcutta, however, Amit is in touch with Jogomaya's college-going son, Joti. It is always possible to reach Labonyo, but he will not. Labonyo and Amit have convinced themselves that their love is not for the real world.

In a way, at the end, Labonyo has created the new Amit, he speaks like her. At their last meeting, in Shillong, she had tells him:

> Don't give me a ring, no reminder is necessary. Let my love be pure, unbeheld by the world. The world outside won't write on it. (Translated)

Labonyo's disinclination to test her love and Amit's in the roads of ordinary life sets the stage for their farewells. Their love frees both from their not-fully-self-aware existences, teaches them to take on the celebrated burden of living; but they won't risk losing their one, most precious, most necessary source of the purest joy and keenest grief. Amit marries Ketaki and Labonyo is to marry Shobhonlal next summer.

Labonyo of *Shesher Kobita* is a distinctive contribution of Tagore to modern Bengali literature. Through her, Tagore introduces into Bengali literature, the figure of the 'beloved as friend', a celebration of camaraderie. When women characters, especially heroines, belonged to set types drawn from the cultural/religious reservoir, Labonyo ushers in a change that erstwhile Bengali literature was desperately in need of. She breaks the mould in many senses. She is not the heroine who the hero marries in the end to live happily ever after with. Nor is she the quintessentially modern romantic heroine. She defies being cast in the mould of any fixed Indian stereotype or archetype. In fact, the meaning and significance of love deepens and acquires greater resonance through the character of Labonyo. In the role of the beloved as friend, a soul mate, Labonyo adds a new dimension to the novel and to women characters in Bengali literature, including Tagore's creations. Labonyo proves that the beloved can be a genuine companion, an intimate friend with whom one can drop all inhibitions and be liberated. It is Labonyo alone who can see through the maze of Amit's self-projections and grasp, his slippery, private self. In fact, Labonyo stands out as a unique woman even in the company of Tagore's other powerful heroines from *Chokher Bali* to *Char Adhyaya.*

Works Cited

Arisika, Razak: "Response", *Journal of Feminist Studies in Religion* 22.1 2006, pp. 99-107.

Collins, Patricia Hill: "What's in a name? Womanism, Black feminism, and Beyond", *Black Scholar* 26.1 (1996), pp. 9-17.

Davis, J. Amanda: "To Build a Nation: Black Women Writers, Black Nationalism, and Violent Reduction of Wholeness", *Frontiers: A Journal of Women Studies* 25.3 (2004), pp. 24-53.

Tagore, Rabindranath: *Sesher Kobita* (*The Last Poem*) Rupa & Co, 2007.

Walker, Alice: In *Dictionary of Literary Biography, Volume 6: American Novelists Since World War II*, Second Series, A Bruccoli Clark Layman Book. (ed.) James E. Kibler Jr. University of Georgie: The Gale Group, 1980, pp. 350-358.

15

Woman Versus Womanliness in Tagore's Last Novellas

Tagore's last novels are more gender specific. "Unconventional relationships—a married woman in love with a younger brother-in-law; a love triangle between a man, his wife and his sister-in-law; an intimate affair between a married man and a distant cousin"—are the subject of Tagore's Novellas *Nastaneer* (The Broken Nest), *Dui Bon* (Two Sisters), and *Malancha* (The Garden and the Gardener). Tagore focuses on the subtle nuances of unsanctioned relationships, exploring feelings of loneliness and worthlessness in middle-class housewives in colonial Bengal. They display Tagore's remarkable understanding of a woman's psyche, with all these three works underlining the incompatibility between husbands and wives, and how the ensuing void lead to forbidden relationships. In Charulata, Sharmila, and Neeraja—the three strong yet vulnerable heroines—Tagore presents emerging 'New Women', with thoughts and desires of their own.

In these three novellas—written between 1901 and 1933—Tagore focuses on the delicate tinges of the unendorsed relationships while exploring feelings of loneliness and unimportance in middle-class housewives in colonial Bengal. They display his remarkable indulgence in a woman's psyche, with all three works emphasising the incompatibility between husbands and wives, and how the ensuing void leads to forbidden relationships. In Charulata, Sharmila and Niraja—the three strong yet defenceless heroines—he presents emerging 'new women and new with a vengeance', with thoughts and desires of their own.

Tagore seems to be agitated on the subject of "conflict of love, more particularly extramarital love". The love triangles explored include Bhupati, Charu of *Nastaneer*, Amal, Shashanka, Sharmila and Urmi in *Dui Bon* and Aditya, Neeraja and Sarala in *Malancha*. He wrote these stories considering the changing notions of the nuclear family, and the changes that the women of the interior family unit were going through. The influence education opened new vistas of romance on the relationships. Each of these stories engages in the woman confronting her limited space. They are ready to face the moral and societal challenges as Tagore's New Women. These stories stand testimony to Tagore's fervent consciousness about the revolution in the domestic space and the emergence of an unconventional version of female selfhood, bordering on dissoluteness. Even if these stories fail to break the conventionality, yet they are unique for the craft and dexterity that outline the subtlety and refinement of unsanctioned attractions. These stories show culpability, pain and trauma that strikingly haunt the contemporary reader. Tagore seems to have been caught in the watershed of transition. He is keenly aware of the winds of change for the New Woman; yet uneasy about the deeper collision on familial and societal structures.

Between *Nastaneer* (1901) and *Dui Bon* (1933) or *Malancha* (1934), there is a space of more than three decades. While there are evident differences between the early and later works of Tagore, these are perhaps less important than the central anxiety, if not obsession, that unites them. There is an investigation of upper-class conjugal relationship and women's problematic place in it. Strain and loneliness in their marital homes push the women to the rim of hysteric insanity bordering with fear psychosis where they learn and ascertain their unidentified sexuality. The same women imprison themselves in stereotypes of domesticity, but still are able to rise and break the shackles. Tagore, in his later fiction, focusing on urban life, was noticeable for their psychological solidity and concerted use of technique. These fictions are described by an almost hackneyed, everyday family life involving sober fiscal planning and calculation: the male protagonists are all engaged in business. The composed surface is then abruptly broken up by a seismal cataclysm similarly in matters of the heart and those of finance. Financial fraud and collapse accompany emotional perfidy and turmoil for both the partners.

> The paradigm of transgressive, often self-destructive, passion of women within a patrician or middle-class milieu can of course be traced back to the domestic fiction of Bankim Chandra Chatterjee. Barring a few exceptions, the Victorian domestic novel had been marked by settled family life and the prudential distrust of ungovernable passion. Thus, it could not have served as a model for Bankim or Tagore. At the same time, Victorian values were a visible 'civilising/colonising' influence on the Bengali middle and upper classes, shaping the ideals of companionate marriage, family, and home. But if Victorian morality gave rise to a new concept of domesticity, Tagore's fictional representation of it exposed the stifling hypocrisy and limitations of that morality. Victorian values may have introduced the notion of companionate marriage to the middle-class Hindu household, but the entire process involved a poeticisation of women. Thus, a prosaic and routine domesticity is turned into a sanctimonious ideal by rhetoric of mystification.

There are certain chief characteristics in Tagore's career as a novelist. After his first two novels, *Bou Thakuranir Haat* (1883) and *Rajarishi* (1887) he never wrote historical romance again—a genre that was extremely popular during his times and the leading names were novelists like Bankim Chandra, Ramesh Chandra Datta and Swarnakumari Devi (Tagore's sister). It is worth mentioning that Tagore, through his novels, wanted to meet the contemporary reality head-on. Secondly, most of his young female protagonists make a more permanent mark on the readers than their male equals, are almost as a rule childless (as discussed in the preceding chapter). Social psychologists infer that in Indian society "motherhood and maternal identity confers upon a woman a purpose that nothing else in her culture can." "To be a mother is, by definition, to be a good wife and in turn a good woman". In Tagore's novels what we come across as widowhood, often a result of childhood marriage to much older husbands, and whom we meet, are young widows who have no ways of attaining any permissible right to motherhood. Their threatening sexuality, which is a genuine problem for colonised male 'self', often wreaks havoc among the family and the society at large. Such widows, offshoots of inequal marriages, were mostly left at the mecry of the dead husbands' family members. They were sexually exploited, used and some of them willingly sought pleasures. The thing that concerns us is why should only a married woman have the right to motherhood; and the woman who are part of these households and part of the society be deprived of this right to motherhood? The results of such pleasure hunts are rapes, numerous abortions and deaths during such illegal termination of pregnancies. This shocking and bizarre exploitation of the widows is still prevalent today in our society.

There is a very important motif in all Tagore's major novels, i.e., the homo-social bonding between male protagonists. Though some would argue that there may be covert suggestions on the part of the novelist of homosexuality in Tagore's novels male friendship does not seek to be homo-erotic but remains strongly homo-social.

In *Dui Bon* Sharmila's (the elder of the two sisters) motherly persona is charted against the beloved-self of Urmimala (the younger sister) and her maternal concern for her husband, juxtaposed with her childlessness. This may thus indicate a mismatched relationship. *Dui Bon* is a two-woman theory novel—mother and beloved as Tagore clearly states at the beginning of it:

> Women are of two classes, such a thing I have heard from some scholars. One class is chiefly mother, and the other beloved. (Translated)

In her persona of mother, at least in the initial stages of the novel, she is allowed the role of an all-controlling woman, and hence, is influential and empowered. Her ubiquitous presence and control on her husband Shashanka's life make her appear a colossal figure amongst all other female protagonists of Tagore's stories and novellas. But Tagore takes refuge in a letter to tell the reader that Shashanka and Sharmila had never really been united, although the fissures were not visible on the surface. Their nuptial relationship is, therefore, pretence and Shashanka openly reprimands her for treating him like a toy in front of the world. Despite her suffering, Sharmila rather masochistically surrenders to the typecast of the woman who is callously left at home by her husband in chase of his commercial venture which for her is the endlessly masculine and heroic struggle with fate.

Urmimala is different, spontaneous, inquisitive, and vivacious. But Nirad wishes to dictate his terms on her completely, cloaking his love of power and money in the form of supercilious ideals according to which he would mould her nature like a scientific procedure in the laboratory. Urmi submits herself to this restrained tyranny, this act of aestivation, much against her nature, although providentially she is not trapped into marriage. Internalising the sermons of Nirad, she would at times rebuke herself and adopt an austere regimen even when he was away in Europe. She thus finds release from this stifling primness in the light-hearted relationship with Shashanka bordering on deceitfulness and betryal. On the other hand, in her disproportionate anxiety for the well-being of her husband, Sharmila develops myopia to the growing intimacy between her husband and her sister. Then she truly thinks like a mother when she discovers the affair between Urmimala and her husband and seeing her own illness and impossibility of recovery from it, she contemplates tying up the knot between her husband and sister. This does not happen because she recovers from her illness and Urmimala leaves for England to study medicine.

Of the three prototypes of marital resonance demarcated in Anna Karenina Tolstoy has set up the Levin-Kitty as perfect because Kitty is not only her husband's partner in love but also in the life of action. With Sharmila's graduation at the end of the novel to ideal wifehood, "Explain your work to me, train me, educate me so that I can be a fit partner of your work", Tagore approximates Kitty's sharing of her husband's work but is actually modelled on the character of his own Chitraganda who seeks to combine partnership in her lover's love life with partnership in his life of action.

Tagore has not only sought to point up the mother image of Sharmila and construct her character on her theory of the motherliness of wife. He has also therorised the necessity of love in life and man's organic attraction for psychophysical fulfillment. The Shashanka-Urmimala relationship grows against the husband wife relationship partly because of Sharmila's failure to meet her husband's psychophysical needs because of her motherly instincts on one hand and her illness on the other. Urmimala finds the meaning of life and realisation through her enticing moves with her sister's husband.

Urmimala is no Binodini who does not mind wrecking the Mahendra-Asha marriage out of jealousy. This portrait by Tagore is that she does not have guilt of wrecking her own sister's married life by flirting with her husband. He has createsd a woman who is famished of psychophysical contentment with her fiance Nirad chooses to quench her hunger from her relationship with Shashank. She is never remiss in her duties to her sick sister, yet when Shashanka professes love to her, saying, "You know for certain that I love you; and, your elder sister, she is a goddess. I do not in my life have greater reverence anybody else. She is no creature of this earth; she is far above us". She makes no protests which means submission.

Niraja's love is also possessive, relentlessly directed equally at the garden, the pet dog and the dependant's son. After the dog's sudden death, when her own child dies during delivery, she is physically shattered and never recovers from it. But even on her sick-bed, with the knowledge of impending death, she is unable to give up her exclusive claim on the garden.

Niraja is an embodiment of love and main focus of the novel is her intensity of love for her husband. Another more interesting aspect of manifestation of her love is her love for the flower garden of the family. She says, "Ever since marriage I learnt that your garden was dear to you as your life, I did not keep any division between garden and myself. Otherwise I would have engaged in fierce quarrel with your garden, I would not tolerate it. It would have been my rival. You know how I have absorbed it in me; I have completely identified myself with it."

This recognition of Niraja with her husband's garden is peripheral compared to Liubov Andryeevna's identification with her ancestral cherry orchard in Chekov's *The Cherry Orchard.* In Niraja's case, her love for husband's garden and her discovery of the flower garden is co-existent and identical with her love for the husband. In Liubov's case the cherry orchard, especially in bloom, is symbolic of hope and rejuvenescence. The orchard, when flourished with white wave of floral beauty in the spring season, symbolises Liubov's dream for a better, more evocative and less splintered life in her tragic and messy spell after husband's death. Niraja's connection with the flower garden too has an artistic element: "Just as one living abroad eagerly waits for letters on special mail days; from season to season they [Niraja and her husband Aditya] have waited for according to amassed welcome to different trees."

If *The Cherry Orchard* has an emblematic connotation for Liubov, Niraja's love for the flower garden has a different dimension—it is closely linked with love for her husband. Niraja's garden fascination has an ontological correlative in love for husband which she can never be lost at any cost. She is personification of jealousy vis-à-vis Sarala [who has been inducted into the house by Aditya.]

The emaciated landed gentry is caught in the inexplicable use of disease in these two novellas. The women are ailing and they are helpless. However, the metaphor is more than just social and is harshly psychological, revealing the incapability of middle-class urbane men and women, trapped in codes of civility, to admit the psychophysical drives behind any love relationship. Niraja learns that her relationship with Aditya has become empty and drained; and her mind turned trivial and harsh by her loss of potency and beauty due to her disease. Her space of freedom is lost in the world around her in her undiagnosed illness. Life, ironically, visits her deathbed in all its susceptibility but has little time for her livid, dying form. Her forlorn afternoons are her time signals. She looks at the quiet garden that she loves so much and beyond it emptiness retreats into emptiness. The isolation and loneliness is rightly captured here. There is a similar inescapability in Sharmila's undiagnosed illness (but, from which she recovers later) brings Urmi to Shashanka together that leads to their fulfillment of psychophysical wants.

Love can hide a longing to dominate or control, expressing itself in thoughtfulness and apprehension. In the eventual analysis, this possessiveness presupposes the ego's attachment to worldly chattels. Perhaps, that is why, in *Malancha*, objects take on a life of their own, suggesting Niraja's jealousy-driven possessiveness. Ramen's advice to Niraja is "to acquire freedom from being tormented by her husband's relationship with Sarala by giving up all her claims. As long as you think your wealth is being snatched away by someone, there is no respite from agony; but once you give up your most precious possession for the sake of the one you love the most, you experience happiness and peace." And, this is amply clear in the following lines:

> If the only freedom is the freedom from possessive desire and if such desire is the necessary pre-condition of love, if the desire to dominate is interchangeable with the desire to be dominated, then what is the way out of this impasse? As Nikhilesh had realised in *Ghare Baire*, "the day I can really release the bird from its cage I will realise that it is the bird who releases me. The one I bind in a cage binds me in my desire and that is bondage stronger than that of chains".

Responding to the indignant probing of Niraja, Aditya describes his love for Sarala as the product of growing up wild together in the forest shade, oblivious of each other's existence. By contrast, their conjugal relationship approximates a punctilious ritual—as Aditya puts it, it was Niraja and not Sarala who aroused poetic feelings in him. Sarala's beauty was irrelevant to Aditya's love for her since he knew Sarala simply as Sarala. In accordance with such an equal relationship, Sarala affirms that Aditya is as much dependent on her as she is on him. This realisation, redolent of Nikhilesh's insight, is echoed later by Aditya when he asks himself whether he had given refuge to Sarala or Sarala had given him refuge.

Tagore shows these women as tormented souls in search for fufilment of their love outside the bondages of marriage. They look for solace in such unastable relationships that turn suicidal and destructive. The instability is apparent in Niraja's dying outburst, in the hysterical weeping of Charu or in the intense repentance of Urmi, and it is equally conveyed through the deformed motherly anxieties of Sharmila. Caught up in this contrary aims and unreal worlds of bonds, the reader recognises the 'faultlines' of pretentious domesticity and identifies with the hysteric anguish of these women's surreptitious lives. By contrast, their counter-parts remain deficient in emotional intensity and are profusely pampered by society into emotional pettiness. These men cannot really share their wives' destinies and there is no question of camaraderie. Thus the abandoned, traumatised women are given spaces of their own, a world created through solitude and pain, where they struggle and survive, love and unlove but still remain free and liberated. In this sense, Tagore remains a feminist before his time.

Works Cited

Chakrbarty, Shirshendu: *Fault Lines of Settled Domesticity.*

Chakrabarti, Santosh: *Studies in Tagore: Critical Essays*, Atlantic Publishers & Dist. 2004.

16

Feminism in Tagore's Dramatic Poems

The world knows him as a poet, philosopher, thinker, painter, musician and social activist, but few know the Nobel Laureate Tagore as a feminist, with gender issues forming the underlying theme in many of his works. From *Chitrangada* to *Chokher Bali*, he was scornful in his comments against gender suppression. He has wonderfully celebrated womanhood in many of his works and his works are relevant even today.

Tagore's works, as we have already discussed—stories, novels, poetry, and drama—all have women characters in the kernel. As plots thicken, the women characters emerge alive and the author's social perception is discovered. He does not cut any reformist image for himself; he is concerned with the umpteen ills that pLagoe our society. He draws attention to the problems and then leaves the rest to the reader to comprehend.

Tagore was naturally sensitised over the predicament of women in Indian society. He wanted to establish the individuality of women because individuality ensures dignity, self-respect and sexual independence of women. From the very beginning of the twentieth century he conceptualised the newer complexities, various ideas and current thoughts of social life of Bengal. There were already signs of break-up of large Bengali joint families and community life. The sense of individual identity became firmer, and there developed a need for determining the individual's relation with society.

The modern women are not only feminists but are a kind of revolt against social conventions. Feminism is not only consciousness of females for equality with males but Tagore seems to be asking "new questions of old texts".

Tagore's feminism as reflected in *Chitrangada*, *Natir Puja* and *Chandalika* and to evaluate these works as per Tuttle's Feminist Theories is considered here.

In the last decade of the nineteenth century, travelling through the rivers and plains of Bengal to look after the family estates, Tagore wrote many short stories, poems, plays and introduced a new form—*Natyakabya* (Dance-Drama) or the dramatic poem. In this genre, like play, there are verse dialogues between characters. This form was borrowed from Western literature. *Chitrangada* is unique. A proper play, in true Greek tradition, is divided into several scenes instead of one. The merit of all the dramatic poems lies in their poetry, and the roots of Tagore are deeply deep-seated in the Indian in the Indian tradition and culture.

Tagore's dance-dramas enter into direct contact with his poetic material, between the intangible and the tangible. They occupy a position where religion, poetry, music and dance find a merger. In his dance-dramas, plain speech progressively develops into finely tuned speech and then draws itself up into emotionally charged songs and the corresponding action is signifying the self: intersections of class, caste and gender issues. Songs and dances in these dramas are an extension of the dialogues and action, not having any separate role to play. In the dance-dramas, dance becomes a part of the songs as the natural outcome of a literary culmination. The dance-dramas illustrate Tagore's bold and perceptive handling of various literary forms and techniques, and the radical nature of his ideological orientation. Unlike previous Bengali dramas, Tagore's dance-dramas emphasise a fusion of lyrical flow and emotional rhythm tightly focused on a core idea.

Tagore liberated dance from the shackles of formal, geometrical patterns of some set movements, tinctured new life and spirit in the dance forms and rendered a supple touch of graceful elegance to them. He conceived of mingling drama with dance in a subtle manner so that it would have a profound imprint on the psyche and mind of the audience. Theatre, songs and dances were finely blended in an unprecedented way in these dance-dramas fusing in themselves Indian tradition and culture as well as Western philosophies.

Integrating several dance forms in his dramas, Tagore's dance-dramas present a unique blend of music, rhythm and expressions. In them, he has freely adopted in his own way the style and techniques from Manipuri, Kathak, Bharatanatyam, and Kathakali, folk dances and even European dances like the ballet. Tagore's dances are yielding, supple, graceful and spontaneous with a poignant effect. In his dance-dramas, the dances do not follow any strict convention or set pattern of the intricate classical dances of the past. Rather, these dances portray the inner worth or essence of the songs through the elegant gestures and expressions. In the dance-dramas, he lets the dances weave the story in an eloquent and poised way creating an elusive union of fiction with romantic imagination. The gestures and expressions of the dance-drama do not need the help of words or speech. The dances aptly express the essence of the songs. "In these dance-dramas, dance is seen as soul's mirror that gives expression to the soul's yearnings and aspirations, the ecstasies and agonies, the dreams and frustrations. The dance-dramas of Tagore, a genre quite unique in his time and milieu, portray the radical nature of Tagore's conception of women and the maturation of their selfhood."

The story of *Chitrangada* is a simple one, narrated in 13 shlokas—eleven in Adhyaya 207 and two more in Adhyaya 209—of the Adi parva of the *Mahabharata*. The timeframe of *Chitrangada* extends to one year. The imaginative pen of Tagore turns these short episodes of thirteen shlokas into a dramatic poem of 1,014, with eleven scenes, set in an unrhymed metre called payar—a numerical metre of 14 letters and regular rhyme.

> On 25 February 1940, about the genesis of *Chitrangada*, Tagore said: "many years ago I was going by train from Santiniketan in the direction of Calcutta. I think it was the month of Chaitra (March-April). Along the edge of the railway tracks there was a forest of wild trees. Innumerable yellow, purple, white flowers were blooming. Seeing them it occurred to me that after sometime the sun will be quite hot and this colourful illusion of flowers will wither—then in the fields of the village, on the branches of the trees there will be mangoes—the very nature of the trees introduces its treasure of juice concealed within the fruits. Suddenly, it seemed to me that if a beautiful woman realised that she was loved for the illusion of her youth alone then she might hate her beauty as she would consider her a rival of her own self! A momentary infatuation calls for an external appearance procured as a blessing from Basanta (Spring) to fulfil biological need. A character within benefits the beloved and the lover and helps their voyage together. Such a character is the true introduction to the soul, which does not get tired and tarnished despite exposure to a dusty environment. The force of character is the primary sustenance of life; it does not depend upon the immediate purpose of the world. I felt giving a dramatic shape to this idea and I remembered the story of Chitrangada from the *Mahabharata*. This story with some modifications remained in my mind for quite some time. Finally, I found time to write the same in a lonely town of Pandua in Orissa.

Chitrangada is a dramatic poem wherein Tagore, the poet ever in quest of truth, expresses his views on truth and beauty in a poetic style and dramatic manner. Tagore's biographer, Krishna Kripalani, writes on *Chitrangada*:

> ...a lyrical drama par excellence, the breath of spring blows through every line of it, making it languorous with the ecstasy of sensuous delight. Indeed, the theme is the enchantment of spring and the power of its spell on the senses, and Spring is itself one of the characters in the play, which is one of Tagore's best, and perhaps the only one that is flawless, if anything made by man can be called flawless. Not a line would one like to take away from it; one wishes it were longer—in the original Bengali where every utterance quivers with lyrical passion held in masterly restraint. The play is in blank verse, his last great experiment in that form.
>
> The play is very characteristic of the author, in the sense that it does not embody a seasonal mood or idea which he outgrew but represents a basic and permanent attitude of his mind and philosophy—his unification of man and nature, the latter almost an active participant in the drama of life, and his concern with the perennial question, what is beauty; what is love; what is true and enduring basis of man-woman relationship?

The play succeeds not much as a play but as enchanting and significant poetry. It succeeds because of the inner laws of art, the laws of beauty, and this beauty we encounter in the persistent veracity of the poet's vision and in the perfection of the structure as a whole. *Chitrangada* is great poetry because of its delicate but bold psychological construct, glorious description, tenderness and grandeur of the passion, evocative images and metaphors and for its music and melody.

Tagore challenges the traditional view of woman as the weaker sex. His *Chitrangada* is as strong as a man. She is an expert in riding, hunting, duel and war. She has an ambition to challenge

Arjuna in a single combat. When Arjuna in the forest rejects her and when she narrates this to Basanta and Madana, one finds how beautifully she understands that she is a woman:

> One day, alone had I set out in search of a deer,
> in the deep forest, on the banks of the river Purna.
> tying up my horse with a tree,
> following the pug marks of a deer,
> I proceeded on a crooked forest path
> difficult to tread upon,
> darkness echoed ever
> with the chirping of crickets.
> Going on further down, suddenly I saw,
> obstructing the tapered path,
> sleeping on the ground,
> a man tousled but resolute.
> In a tone of scorn, I asked him to move away—
> neither did he move nor did he look at me.
> With anxiety, rage and conceit,
> I goaded him with the edge of the bow—
> with the speed of an arrow
> that straight and large body shot up
> and stood before me—
> like a fire resting in the ashes,
> at once flashing up in a flame when fuelled.
> He stared at my face for a moment—
> seeing this child-like figure of mine,
> the anger in the eyes vanished in an instant
> on the edge of the lips, danced a line of smile—
> serene, simple, concealing curiosity.
> I have learned the arts of men,
> adopted the dress of men, stayed with them,
> but seeing his face,
> seeing his self-confident and firm image,
> instantly I remembered that I am a woman.
> At that moment,
> Little did I realise that there stood in front of me
> a man!
> (Translated)

She does not go back home dejected. She tries to show her strength and power by gaining perfect beauty from Madana. She seeks revenge of her insult of rejection by making him to surrender before her borrowed beauty. But he gives her strength by making her come out of her garb of a beautiful woman, the moment she wins him over, which she has donned to woo Arjunaa. The indomitable spirit in *Chitrangada* makes her immortal in his works.

Chitrangada is an ingeminating tale of Tagore's breakthrough feminist dance-drama. Act I opens with the King and Queen of Manipur praying for a son and receiving Chitrangada, a daughter. They rear her as a son. In Scene II, the princess, now the ruler of her kingdom, is out hunting in the forest with her friends, when she encounters the legendary hero, Arjunaa, protagonist of the *Mahabharata*, she falls in love. Dressed as a woman, she offers herself to Arjunaa but, he refuses her on grounds of avowed celibacy. Although she is left in tears, the warrior in her remains undefeated. She asks *Madana*, Cupid, the God of Love, for the weapon she needs, Beauty, for one year. Act II opens with a transformed Chitrangada marvelling at her beauty, at feelings that she had never had before. Arjunaa, bewitched by her beauty, breaks his vow of celibacy and declares his pride in his manhood. Chitrangada's rival is now her own body, and she realises the bitterness of her victory. She also watches her hero belittle himself. In desperation, she goes to *Madana* who assures her that she needs to play the game a while longer. Arjunaa also tires of this love when suddenly he encounters villagers getting ready to fight off prowlers. He learns from them of the woman who rules Manipur, one who loves like a mother and fights like a tigress, a King. He longs to meet his equal. It is time for Chitrangada to return her "stolen" beauty to *Madana*. In the last act, Chitrangada, the Warrior Princess, enters her own court and demands the right and power to be an equal in prosperity and adversity if Arjuna still wants to marry her. Arjuna accepts her on her terms. Chitrangada confessing the truth about her beauty reveals herself as the princess and asserts:

> I am Chintrangada,
> Not a goddess, but not an ordinary woman either.
> Worth worshipping am I not;
> to be ignored and kept in the wings, that also am I not.
> If allowed to share
> the perilous path and perplexing worries,
> I would be helpful in all your difficulties.
> You will know me if I am your companion
> In all your joys and sorrows.

Vyasa's Chitrangada is not only brought up as a son but is also attractive enough to be appealing to Arjuna, who approaches her father for her hand in marriage. In spite of her being brought up as a successor to the throne, she does not have much of a role in the story as well as the matter of her own marriage, which is settled between the two men, on the condition set forth by the father of the bride. Chitrangada is a woman who seeks and rules her own destiny and pursues her goal with the determination of a single-minded warrior that she is trained to be:

> In a sense, both Arjunaa and Chitrangada as portrayed by Tagore as images of his own mind—modern but steeped in the traditions of the Indian culture. Both of them pursue their love on their own, seeking the help of the deities known to be kind, and eventually drifting towards the quest of truth, which is revealed at the end. The quest for truth (*satya*) of the self was a lifelong mission of Tagore, and a path he pursued was that of beneficence (*shiv*) and beauty (*sundar*).

Tagore makes strong argument for gender equality in Chitrangada, where the princess makes it amply obvious to the rather imprudent, sexist and love-struck Arjunaa that she will marry him only if he takes for what she is—neither a goddess nor a doormat but an equal in every way, a partner who will share joys and fears and stand shoulder to shoulder in all battles.

Tagore's *Chitrangada* conforms to Lisa Tuttle's feminist theory of asking "new questions of old texts." She cites the goals of feminist criticism as: (1) To develop and uncover a female tradition of writing, (2) to interpret symbolism of women's writing so that it will not be lost or ignored by the male point of view, (3) to rediscover old texts, (4) to resist sexism in literature, and (5) to increase awareness of the sexual politics of language and style.

A few years after the publication of *Chitrangada* some Bengali critics had found it obscene and corrupt and had held Tagore responsible for 'attributing glory to sin'.

Tagore envisions Chitrangada as an ideal consort of the man of her choice—a woman true to her own identity, conscious of her desires, aware of her potentials, ready for her vocation—not only understanding her partner's needs but aware of her own needs as a fulfilled person. She has pride in herself, in her own identity as a warrior princess, the saviour of her subjects, in her womanhood as well as in her vocation. She wants Arjuna as an ideal companion equal to her in all respects, someone who would respect her for who she is. Yet she is also conscious of her multifariousness; in Surupa, the alter ego of Kurupa, we find the wishful woman who changes herself to woo her beloved man. She acts as the agent rather than a goal and her decision to change herself is her own. As Kurupa, Chitrangada also exercises her choice and agency when she determines the time when she would unmask herself before Arjuna and reveal her true identity. She becomes the ideal woman in tune with her own identity, her desires and her womanhood. She possesses the power and agency to determine her own fate. Tagore's idea of femininity shows a remarkable fusion of Western and Eastern ideas in his reconstruction of the character of Chitrangada here: the older Indian idea of wife as a partner in the duties of family life (*sahadharmini*) had developed, under Western influence, into the romantic concept of a comrade in perilous action.

In the touching tale, *Notir Puja*, Tagore relates about a young girl in ancient India, not too high on the social hierarchy, but resolute and brave enough to defy the royal diktat. She knows that she would have to pay a price for her deed. Yet she does not flinch away. She gives up her life for what she considers to be her duty.

Notir Puja is a ballad, but its dramatic qualities have inspired people to act it out on stage. It is still a hugely popular dance-drama. Bimbisara, the King of Magadha, had a stupa built in a corner of the palace garden, on a tiny toenail of Gautama Buddha. Prayers were offered there every evening and lamps were lit by the women of the royal household. After Bimbisara, when Ajatashatru became the king, he ruthlessly put to sword all those who worshipped the Buddha and put to torch all sacred Buddhist scriptures. He banned the worship of the Buddha in his kingdom. Sreemati was a court dancer. She was an ardent follower of Gautama Buddha. She could not bear to see no lamps lit at the Stupa and resolved to do the puja on her own. She went to all women of the Royal household, to all the queens and intellectuals asking them to accompany her. All of them refused for fear of death. So she went alone and completed the puja. Seeing the light of a lamp under the stupa, the guards rushed in and put her to death, as per the royal diktat.

Srimati in *Notir Puja* makes supreme sacrifice which is an incredible one. She has equalled herself with the males who sacrificed for the noble cause of religion. Thomas A. Becket in Eliot's *Murder in the Cathedral* makes deliberate efforts to become martyr. If one compares his sacrifice with Srimati one may conclude that 'Srimati is superior.' He is a priest of high rank and she is a court dancer of low rank. Srimati becomes a model martyr. Her religious sense is superior to those who just pretend to be religious.

I would like to draw a distinction between the 'real' Beckett and the 'real' Canterbury Chaucer's pilgrims went to, one that still exists. Again there is distinction between Eliot's Beckett which is his alter ego reflecting his inner spiritual struggle from whence comes the selfishness (the desire to be a martyr, of the fourth tempter) and the real Beckett who was not like that. On the other hand, the comparison between Srimati and Beckett in terms of position and class and gender cannot implicitly be the comparison between Tagore and Eliot, if we grant the validity of literature and martyrdom at all. The two primary issues must not be confused, the character with its historical genesis and different historical contingencies and exigencies on the same plane. Srimati is caught in religious conflict, Beckett in a battle between religion and state—the two are different in its grounds. My view is, that both Eliot and Tagore are actually (if the issue is considered to be ideology) hypocrites, as Eliot subverts a system he adopted/converted to, Anglicanism, through his play, and Tagore pretends to be for women, the untouchables and Buddhism through his writings when he was not for any of these things, actually. I hold greater value for the brilliant lives of Srimati and Beckett for the motives of history and not that what Tagore and Eliot ascribed to them.

Another point, it is understood that martyrs in their time and space as noble souls died for what they believed right, what they thought with conviction but in today's world aren't they, when used by Eliot and Tagore, examples of retrogression? They did not want the world to change and tried taking it back into the past but why this fear of present—shown as degenerate—and the future as something that may be even worse in both of them, unless corrected by them. There is no healthy mix of the past, present and future outside of their works. According to them, no awareness that the day may come when historical wrongs will be righted by others or rather, it is that fear that others may do it that makes them both typical patriarchal figures of authoritarian control. By laying down how it should go in the future, whether Tagore in his essays like the collection, 'Creative Unity' or Eliot in his last two treatises on Culture and Christianity have not been to establish any truth. Frankly, Tagore could not predict what was to happen in the third front in India now; that is slowly coming into being, amade up of the Dalits, Communists, Muslims, Christians, Sikhs, Jains, Buddhists, Sects, Techno-communities, Tribes, Atheists, Feminists, LGBT, poor and other unprivileged minorities nor could Eliot predict, the empty churches of Europe of today being replaced by vibrant idiosyncratic followers of Christ who do not care for religion or religions. That is why they seem a bit outdated. The shape of future is going to be different and unfortunately these great writers couldn't see it—they only walked to the tune of an antiquated drum.

In his dance drama *Chandalika* (1938) Tagore explores the intimate links between dance and female self-construction. He opts for the non-conformed icons-warrior, untouchable, and courtesans. The women who danced in his experimental dance-dramas in the 1930s in Bengal in full public view, were far from being confined to the inner precincts of their home, and were called 'impure', 'inauthentic', non-classical yet powerful alternatives of being modern Indians. This shows his feminist orientation in the politics of woman's emancipation in the nationalist era.

Raktakarabi (Red Oleanders) is one of 60 or more plays, dance-dramas and dramatic sketches by Tagore. The play, written in 1923-24, began during a visit to Shillong, Assam, and was stirred by the image of a red oleander plant trampled by pieces of discarded iron that Tagore had come across while walking. A short time later, an oleander branch with a single red flower stuck out through the debris, as if, he noted, "created from the blood of its cruelly pierced breast." It has been suggested that the play's title might appropriately be translated as *Blood-Red Oleanders* to indicate the beautiful but toxic nature of the flower and its association with beauty and death in the play. The writing process was not an easy one and involved some 10 drafts and various titles such as *Yakshapuri* (a mythical city of unparalleled wealth) and *Nandini* (after the heroine who seeks to tear down the barrier behind which the king is secluded).

Tagore's general thematic concerns arise from the view of reality. A. Mukherjee outlines the following dramatic progress of a typical Tagore protagonist:

> ...a human being, because of the narrow barriers of selfhood that he has woven round himself, continues for a while to thrive within that barrier till "the touch of the eternal" or, in other words, the sense of an impending realisation comes to him (mostly through an innocent girl or apparently some such ineffective character) and makes him victorious over his pervious infinities [sic]. While undergoing this process, hesitancy first appears in him; he then sees the first glimmer of the true knowledge and then the struggle intensifies till he is able to defeat the selfhood in him.

This moment towards true knowledge and self-awareness [and the associated self-negation], we find in the characters of the Raja in

Red Oleanders. He is aided in this journey from darkness to light by his interaction with the agents of good in each play: Nandini in *Red Oleanders*, Chitrangada in *Chitrangada*, and Prakriti in *Chandalika*. In each play, suffering and anguish occupy a central position in this progress by precipitating the conclusion, because of Tagore's belief that it cleanses the spirit and enables man to see with true clarity.

Although Tagore makes his protagonists relinquish their self-centredness on the spiritual level through the process of suffering, on the social level he constantly espoused the causes of individualism. The dichotomy between the individual and the organisation pervades his dramatic poems and monologues. He held that civilisation had begun to ignore the individual by becoming totally masculine and patriarchal in nature, thereby, generating more wars and strife among people. He had a great respect for the feminine principle; in his opinion woman had sensitivity, a sympathetic quality, an instinctive spirituality and a freshness of mind that eclipsed the more earthly desires and attributes of the opposite sex. He writes, "In our country a woman is accepted as the symbol strength in every aspiration of man." It comes as no surprise, therefore, to find women such as Nandini, Prakriti, Chirangada, and Sumati in his dance-dramas completely dominating the stage with their gentle, yet powerful personalities. The other omnipresent force in his dramas is an unseen one, that of the natural world.

In the final analysis, Tagore's dramas as well as dance-dramas reveal a strong underlined current of optimism. The affirmative attitude to life, the broad humanism, the conviction about the inviolable relationship between man and his maker, the deep faith in woman and the beauty of nature, all contribute to the pervasive sense of harmony and the invincible spirit of hope in his plays.

Dance-dramas written by Tagore can be used as points of entry into a discourse on feminism. In *Chandalika* he uses dance as a subtle form of self-expression for Prakriti; without the dances the desire for expression in she would remain inarticulate. It is through the free and supple movements of the body that she as a woman expressly articulates her desires—emotional, physical and spiritual—at once liberating the female dancing body from the strict rules of classical dance as well as traditional society that viewed dance as impure and demoralising. It is through dance that she gains her freedom from the constricting strictures of "pure/impure, body/soul, ethical/unethical, self/other that bind her".

Prakriti in *Chandalika* stands for the revolt against conventions. She proves that a woman has equal right to choose her life partner. She does not care for caste, creed and religion for the fulfilment of her ambitions. Tagore's women characters are as conscious as modern-day ladies. They try to gain self-improvement. He has given priority and precedence to his female characters over his male protagonists. Prakiti's perception and realisation instill in her mind the strength to venture further to gain Ananda. She brings him under the control of black magic. She withdraws the magical effect from Ananda out of sympathy. Thus she becomes stronger than Ananda.

In *Chandalika*, the dialectics of Prakriti's selfhood and desire get problematised by the intersection of class and caste with gender. This adds not only to the complexities of her selfhood but also problematises the accomplishment of her selfhood through the expression of her desire for Ananda. For her, the socioculturally imposed selfhood is that of an untouchable, an outcaste; her desire and yearning would only be sanctioned if it expresses within her caste and class. To wish for the love of a monk is like reaching out for the stars for the untouchable girl. It is a taboo no one should dare to traverse. Rejected by others for her caste, her untouchable status, Prakriti at first learns to negate her societal self identity; but nevertheless, she questions the worth and equality of her social standing and silently rages against the Almighty for this unjustness. She remains a victim to her socioculturally determined selfhood as she internalises the social stigma attached to her caste and class. Yet her questionings show her inner consciousness of her self as a human, and thus foreground her agency and power that remain as a latent force inside herself till Ananda awakens this slumbering, latent selfhood and ignites her passion for him.

It is through Ananda that Prakriti first learns to see herself as a human being in her own right. She learns the meaning of dignity; she learns what it is to be a woman, to serve others as an equal. With her awareness of herself as a woman comes the first awakening of desire, which turns into compulsive passion for the man who has shown her respect as a human being for the first time in her life. She falls in love with the ascetic as a disciple loves her God. By giving water to the thirsty monk, she has satisfied her own thirst for self-esteem. It is a kind of cleansing from the antithetical disgrace of being an outcaste. Ananda has given her the power to serve others, the power to give life (water), nourishment to thirsty travellers. It is in his eyes, that Prakriti has seen herself as an equal to all the other human beings. She now identifies herself with a human being. She gets an awareness of her identity as a woman when her passion for him gets stirred. Her longing for the monk is the elemental desire of the woman, Prakriti, for the man, Purush, and it comes only with her awareness of her still nascent womanhood. With her desire as a female comes courage, a daring even to bring Ananda back to her at any cost, by any means. She now takes the help of Maya, her mother, an exponent of black magic. The most potent realisation of her selfhood comes when she calls the post Ananda episode as her 'new birth'. She is in euphoria about what she thinks of as a kind of baptism into humanity and her female desirous self: "it's a new birth for me, a new birth, my new birth… my body awoke with a jolt/ my soul got conscious all of a sudden". This realisation of Prakriti's selfhood is intermingled with the conscious negation of her socially imposed caste and class as well as an acknowledgement of herself as a woman proud for her sense of worth But when Maya's black magic forces Ananda to her door, she realises that her desire is not for the person that the monk represents but for the affirmation of her own identity as a female self equal to others in all respects. Through material desire she reaches a spiritual desire. Ananda's request, "Give me water," besides indicating his physical need symbolises water's regenerative image common in many religious traditions.

In the Indian context, a holy man asking for water from an untouchable violated a social as well as a religious norm. To receive and to give food or water were sacrilegious for both. The monk's extraordinarily radical request awakens Prakriti's awareness of her own innate Self. Through the universal image of water, Tagore intertwines the ideological revolution reflected in the social, religious, and political scene of his own time. Prakriti's self-assertion imbued in desire is manifested in her love for the young monk. Infused by Eros, Prakriti's love ascends and through dedication and repentance to liberation.

Tagore's Chitrangada, Srimati and Prakriti have significant status. They are shown as self-sufficient and strong. They emerge victorious. Chitrangada proves her ability by defeating Arjuna in the battle of romance. Srimati proves her superiority by making supreme sacrifice for the noble cause of religion. Prakriti shows her strength by making Ananda come to her doorsteps begging for love. Thus Tagore's women characters are superior to other ordinary women in the society. They are role models for the women. Suffering women can improve their circumstances by imitating the women characters of Tagore. They may realise their strength and may improve their condition.

The Bengali Renaissance brought with it a new approach to the concept of women in society. In the plethora of writings, inspired by the various movements that sought to address the condition of women in society like, widow remarriage, abolition of sati, abolition of child marriage and *kulinism*, the initiatives taken for women's education, the whole sociocultural and familial view of women underwent a drastic change. In the writings of Tagore too there were no omissions.

Much has been said about the way Tagore views his women in his poems, essays, novels and drama. Yet it is his dance-dramas, a genre quite unique in his time and milieu, which portray the radical nature of his idea of women and the maturation of their selfhood. These three dance-dramas thus profusely demonstrate the feminist proclivities that Tagore's women portray. Significantly, Tagore uses the dance form in a subtly nuanced manner—he explores the intimate links between dance and the processes of female identity formation in Bengal. These dance-dramas examine alternative forms, non-classical artistic experimentations in the territory of theatre-dance inspired by the Western traditions of theatre and the folk theatre tradition in Bengal as well as in India, focusing on dancing bodies that actively engaged with, and wrote different meanings for, the socio-political space they inhabited. They open up a space in which representation of Indian women through bodily performance troubles notions of cultural purity and origin and offers instead 'impure' but nevertheless powerful cultural texts.

In *Shyama*, the identity of Shyama is left vague and formless; she is *rajpuranandini*, an inmate of the king's palace, where she has the power to wear the *Rajanguriyo*. She also has some authority over the Nagar Kotal, the law-keeper of the city. In the original story from which Tagore had taken the story, she is a Nati, a courtesan in the king's court; but the word *rajpuranandini* problematises the concept of selfhood in Shyama. Is she a paramour of the king, or even a daasi, a servant-maid or merely a relative of the king? What is more important is her power to exercise her choice in choosing her partner. She gets attracted to Bajrasen, the merchant, a foreigner escaping the king's courtiers. She knows the extent of the lethal game that she will play with the young Uttiya who loves and adores her silently from a distance. When she gives him the ring embossed with the king's name, and asks him indirectly to sacrifice himself on behalf of Bajrasen, both of them are fully aware of the terrible outcome. Yet she purposely sacrifices Uttiya's life for her desire for Bajrasen.

Significantly, in all three of these dance-dramas, the women, are fully conscious of their desires as women, and they do not shy away from admitting their desire; indeed they even travel great lengths to fulfil their desires. Though Tagore sets his dance-dramas in a historical religious context, yet he accentuates and openly shows this facet of female desire which is a taboo subject. Shyama sacrifices Uttiya to get Bajrasen as a lover, and is ready to flee with him to unknown lands but her love and her desire are foiled when Bajrasen himself rejects her as a sinful woman. The poignancy of her unrequited desire and self-determinism comes out forcefully in the final dialogues between Shyama and Bajrasen:

> I have not wronged you, I am a sinner in God's eyes, if He shows his wrath, I would silently accept it; butif you do not show sympathy, I can't bear it. Bajrasen replies: Even then you

> won't leave me. Shyama replies: "I have sinned for you, and you are twinging my soul, I won't let you go.

Clearly, Bajrasen uses brutality on Shyama—this is the same Bajrasen that Shyama loves and whom he rescues from death by sacrificing Uttiya. Yet till the end, she remains loyal to Bajrasen even when he repulses and rejects her so harshly.

Morally Shyama's sin might not be condoned, yet, what comes out of this dance drama is that Shyama does not shirk from or hesitate to acknowledge her own desires and thus acts as an agent with a choice of her own. This is what makes her a radical figure, self-conscious of her choice—accepting full blame for her own actions. The rendering of Shyama goes beyond the typecast of the silent submissive selfless women who were considered the epitome of virtue, the idyll of the eternal feminine, the perfect woman that was hammered in women in contemporary India. Significantly, she retains her dignity and the audience's sympathy till the end; while it is Bajrasen who comes out as a heartless monster, one who is unable to appreciate what Shyama has done for him, unable to show pity and yet more unable to recognise her all-consuming love for him, a love that makes her forget the norms of ethics and morality imposed by society.

Tagore's dance-dramas have poetic worth, the subtle and the substantial, between the intangible reality of poetry and the tangible unreality of our daily lives. They engage a position where religion, poetry, music and dance merge into one another. They explore the intimate links between dance and the processes of identity formation, and examine alternative, non-classical artistic experiments in the realm of theatre dance focusing on dancing bodies that are actively engaged with, and write different meanings for, the socio-political space they inhabited.

One of the most significant characteristics of these three female protagonists is their determination to go any lengths in order to fulfil their desires; yet they are not illusive, nor gullible. They exercise power and action in their choices in life and as self assured, mature women, conscious of their selfhood and female desire; they take full responsibility for their own deeds. All of them have come to know the consciousness of their selfhood through pain and anguish. Their journey is a spiritual journey through desire to discover their own selves and their spiritual strength. They are not a departure from the other Tagorean heroines. They are true Tagorean discovery.

Works Cited

Bardhan, Kalpana: *Of Love, Nature And Devotion: Selected Songs Of Tagore*. New Delhi: Oxford University Press, 2008.

Chakraborty, Kaustav (ed.) : *Indian Drama in English*, PHI Learning Pvt Ltd., New Delhi.

Das, Sisir Kr. (ed.) : *The English Writings of Tagore*, Vol. 1, Poems, New Delhi: Sahitya Academy,1994.

Parekh, Shailesh: *Chitrangada and Other Dramatic Poems*, Rupa & Co, 2007.

Purkayastha, Prarthana: Warrior, Untouchable, Courtesan: Fringe Women in Tagore's Dance-dramas*: South Asia Research*, Vol.29 (3), Sage Publications Ltd., 2009, p. 255.

Rao, Shyamala B.: *Indian Writing in English*: T*agore and His Chandalika. A Critical Study*, New Delhi: Sterling Publishers.

17

Challenges of Women and Their Quest for Fulfilment

> Why shall you not give the woman
> Her right to conquer her fate, O God?
> (*Sabala* (The Strong Woman) in *Mahuya*, translated)

In the short stories of *Galpaguccha*, Tagore has portrayed social problems and their impact on the life of the individual, the interaction of the individual and the family, the flight of the individual to free herself from the numerous ill-begotten customs crushing the flow of the normal life, the marginalisation of women in family life in particular and society in general and, many such problems afflicting the life of the individual and society.

Though born of a traditional Indian mother in a traditional Indian family, nurtured on the Indian mythologies and epics, Tagore's outlook, his feminism and thought process are all results of Western spirit. The age when Tagore wrote his stories, women's emancipation and liberation were a far-cry from today's world. He waged a war consciously against the injustice meted out to the women in our society through his stories. His women are modern and modern with vengeance—they are doting mothers, loving daughters, mysterious lovers and above all, they are mentally enlightened, if not, typically traditional.

Tagore advanced the women's cause by showing rebellion by his heroines. Individualism is a marked trait in the female characters. They are crusader of individual freedom. Tagore valued women's individually ever since he wrote *Chokher Bali* (The Eyesore) and *Ghater Katha*. He oscillated between traditionality and bold unconventionality on the gender question in his works.

Tagore's heroines are not extravagantly traditional. They are the 'new woman'. They undergo emotional crises. They want love, affection, self-expression and freedom of thought. His progressivist thinking was vehemently protested in his age—but what the great seer could feel and write more than a century before have come true in the modern times.

The identity crises faced by the female protagonists of Tagore's stories are overcome by their distinctiveness, by the display of boldness and dare and the author advocates for their rights. While making an exploration of individual personality he makes his heroines highly susceptible to love and emotions. They are not materialistic and their quest for love lies in the fulfilment of their familial duties. The basic ingredient of their characters is determinism, and that manifests itself in their love-relationship. With the emergence of the individualised, emancipated women in the West, Tagore's women also emerge in this new light. "Love makes Shakespeare's heroines adventurous, Tagore's adventurous and reckless."

In Indian society the presence of child-widows became inevitable in the middle-class homes because of the custom of unequal marriage between tender-aged girls and older men. Then on one hand, their harsh lifestyle brought them untold misery, on the other their natural youthful growth and negligence from their partners and repressed sexual urges helped develop a socially unsanctioned illicit sex-relationship with the younger male members of the family.

Judging by a lecture he gave on Hindu Marriage in 1887, his inner struggle about Tagore's own marriage emerged strong. The lecture was a reasoned appeal, moderated, even cautious, for the abandonment of child marriage, several decades before the idea was accepted in the educated Bengali society.

Tagore's wife gave birth to his first daughter Madhurilatha (Bela) in October 1886, when Mrinalini was about 13 years old. Tagore never mentioned the event in any of his letters or anywhere in his works. Child marriages were prevalent in the Tagore household and he has himself condemned his two daughters Bela and Renuka to the same fate. By 1901, there was no social pressure for early arranged marriages in Brahmo circles, rather the reverse. Then, was Tagore conscious of the grotesque contradiction? Was this the same Tagore who attacked early marriage and the 'joint family' in 1887? It is difficult to know! So there he was: in his fiction portraying the searing agony of arranged marriages between older men and a barely-more-than-child-bride while in his life he was consigning his daughters to precisely the same relationship with the same potential for disaster.

No discussion of Tagore's female protagonists is complete without a referring to the male characters. The multi-dimensionalism of Tagore's women in the plethora of his literary works has left his male characters in the shadow. The male characters add to the sociofamilial constrictions under which the women live, and they should be studied, especially for their roles in shaping the destiny of women. They play crucial roles by their positive / negative / indifferent approach to the problems. They make, mar and change the direction of the life-force of those who are close to them. Their indifference and their clumsy handling of situations or inability to understand the opposite sex spell doom for themselves and others.

The male characters that Tagore has created in his short stories are diverse, varied and multi-hued, and of the different categories. They can be classified in the following heads:

i. Strong-spirited personalities
ii. Weak-kneed cowards / chauvinistic / unassertive, self-effacing / compromising / uncertain
iii. Unconcerned husbands / unfeeling
iv. Loving husbands
v. Lovers: apathetic / corporeal / platonic / earnest
vi. I ntellectuals / responsive
vii. Effeminate / having woman fixation

The most important peculiarity of Tagore's short stories is that the characters are culled from the socio-domestic milieu and not from the political arena, and so the men are identified in terms of interpersonal relationships. They are brothers, fathers, husbands and lovers.

Tagore's portraits of women go against the literary conventions of his day. He generally portrayed women not just as symbols of goodness but as living beings with feelings and emotions.

Tagore's women identify with three cycles of women given by the feminist writer Alice Walker. First are those "who were cruelly exploited, spirits and bodies mutilated, relegated to the narrowest and confining lives, sometimes driven to madness." Kumudini of *Jogajog* (Communication), Mrinal of *Streer Patro* (The Wife's Letter), Nirupama, Haimanthi, Sashi, Kadambini, Mahamaya, Hemashashi et. al. fall in this category. But Tagore's women are different because they are rebels; they fight back and escape from the society for their freedom. Alice's second cycle comprises those "who are not so much physically as psychically abused". Tagore's majority of women fit into this category because they are women of substance and they are faced with emotional crises and challenges from time to time. In the third cycle are those women who have gained a new consciousness and pride, "their right to be themselves and to shape the world" and Mrinal, Anila and Charulatha, Sohini, Damini, Urmimala, Niraja, Sarala, fall in this cycle. His stories contain women of all the three cycles.

Then where is identity of woman as a woman? She is like a character in a drama playing different roles and her actual persona is lost somewhere behind the curtains. Some modern day critics argue that even male members of the society play their roles as fathers, brothers, husbands and lovers. Yet, the point of debate arises when they become the adjudicators, when they prescribe and proscribe roles for the women in the society; then it is time for revolution.

Women-centric art claims to be reaching out towards the light—more freedom and empowerment to the women are the only objectives. Tagore's art did not imitate contemporary society as a whole, but about a century later, the modern life is imitating art. It is not art imitating life but life imitating art.

> the palm goes
> always to the light;
> who most shall advance the light—
> call it what you may!
> (William Carlos Williams)

Works Cited

Dutta, Krishna. & Robinson, Andrew: *The Myriad-minded Man: Tagore*, Rupa & Co., 2003, p.131.

Guerin Earle Labor, Lee Morgan, J.C. Reesman & Willingham: *A Handbook of Critical Approaches to Literature*, OUP, 2005, pp.265-266.

18

No Last Word

Commenting on Tagore's short story Pramathanath Bishi notices a tension between "a longing to enter the human world of happiness and sadness, meeting and parting, and a longing to rove freely in a world of beauty". The former mainly finds its expression in the stories, the latter in the poems: but he stresses that they are not 'watertight compartments' and, neither are they strikingly opposites.

The Selidah years were prolific in poems, plays, songs, musical dramas and essays, many of them published in a new family magazine *Sadhana*, of which Tagore was the chief contributor and later its editor. But to these forms he added a new form, the short story. Between 1891 and 1901 he wrote 59 short stories, set in both the villages and towns of Bengal and in Calcutta, dealing with characters at every level in society. "The best have pathos or ironic humour which is inimitable. Edward Thompson, having translated a number of them, was convinced that they were among the world's great short stories".

In Tagore's stories the realism and the idealism are present. His ultimate artistic and spiritual goal is to reconcile realism with idealism. In *My Reminiscences*, he identifies this goal as the "subject on which all my writings have dwelt—the joy of attaining the Infinite within the Finite". There are many poems and songs where it is achieved where the *sukh-dukh* (happiness-sadness) of mortal life is in ideal harmony with the Spirit that 'rolls through all things.' It is achieved in the short stories.

One needs to distinguish between the content and art of the stories. The essence of their content seems to be a conflict of Real and the Ideal (*sthal* and *jal*). They belong to the Ghat, a reality, to the meeting-place of land and water, to a place more of sorrow and tears. His characters weep because of a conflict between goodness and cruelty, innocence and the world, sensitivity and insensitivity, depth and shallowness. "Sensitive characters, Ratan in *Postmaster*, granddaughter in *Thakurda*, Mrinal in *Streer Patro*, Nirupama in *Denapowna* Shashikala in *Didi*, Nilkanta in *Athithi* and many more weep because their feelings have been hurt; those who have the potential for change and growth, like the narrators of Thakurda, Bhupathi, Amal, Nibaran et al. weep when they realise that their actions have been at odds with kindness and goodness." The sky weeps heavy monsoon tears in *Jibito O Mrito*, *Chuti*, *Shesher Ratri* as if in sympathy with the tension that always exist between separation and harmony, malice and kindness, world and spirit.

In the *Sabujpatra Phase*—in which Tagore accords an exalting welcome to youth in the *Balaka* (The Flight of Wild Geese) sequence of poems—he swerves away from the usual socio-familial image of the Indian woman—the images of mother, the daughter, the suffering daughter-in-law—and sets a new value judgement for the woman. The aging poet's salutation to youth has its appearance in the notion of the rebel woman who does not accept her husband's neglect lying down, but revolts silently. The poet's travel abroad and exposure to the socio-familial life-pattern of the West and the idea he formed about the liberated woman moulded his reformist outlook. The Indian woman, at the beginning of the twentieth century, knows no divorce, nor does she revolt, yet ends up in taking a kind of step that Mrinal takes. But Tagore's women in a number of short stories written in the *Sabujpatra Phase*—Mrinal of *Streer Patro*, Kalyani of *Aparichita*, Anila of *Poila Number*, Nirupama of *Denapowna*, Haimanti of *Haimanti*, et al—show an individuality as yet unheard of in contemporary Bangla literature and even in life itself. Gurudev, like a seer anticipates the shape of things to come in the century ahead.

Tagorean protagonists, male and female, suffer, fall and are doomed because of excess. Excess of traditionalism, conventionality, extroversion, greed, innocence, ignorance, passion—all nimiety mar these characters. Shakespearean heroes and heroines fall because of the fault in their characters, Tagore's because of surplusage.

At the more factual and historical level of content, many stories hinge on a conflict between one or the more of the pairs of opposites: modern and Westernised, values and traditional patterns of life, unity and division, spirit and world, female and male, imagination with pragmatism, idealism with realism. With Tagore the conflict lies sometimes sympathising with the former, for example, child-marriage or female education, and sometimes with the latter, older patterns of diehard truthfulness of Ramkanayi, and sometimes holding himself ironically and quizzically aloof. This detachment makes his stories unique. He never preaches, sermonises or makes comments but shows. Maru Lago, in her study of the stories, sees them "essentially as a product of the clash between the new and the old, town and country that characterise the evolution of nineteenth century Bengal". Tagore's art lies here in the balancing act, in the reconciliation of the opposites.

> Tagore's art is vulnerable. Nearly all his writings are vulnerable to criticism, philistinism or contempt, because of his willingness

> to wear his heart on his sleeve, to take on themes that other writers would find sentimental, embarrassing or grandiose and his refusal to cloak his utterances in cleverness, urbanity or double-talk. His stories are his most vulnerable productions of all, and some of them attracted scathing comments when they first appeared. His stories are poeticised. Tagore succumbed to this kind of criticism and abandoned the editorship of *Sadhana* and gave up writing stories completely in 1896 and 1897.

Tagore's comments on his stories later in life show that he was aware of their weaknesses. He knew that not all of them would bear comparison with the best European stories—especially the French and Russian writers. He defended himself by pointing out that he had to play the demanding role of a pioneer in the art of writing short stories in Bangla. In his interview with Buddhadeva Bose he said:

> You speak about my language, and say that even in my prose I am a poet. But if my language sometimes goes beyond what is appropriate in a story, you can't blame me for that, for I had to create my Bengali prose myself. My language was not there, heaped-up and ready-made... I had to create the prose of my stories as I went along. You often speak of Maupassant and other foreign writers: their language was already made for them. If they had to create their language as they wrote, I wonder how they would have fared.

It is not true that there was no Bangla prose to speak of before Tagore: Bankim Chandra Chatterjee was a master stylist, even if his dry compact style was not a model that the lyrically inclined Tagore could naturally adopt. It also a fact that other Bangla writers started to write short stories at the same time as Tagore—particularly Nagaendranath Gupta (1861-1940)—so Tagore was not totally alone. But he was the first Bangla writer to think of the short story as a serious art-form, rather than merely as an entertaining way to fill up the pages of periodicals; the first to write about real, contemporary life rather than romanticised history or myth; and although some British and American models were available to him—and his brother Jyotirindranath perhaps gave him some acquaintance with French—the manner and origin of Western short stories were really too remote from Bengal to be of much relevance.

> In Tagore's art—in his most realistic, prosaic, ironic or skeptical art—there is the transcendental Spirit that Indian through the ages have attempted to know. The sages who wrote the *Upanishads* in the seclusion of their forest hermitages realised there must be a supreme cosmic force behind the *Samsara* (World) of mortal existence, the *Maya* (Illusion) of sense-perception, or the *Swargaloka* (Heaven) of Vedic and Hindu Gods; and Tagore's spiritual endeavours were in direct descent from theirs. He took it for granted that higher levels of human consciousness. As a romantic artist, Tagore strove to do this through art rather than through meditation of mysticism: but in this he was extending the central Indian tradition, not diverging from it.

Tagore inherited the spiritual bend of his mind from the 'Maharshi' but his realism, the earth-bound scepticism from his grandfather Prince Dwarkanath. He feels all the works, desires, hopes and conflicts of mankind as notes of a single melody whose mood is unbearably still and sad as darkness descends. This is the timeless spirit that lies behind the veil of the mortal life:

> The essence of the matter is this: those men are small and their lives are fleeting, yet the stream of life, with its good and bad and its happiness and sadness, flows and will eternally flow with its ancient solemn murmur. On the edge of the town and in the darkness of the evening that constant murmuring sound can be heard.

One has to look further than the content of the stories, for they are linked to Tagore's perceptions of the spirit at the deepest levels of style and expression. In his Bangla prose one finds both complexity and simplicity. One finds passages of sensitive description or feeling, and long and elaborate sentences unprecedented in Bangla prose; again there is a direct, simple, sometimes, almost a bold manner of narration, then he is also accused of writing poetic prose. It is the latter quality that is present in the translation most forcibly:

> Tagore's long sentence, with their relatives and correlations, strings of participates, and parallelism of phrasing—at their best, broad and grand as a Bengali river—requires its original orchestration, whereas in the translation of his simple mode probably less is lost. But perhaps an overall vitality and energy will be sensed, running through all the stories; and perhaps their counter-vailing simplicity will be felt, even in translation, not only as an aspect of their realism, but of their poetry.

Tagore's narrative technique is swift, dense, stylish and lucid. His plain and direct utterances lend strength to his stories. Though his language in some of the stories are poetic, but at the same time racy and beautiful.

During more than half a century of incessant creative activity Tagore produced about 100 short stories, a large number of plays and playlets, a dozen novels and as regards poems, their name is legion. There is no other writer in India whose output is equally large. It has to be remembered that he conquered the Western world and wrested the Nobel Prize on the strength of a modest volume containing only 103 short prose-poems *Gitanjali*. One is struck by the variety, the abundance and the dynamism. Artist of life, he was more than a mere writer. Not just one of the makers of the modern Indian literature, Tagore was also a maker of the modern Indian mind and civilisation. A Renaissance figure, he has been called a Complete Man.

At the centre of a ceaseless, copious at times, unequal creativity stands a person. A life full of events, the shift from a regional milieu to the boundless sky does not escape notice. To which was he more loyal: to the sky or the nest, the wings or the roots? A seeker of the surplus and the beyond, he also claimed to be a poet of the earth, *ami prithivir kobi* (I am the poet of the earth).

Creativity such as Tagore's may not be schematised. The peaks are many and to put them in order is a tough job. In any case he is more the other than the poet of *Gitanjali*. Like the note of modernism in his stories, even in *Gitanjali*, the protestant note cannot be overlooked: "Leave this chanting and singing and telling beads. Open your eyes and see your God is not before thee!" Not God of temple, church and mosque, but Nature, or God in Nature, his *jiban-debata* (Life-God), spoke to him more freely, not only of joy but also of agony. The pastoral poet could warn. In fact, he uses the pastoral, which is perennial for him, to criticise the distempers of the contemporary world. Not that he turned a blind eye to, society and history.

Tagore's writings are significant because of their abiding literary value at home and abroad. His novels are riveted to the socio-familial problems of the times, and their merit lies in their transcendence of the immediate time and place and their relevance to the present-day Indian society. His study of the women form the psychological angle reveals and ever-sensitive mind, keen perception and clarity of vision which make his writings exceptional.

Beginning with historical romances, *Bou Thakuranir Haat*, *Rajarshi*, and Tagore moved to psychological novel of frank social realism, with little or no romance. Skirting the danger zones of marital and extra-marital relationships, he manages to end on a conventional note. In *Chokher Bali*, Binodini becomes almost a *Sanyasini*, Bimala in *Ghare Baire* returns to her husband Nikhilesh, after a brief fling of freedom in the outside world. Kumudini in *Jogajog* goes back to Modhusudan, with whom she has nothing in common except an arranged marriage, and his *Naukabandi* is quite tame. Was Tagore a progressive within bounds? The traditionalists found him too modern, the moderns found him too traditional. Tagore had views of his own, which he put forth through the characters and situations. His *Gora* is a kind of mouthpiece for him. There is a dimension of discovery or self-discovery wanting in other novels and stories. In *Ghare Baire*, the author's dislike of the anarchist, abnormal Sandip is as clear as his preference for the sober, unprotesting Nikhilesh. His antipathy to underground extremism is even sharper in his later stories. It is clear that the creator of *Gora* could also materialise though late in life. Tagore's short stories, washed in the beauty of pathos, closer to the life of the folk, are less faulted than his other forms of writing. His last stories, in particular, take a sharp, modern turn.

This book will remain incomplete if a word of his dream hermitage *Shantiniketan* (The abode of peace) is not mentioned. As a teacher he never forgot the children. His concern for their need for joy, love and freedom, was genuine. He believed in Nature as well as art, and was eager to see education rooted in the native soil, the rural environment. He did not really care much for collegiate or university education. He preferred a Centre of Culture and later, a World Fellowship of artists and thinkers. It was not very easy for such a perfectionist prescription to be a school's daily food and one has a feeling that his ideas, not for the common soul, have not had a full and fair trial. Indian Renaissance is mirrored in Shantiniketan. Its greatest gift has been a dream and a legend, an enchantment's touch.

In a lecture given in Calcutta in February, 1936, Tagore expressed his view on education:

> That education is a living, not a mechanical process, is a truth as freely admitted as it is persistently ignored.

Again in a letter written to the prince of Tripura in April 1902 Gurudev wrote about his dream abode Shantiniketan:

> I wish to keep my students away from all the luxuries of European life and any blind infatuation with Europe and this lead them in the ways of the sacred and unsullied Indian tradition of poverty.

Prabaha (The Stream) of life is intimately bound up with Tagore's own creative life as well as with the laws of Nature and humanity. It was in the 1890s that he began to express his profound sense of a *jiban-debata* (Life-God) guiding, impelling and harmonising all his creative and practical endeavours. The following letter to his niece Indira Devi, is an extreme statement of an inspirational, deterministic theory of artistic creativity: the poet impelled by God who is himself a poet:

> To this poet, who fashions my life out of all my good and bad, strong and weak points, I have given the name of *jiban-debata* in my poetry. I do not just think that he forms all the separate fragments of my being into a unity, so as to bring it into consonance with the universe; I also believe he has brought me to this present life from some previous existence, via a strange stage of forgetfulness; and that a strong memory (derived from his power) of my flowing journey through the universe continues to remain subtly within me. That is why I feel so ancient a harmony with the trees and animals and birds of this world; that is why I do not find the vastness and mystery of the world either alien or terrifying.

Tagore's artistic philosophy he could never quite abandon—though his relationship with his *jiban-debata* (Life-God) grew steadily more bewildered and humble. Growing, changing, there is a sense of the 'not-yet' about him till the end.

His sense of solitary and the non-conformist are so basic and overpowering that his quest away goes on and on and Tagore speaks thus, as a parting word:

> When I go from hence let this be my parting word, that
> What I have seen is unsurpassable.
> I have tasted of the hidden honey of this lotus that
> expands on the ocean of light, and thus am I blessed—
> let this be my parting word.
> In this playhouse of infinite forms I had my play and
> Here have I caught sight of Him that is formless.
> My whole body and my limbs have thrilled with His touch
> Who is beyond touch; and if the end comes here, let it
> Come—let this be my parting word.
>
> (*Gitanjali*)

Works Cited

Dutta, Krishna. & Robinson, Andrew: *The Myriad-minded Man: Tagore*, Rupa & Co., 2003.

Radice, William: *Selected Short Stories: Tagore*, Penguin Books.

Lago, Mary M: *Rabindranath Tagore*. Boston: Twayne Publishers, 1976.

Tagore Rabindranath: *Atma-parichay*, Visva Bharati, 1969, p.7-8.

____ : "Galpaguchcha", Vol.iv, *Granthaparichaya*, p.307.

____ *: My Reminiscences*, London, 1917, p.238.

____ *: Kabya-Grantha* (*Collected Poems*) 1903.

Bibliography

Books by Tagore

Banerjee Hiranmoy: New Delhi, 1971.

Broken Ties and Other Stories, London, 1925.

Chinnapatrabali (*Torn Leaves*), 1960.

Collected Poems and Plays, London, 1936.

Creative Unity, London, 1922 (Essays).

Devi Jnanadanandini: Smriti Katha, Sharadiya Ekashan, 1990.

Essay entitled "Bharathbarsher Itihas' (Indian History).

Galpaguchcha, Vols. I and II, published by Amulyanarayana Ray at the Majumdar Agency and printed by Debendranath Bhattacharya at the Adi Brahmo Samaj Press, Calcutta, 1900 and 1901.

Gora, W.W. Pearson. Surendranath Tagore (Novel) Trans., London, 1924.

Mashi & Other Stories, London, 1918.

Mrinalini Devi, Vishwa Bharathi, 1974.

My Boyhood Days, Marjorie Skyes trans., Calcutta, 1940.

My Reminiscences, London, 1991.

Rabindrachanabali (*Collected Works of Tagore*) Vishwa Bharathi, 1939-48.

Rabindrajibani, Vol.3, 196.

Sesher Kobita (The Last Poem), Rupa & Co, 2007.

The Religion of Man, Rupa & Co. 2005.

Towards Universal Man (Essays), 1961.

Other Books

Adhikari, Sachindranath: *Selidah O Tagore*, 1974.

"Alice Walker", *In Contemporary Authors Online.*

"Alice Walker", In *Dictionary of Literary Biography,* Volume 143: American Novelists Since Bardhan, Kalpana, *Of Love, Nature and Devotion: Selected Songs of Tagore.* New Delhi: Oxford University Press, 2008.

"Alice Walker", In *Dictionary of Literary Biography,* Volume 6: *American Novelists Since World War II.* Second Series. A Bruccoli Clark Layman Book. Ed. James E. Kibler Jr. University of Georgie: The Gale Group, 1980. 350-358.

Basu, Shankar: *Chekov and Tagore: A Comparative Study of their Short Stories,* Sterling Publishers, New Delhi, 1985.

Bhattacharya, Upendranath: *Tagoreer Chhotagalpa O Upanyas,* 1988.

Bishi, Pramathanath: *Tagoreer Chhotagalpa,* 1985.

Bose, Buddhadeva: *Prababdha Sankalan,* Calcutta, 1966.

Boumelha, Penny: *Thomas Hardy and Women,* 1982.

Chakrabarti, Kalidas: *Chota Galpa,* published by him and printed by him at the Adi Brahmo Samah Press, Calcutta, 1894.

Chakrabarti, Santosh: *Studies in Tagore: Critical Essays,* Atlantic Publishers & Distributors, 2004.

Chakraborty, Kaustav: (ed.), *Indian Drama in English,* PHI learning Pvt Ltd., New Delhi.

Chakrbarty, Shirshendu: *Fault Lines of Settled Domesticity.* Research Paper.

Chaliha, Jaya: "Tales from Tagoreana." *India Today* 10 July 2000.

Chatterjee, Joya: *Bengal Divided,* Cambridge University Press, First Paperback Indian Edition, 1996.

Chaudhuri, Indra Nath: Theatric Form of Tagore's Dance Drama and Its Symbolism, Chaudhuri, Bhudeb and K. G. Subramanyan (eds.) *Rabindranth Tagore and the Challenges of Today,* Shimla: Indian Institute of Advanced Study, 1988.

Chauduri, N.C.: *Autobiography.*

Collins, Patricia Hill: "What's in a name? Womanism, Black feminism, and Beyond.", *Black Scholar* 26.1 (1996), pp. 9-17.

Davis, Amanda J: "To Build a Nation: Black Women Writers, Black Nationalism, and Violent Reduction of Wholeness", Frontiers: A Journal of Women Studies 25.3, 2004

Deb, Chitra: *Thakurbarir Andarmahal,*Calcutta: Ananda Publishers, 1983.

Debi, Ashapurna: *Pratham Pratisruti,*Calcutta, Mitra O Ghosh Publishers, 1964.

Dutta, Krishna. & Robinson, Andrew: *Tagore: The Myriad-Minded Man,* Rupa & Co. 2003.

Dwivedi, A.N.: *Kamal Das and Her Poetry,* Doaba House, Delhi, 1983.

Forbes, Geraldine: *Women in Modern India*, Cambridge University Press, India 1996.

Forster, E.M: *Daily News and Leader*, 11 Nov 1914.

Gangopadhyay, Narayan: *Kathakobid Rabundranath* (Tagore the Story-teller).

Ghose, J.C: Bengali Vocabulary.

Ghose, Sisirkumar: *Makers of India Literature*, Tagore, Sahitya Academy, 1990.

Guerin & Others: *A Handbook of Critical Approaches to Literature.*

Hughes, Ted (ed.) : *The Collected of Poems*, New York: Harper and Row Publishers, 1981.

Iyengar, Srinivas K.R.: *Indian Writing in English*, Asia Publishing House, 1973.

Karlekar, Malavika: *Voices from within*, New Delhi: Oxford University Press, 1993, p.59.

Lago, Mary. & Dutta Krishna: *Selected Short Stories*, Trans. London 1991.

Mahajan, V.D: *India Since 1526*, S.Chand & Co., 2001.

McNay, Lois: *Foucault and Feminism*, California: Notheastern University 1992.

Mitra. Ashok: *Chaturanga*, Quartet, Bengali Classic, (Uncle, Sachis, Damini and Scribilas).

Nasreen, Taslima: *Nirbachito Column*,Calcutta: Ananda Publishers, 1992.

Parekh, Shailesh: *Chitrangada and Other Dramatic Poems*: Rupa & Co, 2007.

Prayer, Mario: "Shakti and Womanhood in Tagore's criticism of Nationalism", *Journal of South Asia Women Studies*, International Symposium, 18th October 2004, originally printed in 13th October, 2003, JSAWS, Vol.9, No.1.

Purkayastha, Prarthana: *Warrior, Untouchable, Courtesan: Fringe Women In Tagore's* Dance-dramas*: South Asia Research*, Vol.29 (3), Sage Publications Ltd., 2009.

Radice, William: *Tagore: Selected Short Stories*, Penguin Books, 1994.

Rao, B. Shyamala: *Indian Writing in English, Tagore and His Chandalika: A Critical Study*. New Delhi, Sterling Publishers.

Ray, Niharranjan: *Rabindra-Sahityer Bhumika*, Calcutta, 1962.

Razak, Arisika: "Response." *Journal of Feminist Studies in Religion* 22.1 (2006) : 99-107.

Seal, Bajendranath: *New Essays in Criticism*, Calcutta, 1903.

Sen, Amartya: *Development as Freedom*, New Delhi: Oxford University Press.

Sen, Rajani Ranjan: *Glimpses of Bengal Life*, translated and introduced by him, G.A. Nateson & co., Madras, 1913.

Shirley, Walker: *The Poetry of Judith Wright*, Edward Arnold (Australia) Pty. Ltd., 1980-91.

Sidhanta Nirmalkumar: "Tagore's Short Stories." *Tagore: 1861-1961: A Centenary Volume.* New Delhi: Sahitya Akademi, 1961.

Tagore, Debendranath: *Atmajibani,* Arabinda Mitra and Ashim Ahmed, Calcutta, 1988.

Tagore, Surendranath: Trans. of *Ghare-Baire* (*Home and the World*), Macmillan, 1992.

Tagore, Rabindranath: Illustrator, Publisher, SAH, 2009.

Weedon, Chris: *Feminist Practice and Post-Structuralist.*

Williams, Tennessee: *Complete Plays*: Penugin, 1984.

Index